CAMPUS MELTDOWN
The Deepening Crisis in Australian Universities

CAMPUS MELTDOWN

THE DEEPENING CRISIS IN AUSTRALIAN UNIVERSITIES

William O. Coleman

Editor

Connor Court Publishing

Connor Court Publishing Pty Ltd

Copyright © William Coleman 2019

ALL RIGHTS RESERVED. This book contains material protected under International and Federal Copyright Laws and Treaties. Any unauthorised reprint or use of this material is prohibited. No part of this book may be reproduced or transmitted in any form or by any means, electronic or mechanical, including photocopying, recording, or by any information storage and retrieval system without express written permission from the publisher.

PO Box 7257
Redland Bay QLD 4165
sales@connorcourt.com
www.connorcourt.com

ISBN: 9781925826494

Cover design by Maria Giordano

Printed in Australia

CONTENTS

Foreword
Henry Ergas   vii

1. Fear and Loathing in Aus U
   William O. Coleman   1

2. The Administration of Australian Universities:
   A National Scandal? or Amiss in Funderland?
   James Allan   23

3. You Can't Say That
   Steven Schwartz   43

4. Law Schools in Australia and the 'Free Speech' Turmoil
   Michael Sexton   63

5. From Realism to Surrealism: The Study of International
   Relations and the Closing of the Australian Mind
   David Martin Jones   73

6. 'And Gladly Teach': The Destruction of the University
   Teaching Culture on the Contemporary Australian Campus
   Barry Spurr   99

7. Teaching Quality in Australian Universities: Present
   Measures, Politics, and Possibilities
   Gigi Foster   121

8. Same Policies, a Different Country: How English Universities have Developed in an Era of Loans, Growth and Globalism
Alison Wolf   145

9. A Canadian Perspective on Higher Education in Australia
Charles M. Beach and Frank Milne   173

10. Then and Now
Peter Drake   207

11. Culture, Utility, and Critique: The Idea of a University in Australia
Stephen A. Chavura   213

12. The Academic Social Welfare Dysfunction
Ruth F. G. Williams   233

13. The Exposed Academic and the Disappearance of Disciplines in the Managerial University
John Lodewijks   259

14. Introducing Competition Policy into Higher Education: Potential to Create Genuine Diversity
Paul Oslington   273

Acknowledgements   285

Contributors   287

Foreword

Henry Ergas

Whether our universities have ever lived up to their lofty ideals is difficult to say. What is clear is that the gap between aspiration and reality has rarely been as great as it is today.

With this judgment there is the risk of falling into the trap of 'declinism'; elevating a rosily remembered past over the jarring present. But even bearing that risk in mind, it is striking how rare it is to meet an Australian student who has experienced that sharpened sense of challenge, the impression of being seized by momentous ideas, which at least some of us felt decades ago when sitting in the lecture hall.

As for university life, it seems to have withered away. With so many students working part-time, academics routinely address empty classrooms, eliminating the interaction central to teaching and learning. The growing numbers of foreign students, who often struggle with English and so tend to associate with their co-lingual peers, compounds social fragmentation.

Nor do the universities seem especially interested in creating an atmosphere of intellectual excitement. Governed by a depthless pragmatism, their goals are as rigidly determined by the struggle to secure a niche in the global rankings as the caricatural hedge fund managers' are by the drive for a larger bonus. Teaching gets little weight in the factors that affect those rankings, with the result that it is palmed off to a burgeoning, often under-qualified, army of temporary staff.

Perhaps the most depressing component of this desolate scene are the academics themselves. There is much to criticise in higher education in North America and continental Europe; but anyone familiar with those countries' great universities would agree that teaching remains, first and foremost, a calling, which confers dignity on those who engage in it, commands public respect, and imposes stringent and well-understood obligations.

In contrast, Australian academics, while often hard working and productive, appear gripped by an uneasy combination of complacency and resentment, smugness and exasperation. Faced with ever-expanding university bureaucracy which pays itself salaries far higher than those of its counterparts at far more prestigious universities overseas, the vocation has, for many academics, degenerated into a mere job.

The result is not even the 'fair average quality' that W. K. Hancock lambasted. Nowhere is that clearer than at postgraduate level. Apparently, some forty Australian universities award doctorates; but in most disciplines the best students are rightly encouraged to go abroad. At the same time, Australian programs rarely attract foreign students, who have the option of studying at leading universities in Europe or the United States.

No doubt all this may seem par for the course to those familiar with the history of higher education. It is, after all, hardly unprecedented for universities to experience crisis, stagnation or decline.

Indeed, already in 1346, barely a century after a great wave of university foundations, Pope Clement VI suggested that universities were consumed by arrogance, and wasting their time in never-ending staff meetings devoted to bickering over ranks, titles and emoluments. As for what they called scholarship, it consisted of incomprehensible prose destined to vanish like the fog it evoked.

Clement's complaints proved merely the first in a sequence that has repeated itself, with varying degrees of irritation and accuracy, ever since.

This might be seen as the price of academic freedom. The university, it is worth remembering, was not a Western invention. Rather, it was pioneered in the Islamic world and transferred into Christendom in the great process of cultural transmission that underpinned the emergence of Scholasticism. But if the Islamic academies, despite the brilliance of individual scholars, never developed into enduring centres of intellectual excellence, it was at least partly because they lacked the institutional autonomy their Western equivalents secured and largely retained.

However, that institutional autonomy has also made them vulnerable to the pathologies which economists term 'principal-agent problems,' particularly when they enjoy secure funding and insulation from competition. Diagnosing those problems is at the heart of many of this book's essays; while the assessments differ, the seriousness of the condition, and the urgency of dealing with it, are palpable.

Somewhere Marx remarks that the bourgeoisie in its decline reproduces every irrationality against which it once fought. And the universities, he might have added, become the vehicle by which the rot is legitimised, spread and entrenched – not least by those who proclaim themselves Marxists.

We should be grateful to this book's authors, and particularly to its editor, William Coleman, for so clearly sounding the alarm.

1

Fear and Loathing on Aus U

William O. Coleman

Crystal was scanning the Egyptian blue sheets of the exam paper in front of her. She had failed this course three times before, and – now contemplating the questions before her – she saw she was heading for a fourth. She would pay out the lecturer on the online student course assessment once the exam was over. But – however gratifying that might be – it would not get her a pass, would it? True: the exam – in 'Advanced Communication Mimetics' – was all multiple choice. And true: even though the exam had been proceeding over an hour, on past experience she could still walk out now, and have another exam scheduled. But that would simply be putting off the problem. She really needed something to wipe out the course co-ordinator. And she thought she had it ...

The Dean was proofing her latest paper when an email popped up from Student Relations reporting a complaint of a student about an academic. The paper's destination – The Swedish Journal of Counselling Discourses *– was not highly ranked, though she had arranged to have it bumped up to an A grade at the next meeting of the Australian Council of Deans of Human Sciences. Anyway, this email was welcome news; it might dispose of a tiresome appointment. It was bad enough that years ago the accused academic had been convicted of aggravated assault, even if he was later acquitted on appeal. But his recent declaration on Q&A that 'The Abrahamic religions are a cancer on the human race' was a nuisance. The detection of a Discovery Grant ending up in his personal bank account really should have finished him off; too bad the university had thought it best to bury* *that pile of dirty laundry. But this complaint should do the trick. Its nature, however, dictated delicate handling, and a phone call would be appropriate.*

When his EA's phone rang the Vice-Chancellor had been savouring The Universities Education Supplement *congratulating him on his 'transformational leadership' of the 'relaunched' Central Victoria University. The motto had been replaced (to 'Change Now!'), the logo refreshed, and – the masterstroke – the name changed from the old 'University of Central Victoria'. So he would be 'unavailable' for the incoming call. Anyway, the first graduation ceremony of the year was due to start in 25 minutes. And he couldn't miss this one: it would confer an honorary doctorate on an ABC breakfast television compere. But, ... hang on, ... where exactly was Chapman Hall, anyway?*

The prologue above is a phantasmagoria inspired by authentic materials; a syrup of a mordant sap drawn from the present writer's experience of 11 academic appointments over 30 years, mostly in Australia, some abroad.

Such a prologue demands some prompt gesture of redress to the 'invisible college' that silently strives amongst the hurdy gurdy of the Australian campus: it requires an acknowledgement of the administrators of integrity who endure at their posts; of the students who wish to learn; and the academics who love their subject. In that silent college one should also include the still lively department, the faculties that defy subversion by Chancery bureaucrats, and even the odd entire university that cleaves yet to methods of teaching tested by long experience. But this book is not about you, the members of that college. You are, in one sense, unimportant. Your concerns weigh very lightly in the counsels that direct higher education; and you are now distinctly untypical of the largely homogeneous Australian tertiary education 'sector'.[1]

This book is about the typical Australian university; Aus U: the brightest and shiniest lie in Australian life.

---

[1] It has been said that 'Australia only has one university which is located across 220 campuses'. A slight exaggeration.

The malady

Students

One definition of a lie is 'something intended to convey a false impression'. A Potemkin Village is a lie. Australian universities are some of the most expensive Potemkin villages ever contrived. Stroll through those campuses; consider those wide tree-lined avenues, with interspersing handsome 'lecture theatres'. Lectures are on. But nobody's there. Or almost nobody. Open those double-swing doors and peer inside. Behold a room engaged for a course of 250 students, but perhaps only 20 students desolately scattered across the expanse of auditorium seating.

Why aren't students there? Because skipping lecture attendance is actively facilitated by many Australian universities, and virtually encouraged by some. And take heed: the absent students are not at home downloading the lecture in 'off campus study'. If they are doing anything, they are at paid work. Often full-time work. This disengagement of students is both a cause and a consequence of the thinness of student life at Aus U. Massed numbers on the massive campuses – that have been so avidly sought by Vice-Chancellors, education bureaucrats and ministers – do not provide a very congenial environment. Would you care to live in the 60 storey student 'residence' that is now currently projected for Melbourne? Another consequence and cause of this disengagement is the vanishing sense of studentship; the sense of being a member of a guild, or having a vocation. Students, in other words, aren't what they used to be (chapter 10). That Diploma of Property Strategy of yours is just one thread in the weave of wonderful you; along with being a State finalist in the tango championship; your entry in under-21 Motocross; being driver on Thursday night's soup van patrol; and managing that ensemble of weekend DJs.

Thus Australian universities brim with students who don't care about being students. But still they flood in. Why? To improve their career prospects, of course. Has it not been remorselessly pressed that studies demonstrate that a university degree is the 'best investment to be had '? These studies, however, are flawed.

1. They are old. Twenty years ago the number of students in Australia was half what it is today (see Banks 2018). Not surprisingly the average 'graduate premium has been sagging in the face of exploding degree numbers.[2] (Newer studies have been advanced but they still of necessity deal with old data.)

2. They are dogged by the omission of key variables. Talent, self-discipline, aspiration, socialisation: these are the great explainers of career success. And there is no better available measure than these, traditionally, than completing a degree. It is by proxying for these attributes that degrees 'explain' high incomes. This truth – that the completion of a degree simply signals attributes rather than cultivates them – is underlined by recent studies that reveal that student success in thinking and problem-solving barely increases over an undergraduate degree.

3. They are concerned with the *average* return on a degree, and thereby efface the range of returns. To make the point, a positive return *on average* for a Bachelor of X is perfectly consistent with 60% of such graduates earning a positive return, and 40% a negative one. Unemployment rates of about 30% of graduates only bring home how poorly many degrees serve many of their holders (see Norton and Cherastidtham 2018).[3]

In any case, the 'best investment' studies typically concern the 'private' rate of return on a degree. The private rate of return is an

---

[2] In vocational education women who undertake VET training have in recent years earned 1.8% *less* than those who enter employment straight from high school. Males earn only 2.1% more (12 November 2018, *Australian Financial Review*, 16).

[3] It might be asked, 'doesn't the willingness to incur student debt indicate a return?' But student studies are financed by government loans supplied on distinctly concessional terms. To take an extreme case: an Australian graduate living as an expatriate will pay nothing back at all. Foreign students do not, of course, have the benefit of such concessional loans. But for foreign students the payoff for study in Australia is not educational as such: it is access to work-visas, immigration, and the bogus lure of a 'top 100 university'. The employment rate in Australia of male graduates born in China is remarkably low: not even two-thirds in 2016 (see Birrell 2018, Table 4).

entirely different animal to the social return – that measures the net change in *society's* income from a degree. It is easy to create a private return for a qualification that has zero social return: a simple way is make some degree a legal requirement for some profession. To illustrate: make the completion a two-year Masters of Education a legal requirement to practise as a school teacher. This qualification is socially worthless, but the legal requirement means that anyone with talent for teaching must have this piece of paper if they are to unlock a reward for their talent.

But still they flood in. Nobody seems to mind; or care. ... And, if everybody else has this piece of paper bearing 'Bachelor of X', why don't you have one?

Academics

Now give a moment's thought to the academic discoursing to those rows of empty seats. Once universities recognised that the pregnant encounter of the student with the academic almost *was* a university education (chapter 6). But the academic has endured the death of the teacher as a role of any significance; and plunged from a once near Jungian archetype to what Australian universities now call a 'learning resource'. A kind of human app. A human tool, indeed. Like any app it is subject to online 'reviews', in the form of brusque and barbed 'student evaluations'. Such student evaluations can be used or misused, or abused (chapter 7). They are, in fact, abused. Online assessment may be submitted by a drunk and stoned student at 2.00 am. Officially sponsored student associations may – and have – organised students to submit mocking comments of the physique of lecturers. This is workplace bullying; it is called 'student assessment'. Putting aside such grosser abuses as these, the stress on evaluations ignores certain banal truths of many 19-year-old minds: good teaching means 'an entertaining performance'; or, failing that, high marks without much work.

A second ordeal of academics is the decline, to the brink of extinction, of the natural habitat of the genuine academic: 'the department'. It was the hub of scholarly fellowship – along with other now deceased marks of the academic terrain, the tea room, and staff dining room. It was the locus of the 'oral traditions', the germ of intellectual life; the vehicle of essential tacit knowledge of the discipline. And it was the atomic unit of organisation of the institution; the cell of the university organism. In a sense, departments *were* the university. But now they are dead. Or as good as dead. They were a fatality of over-centralisation. Amalgamations in the 1990s made them too large to constitute genuine intellectual communities. And their powers have been removed to the Chancery or Dean's office, leaving them minor administrative agencies. Call them DINOs.

But don't be too ready to console academics. Do not assume most academics regret what has come to pass. No: many have welcomed flight from the essential, defining activity – teaching – into more preferred pastures. About one in six academic appointments now do no teaching (or administration) at all; they are 'research appointments'. The surge in these appointments doubtless reflects the relish of the Department of Y to pay for someone from, say, Slovakia to sit in a room all day in an Australian suburb to produce papers on, say, French labour markets, by means of electronic liaison with their, say, Turkish co-author; and thereby win plaudits for the 'high research performance' of the Department of Y.

But that brings us to the cult of 'research'.

Research

There is parallel between the masses of students and their poverty of learning, and between academics and their research. Today a giganto-mania of publication co-exists with an enfeeblement of achievement.

In empirical sciences the 'replication crisis' has revealed how tenuous so much research is. Extending over social sciences and humanities there is a monotony, mediocrity and triviality, already lamented three decades ago by Russell Jacoby. Amongst all this busyness of 'research' the Russell Jacoby question is, 'where is the intellectual excitement?' The truth is that intellectual excitement is rather beside the point. All are in search of the pseudo-prestige of the 'highly ranked' journal. Ranking a very much a gamed racket. Within a discipline, 'research assessment exercises' are run by cliques. And across disciplines, these 'exercises' are rigged to demote pariah disciplines, such as economics (see chapters 11 and 12) and promote the much doted on STEM subjects, and medicine.

The dysfunction of academic research has been spectacularly exposed in numerous refereeing scandals, in which junk papers have been awarded the hallowed benediction of a 'refereed publication'. The milder of these scandals betray no worse than a dismal vulnerability of referees to fashionable pseudo-scientific patter (Bogdanov affair). Science, with a capital S, is human, all too human. More damaging is the fake data from fake experiments that have successfully leapt the refereeing hurdle into the journal page. Thus, the much published, but bogus, 'experiments' of Diederik Stapel (Bhattacharjee 2013). The publication of his 'results' might be exonerated as instancing no more than the helplessness of good faith in the face of carefully crafted falsehood; falsehood without even an April Fool's Day joke give-away. But such an exoneration would miss that part of the success of Stapel's that lay in the appeal they made to preconceptions of referees. Thus the result, that vegetarians are nicer than meat-eaters, excitedly reported by the Dutch media.

Still more telling are the outright hoaxes – *with* April Fool's Day joke seasoning deliberately added – that have been solemnly accepted. The best known involve the humanities. The Sokal hoaxes of the 1990s targeted post-modernism. More recently, Lindsay, Pluckrose, Boghossian have succeeded in having seven sham papers accepted 'by ostensibly serious peer-reviewed journals' and only six rejected. And these hoaxes encompass the natural sciences. Thus the submission of several hundred faked papers to peer-reviewed science journals, each of which 'deliberately inserted unscientific material to test whether or not it would be caught by the journals' peer reviewers'. Half the time, they were not.

Perhaps worst – because it exposes a lack of good faith – is the state of acute corruption that exists between certain journal editors and certain authors.

Capping it all is the profusion of fake journals, documented by the *Cabell's New Predatory Journal Blacklist*:

> Dear Dr William Coleman,
>
> Greetings!!!
>
> It is our immense pleasure to introduce our new journal: Journal of BioIndicators.
>
> We would like to invite eminent, efficient and supportive adepts of the corresponding field to join our Editorial Board as an Editorial Board Member.
>
> Your contribution can prove great need to our journal to reach greater heights.
>
> Your amalgamation with our journal can be attained by sending your CV, Biography (150 words), Research Interests accompanied by a recent passport size photograph.
>
> Hope for a long lasting scientific relationship.
>
> Sincerely,
>
> Editorial Office, Journal of BioIndicators 160 Rowntree Drive, Room 101 Dover, DE 19904, USA

Perhaps the ultimate charge against the 'cult of research' is that so much research is not merely bad research, not merely trivial research; it is not research at all. In contemplating the masses of self-referential pages of ink produced by some humanities – all that minute activity so mutually gratifying to participants – one is reminded more of primate grooming than 'research'. And, alas, research can be less about seeking the truth, than hiding from it. In sorry accord with that suggestion, today's campus seems to be most animated by dogma, censorship, bowdlerisation, and inhibition (chapter 3). Universities have become hothouses of Orwellian oxymorons, where 'Safety' means danger – to anyone deemed 'unwelcome'; where 'Diversity' means uniformity – in opinions (chapter 2); and 'Inclusion' means exclusion – of men.

For this state of affairs administration bears a direct responsibility.

Administration

Contemplating the procession of persons to uppermost positions of authority in Australian universities prompts the adaptation of an old jape.

Q: *'What are people who get to the top actually good at?'*
A: *'Getting to the top.'*

The sting in such a jest lies in there existing in academia an evident disconnect between being good at *getting to* the top; and being good *at* the top ....

One could prepare a small volume on ignominious departures of Australian vice-chancellors from their positions. At the same time, some appear to enjoy kingly reigns. And almost all enjoy kingly incomes (chapter 9).

How these extraordinary incomes arise, and are endured, is a good question. The task of a VC is, after all, to run a university; it's not the Manhattan Project. But the point of stressing these incomes here is to underline the stately distance of the VC from those who work in the engine rooms of the university. Within living memory an Australian VC might be seen lunching with staff in the staff club; now they are more likely to be driven around campus by a 'chauffeur', to use the term chosen by one vice-chancellor for their driver.

Function and effect are tied up here. One of the functions of the lavish emoluments of the VC – and his or her team – is to confirm their superiority. A Chancery bureaucrat who has never themselves had a professorial position finds an assurance in an income that dwarfs any professor's. One of the effects of lavish emoluments is disregard of academics: after all, with such an income, what sort of cognitive dissidence would you labour under if you *didn't* think you were worth a quartet of professors? But the (not so surreptitious) contempt by many VCs of academics has other roots; with a surprising frequency they have marginal academic backgrounds; they have been the chair of the Australian Council of this or that, or a nurse.

The appointment in Australia of VCs with weak academic credentials is not actually new, historically speaking. But, at least in the past, VCs commonly (if not always) saw themselves as constituting a binding and connecting figure in their institution; an institution which was properly, by its nature, a conglomerate. Today the preferred relation of VC to academics is that found in technical and research institutes; that of the supremo to the boffin. In this vision the boffins may be skilled, but it is the supremo who is *creative*. That is, of course, a perfect inversion of the reality of the location of creativity on campus. But, in keeping with this vision, the VC in Australia not uncommonly assumes a Napoleonic presentation; imposing, but without ceremony; frank, sudden, and deviceful. Thus they appear to academics, and to their burgeoning legions of administrative functionaries, whose principal purpose is, perhaps, to jump when commanded to by the VC; a talent in which genuine academics are lacking. It is not surprising that these campus Napoleons transform into paper tigers in confronting a superior authority. And the grim pall of managerialism does now extend its reach to a VC. In days past the relationship of Vice-Chancellor and Chancellor was not unlike that of Prime Minister and Governor-General. The VC ran the place, and the Chancellor was a 'reserve power;' to oversee a replacement if some crisis of confidence overwhelmed the VC. Today the much preferred model of the relationship is that of CEO and the Chairman of the Board. Some VCs are explicitly nominated the 'Chief Executive Officer' of the university, and their tenure is almost as chancy as the real thing.

But is this demotion of the VC necessarily an unwelcome development? Might these Councils that now like to play 'Board' – blissfully free of shareholders – be less incompetent than VCs? Councils of the highly ranked universities in Australia often look good 'on paper'. But that invites adapting the jape:

What are those who look good on paper actually good at?

Lack of correction

A final feature of the malady of Aus U is the dearth of criticism that would provide corrective and reforming 'negative feedback'.

Granted, critics have long protested the decline of the Australian university. *Degrees Galore: Australia's Academic Teller Machines* appeared over 20 years ago, edited by a distinguished historian, Frank Crowley (1998). It has been followed by many others (Coady 2000; Hill 2012; Meyers 2012). And to absolutely no effect. This bespeaks the marginalisation of genuine academics from any counsels of state, a thing less taken for granted outside Australia than within it. But, in 'the land of newspapers', one might hope to find a compensating and correcting scrutiny in the media. Not really. Australia has several academic trade journals: but they are 'part of it'. Television media will pursue a corruption story, but anything less palpable is beyond them. Print media does some useful reporting; but, apart from guest op-eds, this media tends to operate as an ally of 'the sector', and is often good for helping-hand headline.

'Uni rankings slip in wake of funding cuts, but experts say Australia is doing OK'
(*Australian Financial Review*, 26 September 2018)

As for the Tertiary Education Quality and Standards, it – need it be said? – is part of the problem, not the solution. It is one of the grosser Orwellian miscreations of the present times. This preposterous Ministry of Standards has been responsible for vandalising some of the best degrees in the country. Granted; there were problems in the (less illiberal) regime that preceded it: degree requirements had been abused. A Certificate in Graphic Design could be parlayed into PhD, without an undergraduate degree along the way ('Only in Australia'). But a better remedy would be an end fetishisation of PhDs (chapter 2), and academic titles.

Finally, there seems little hope in 'policy'. Policy in no way reflects the refraction of public opinion and interests through political parties and their supposed principles. In Australia, policy for higher education – like policy for almost anything – is determined by 'the sector'; namely the suppliers and key bureaucratic agencies. These behemoths fashion amongst themselves arrangements that serve their convenience, indulge their crotchets, and gratify their craving for control; which are then sold to the popinjays that swarm today in Australian politics, who, lacking any ideas or any constituency, are avid for 'policies'. These politicians are scripted by 'the Department', and can be relied to learn their lines.

Diagnosis

The symptoms of this illness immediately suggest a diagnosis: corruption. Either directly, or indirectly, as the underlying disease that permits secondary infections to thrive.

By 'corruption' one may include instances in the most palpable sense of the term. But, more generally, I mean the situation where an 'agent' deceives a 'principal' regarding their relationship with a third party, to the benefit of themselves, and to the cost of the principal.

The 'principals' are those who pay: those who confer resources. Thus the principal is the Government, but ultimately the Community – the tax payer, and the philanthropist. 'Agents' are those who decide how the resources are used; the university administration. The 'third party' is those to whom the resources are applied, or used by: students in the main, but also researchers. To put the idea concretely: tax payers pay university administration to educate, but administration and students enter into a corrupt *modus vivendi* with each other: 'if you pretend to be a university, I'll pretend to be a student'.

Two circumstances of the last two decades have fostered this disorder.

The first turns on the truth that relationships of agency are essential to corruption. And bureaucrats are agents; bureaucracy consists of elongated, ramified and opaque chains of deputation and delegation. The ever intensifying bureaucratisation of universities constitutes a nourishment of corruption.

The second circumstance is the explosion of university revenue. Today there is money to be made on campus; money to burn, money to drown in. Thanks to the explosion of full-paying foreign students the 'price of money' has fallen steeply, and the beneficiaries – universities – have gone on a spree.

Thus the contemporary Australian university amounts to a miscegination of bureaucracy and the dollar. Research is valued for money: research *means* money. Administration will coo over 'research' that brings in money, and curtly convey their disregard for what doesn't. And students are there for money: they mean money.

Foreign students, above all, mean money. But the importunate quest for foreign students leaves the analysis above incomplete, as this quest has introduced to corruption's uncouth country cousin to campus: fraud.

> Using a hidden camera, the ABC went to some of the biggest education agents that recruit for Australian universities in Beijing and found one willing to accept a forged school report and others willingly advising on how to avoid the tough requirements of the IELTS English language test. Posing as a parent whose child wanted an Australian education, the undercover reporter was told by education agent Shinyway – which recruits on behalf of many Australian universities including the University of Sydney, the Australian National University, Monash University and the University of Queensland – that a forged document was fine as long as it looked normal.
>
> (*Australian Financial Review*, 21 April 2015, 3)

'Jack' has been advertising online since 2012. He specialises in finance and accounting, and has 3 years' experience as an 'exam impersonator' at some of the country's top universities. For $3500 he'll outsource his brain to you and sit your exam. For $5000-6000, he says he can do an entire subject – from start to finish.

https://www.sbs.com.au/news/the-feed/pens-for-hire-how-students-cheat-and-how-they-get-away-with-it (10 November 2015)

Here someone is passing off costume jewelry as the real thing. It is not that Australian universities are passing off the bling. They are just making it. Universities, then, are accessories to fraud.

To try to summarise the malady of Australian universities, one might try to use geographical comparisons. For a century after their creation Australian universities did a reasonable job at imitating better provincial universities of the UK. In the second generation subsequent to 1945, the top tier of Australian universities had a reasonable shot at imitating State universities in the US. Today, the appropriate geographical comparison has changed. To Latin America. Historically, it had plenty of universities; plenty of bad ones. What we have experienced over the past 25 years is 'Argentinafication' of the Australian university system. Or the Brazilianisation. Consider this account of the Brazilian university of a century ago:

> ... the curriculum ... mattered little to students, who rarely attended class, or to poorly-qualified teachers who placed a premium on memorisation and oratorical skills. Few students failed and the vast majority received the highest possible grades as a matter of course. (Kirkendall 2002)

Substitute 'presentational' for 'oratorical', and you have today's 'Aus U' down pat.[4]

Explanation

Societal theories

If the disease is corruption, then its immediate origin is traceable to the tainted vessel that bears it: Australian society.

---

[4] The parallel becomes even more acute when it is noted that, despite their deficient education, Brazil's graduates 'moved quickly into judicial and administrative positions'.

Australia is a corrupt society.

Its corporations, its trade unions, its legislatures, its 'iconic' bodies of civic society – from the professions to sport – are roiled by corruption.

But to invoke 'corruption' only begs questions about some general characteristics of Australia, which will take us far away from our topic.

A much more specific culprit may be in a much remarked feature of Australian life: the flatness of its status gradient; a flatness that has been costly to academia, since in traditional prestige hierarchies, learning and scholarship were esteemed. A significant upshot is that, in Australia, a university is deemed, by common consent, too serious a matter to be left to such obvious non-entities as academics. They need to be carefully entrusted to former politicians, mining magnates, and ageing civil servants on the hunt for a retirement gig. Thus the awfulness of Australia's universities might be construed, in part, as one of the 'prices of democracy'. But the United States constitutes a counter-example; its democratic flavour has not prevented it creating the best universities the world has seen. In fact, it has helped it.

The key feature of Australian life that has been subversive of universities is the lack of interest of the Australian community at large in education. Schools, it has been sagely observed, aim to provide no more than a 'basic wage' of education; and the plummeting measures of Australian school pupils' performance – despite ever burgeoning 'funding' – only underlines how marginal genuine education is to vernacular Australian society. The low participation in universities historically is more specifically an indicator of the lack of value placed on higher education. Another indicator of this low value is that Australian university students are overwhelmingly day students; living off-campus but in the same town or city as where they finished high school. In the US, Canada, the UK and, yes, New Zealand, parents are willing to pay so that the undergraduate experience is a distinct chapter in the life of their progeny. But not in Australia.

Another manifestation of the lack of value on education is the vocationalism/professionalism that has been dominant (almost) from the beginning. Attempts in the mid-19th century to transplant to Australia the Oxbridge arts degree as the universal degree quickly failed, and Australian society's disregard of the liberal arts degree has remained an important difference between Australian attitudes and those of Britain, and, of course, the United States. This difference is plausibly traced to an apparent utilitarianism in Australian life (chapter 11). The difficulty with that diagnosis is that 'utilitarianism' places a pre-eminent stress on *consequence*. But an indifference to consequence is a regrettable marker of Australian mentality. The weakness of the liberal arts degree might be more successfully traced to the shallowness in Australia of the sense 'meaning' and 'significance' – the sort of things an arts degree is meant to be about. To illustrate the contention, Australia is fond of dress-ups, but can barely reach to creating drama. Australian life, in other words, has a predilection to the incantational, to symbols bereft of meaning: to 'ritualism'. Universities are vulnerable to this predilection, as ritual has always been conspicuous in universities, on account of its proper Durkheimian use in community-making. But when ritual supplants reality rather than conveys reality, ritual becomes 'ritualism', or 'empty formalism'. We see this empty formalism in inappropriate requirements for PhD qualification (chapter 2). And it may, perhaps, be seen in the torrent of students entering law faculties, a torrent so massively in excess of the modest demand for legal practitioners. This flood is a puzzle – but a law degree probably best serves the ritualistic impulse to 'have a degree'. Another manifestation of ritualism may be detectable. A doleful upshot of this ritualism is the pervasiveness in Australian life of ritualism's stern drill-master, phariseeism. Alas, law schools have been fecund in the nation's proudest Pharisees.

But perhaps the focus in the above paragraphs on Australian particularities is erroneous. After all, the problematic character of the modern university is hardly specific to Australia. Is not the Australian university simply reproducing the calamity observable in the rest of the world, and lamented almost weekly? The decay of 'the student' and 'the teacher' as categories; the intensifying bureaucratisation; even Australia's particular policy moves: all have palpable parallels in other countries (see chapter 8).

But, if Australia has a global sickness, its case is far worse than elsewhere (see chapters 8 and 9). The rest of the Anglophone world reveals nothing like TESQA; there are nothing like VC salaries (see chapter 9).

But perhaps any distinction between 'global' and 'national' causes turns on a false antithesis. Australia's circumstances are such that global forces have an effect that they would not have in larger countries. Globalisation has inevitably demoted the prestige of Australian-specific research. In the unceremonious but unanswerable words of André Gunder Frank ,'Who cares about Australia?'. No one but Australia, pretty much. And not even Australian universities, in these globalised days. 'World class' research is, with a few inevitable exceptions, not research on Australia.

University specific

An alternative to 'societal' theories of university dysfunction is the attempt to locate their malaise in the nature of higher education. Here is a hypothesis of that kind:

There is, and can be, no 'information' regarding higher education.

That is, education is necessarily devoid of any *publicly* accessible and *publicly* derivable knowledge of it. University education is an 'experience good'.[5] You only know anything about that bit you have consumed yourself. But how does that produce problems? One might call on Adam Smith's 'fencing master' who appears in his severe critique of the university teaching of his day. Smith observes that the fencing master may not teach well, but his students 'seldom fail of learning to fence'. Why should not universities transfer knowledge as unproblematically as the fencing master? Smith's answer to this question, I think, misses the main target.[6] The key factor, I suggest, is

---

5 Aspromourgos (2012) contrasts the difficulty of obtaining information about education with the relative ease of product discovery.
6 Smith maintained that the problems of universities arose from teachers not being paid on fee-for-service basis, with a consequent lack of any incentive to teach well.

whether there exists 'information' about whether the knowledge has been transferred or not. To be concrete: imagine that, after the conclusion of your lessons, most of society can't tell if you know how to fence or not. Would this not wreck incentives both to learn and to teach? Society might try to rely on those few who do know if you know. But suppose society finds it difficult to know who knows? In the void of 'knowledge of knowledge' enters fraud. This void has provided space for several other frauds, as the problem of not knowing who knows is not restricted to the transfer of knowledge. Who is to know if a company's debt is worthwhile? Ratings agencies claim to know, and convey what they know. Their claims to know, and to convey what they know, were seriously exposed by the Global Financial Crisis. Who is to know if art is genuine? Authenticators claim to know, and convey what they know. But certificates of authentication have been problematic since the days of Bernard Berenson. Perhaps the issue is best illustrated in medicine, with the Quack. So, in a phrase: when it comes to universities, the quacks have taken over the College of Physicians.

But why now?

Universities germinated in the 13th century when the monastery school went to town. This movement was a response to the birth of a novel social category, one unknown to the Classical world; 'the student'. Thus universities in origin were genuinely student-centred. This new category of social life was evidently seeking something different from the monastery school; but also something different from today's vocationally fixated students. What they were most interested in was *philosophy*. Thus universities were born of an animation sphere of meaning. And so, in terms paradoxical to moderns, universities were invented in the depth of medieval poverty, and flourished in spite of it. Indeed, universities reached the zenith of the genuine prestige in the Middle Ages. Huizinga (1955) declares, 'the two great conceptions of social life which gave form to the Middle Ages' were 'the knight and the doctor': thus Erasmus.

From the Reformation universities commenced a gradual but remorseless recess from society's centre. They reached their nadir in the 18th century, when England's universities were not much more than a refined articulation of the class structure, and when, in Adam Smith's bitter recollection, 'the greater part of the public professors have, for these many years, given up altogether even the pretence of teaching'.

The first source of rescue was the advent of the scientist. Not 'science': the Scientific Revolution, despite Newton, had little directly to do with universities. But, with the professionalisation of science in the 19th century, universities were the most obvious place to put 'scientists', and the word, 'scientist', was first coined by a Cambridge don in the 1830s. Even more important was the concomitant burgeoning of scientific technological research. Such research is always the state's favourite reason for the existence of universities, perhaps because it is the closest thing to power. A trickle of money began to flow into universities, growing seemingly every decade.

There was a second, but broadly correlate, fostering impulse that was first felt in the 19th century. The state discovered the use of universities as a source of expertise. The 'administrative revolution' of the early 19th century; the much sought professionalisation of bureaucracy in the latter 19th century; and the expansion of the state's responsibilities in both scope and space throughout the century: these fostered the conception of universities as both a training ground and finding-aid for governments in need of bureaucratic talent. Balliol College was a model source in Britain. In France, the École Normale Supérieure. Much later, both impulses were key to the creation of the Australian National University.

But it was early in the 20th century that universities first tapped another energy, one that was to prove a powerful, never fading geyser; the impulse to *self-transformation*. The classic arena of this impulse is capitalism, but it appears that it was in the 1920s that American universities began to receive part of the impulse – the decade when US universities first began to receive more applications than they had places; the decade of the tragic self-transformer, Gatsby, who – it will be recalled – claimed to be an 'Oxford man'; and the decade the phrase, 'the American Dream', was coined. Universities became part the American Dream; and thence the world's dream; the fetishisation of education had arrived.

It cannot be denied that, in small ways and large, universities have over the last century usefully served the impulse of self-transformation. But it appears that exploitation of that impulse has become more costly as the impulse has become ever more intense in recent decades. What was an animating 'myth' now partakes of a destructive delusion; that you can turn yourself into whatever you like is, taken literally, a perfectly bogus premise, opening the gate to a thousand futile delusions; including that 40% of the population can be university students in any meaningful sense. The intensification of the impulse has also been damaging in an indirect way. The impulse has played out productively in capitalism so long as it exists, in tension, with self-control. But can such a tension endure? The invitation to be what you wish comes close to an invitation to do as you wish; to do as you please; and to judge as you please. There is no need to labour the total destruction this has had on intellectual authority and, therefore, all learning.

The boiling over the impulse to transform oneself has been accompanied by a waning in the original font of the university: the quest for meaning. We live, of course, in the age of 'the how' rather than 'the why'; the age of the algorithm. This surely has had an enervating effect on cultural achievement: Australian baby boomers have proved an almost completely forgettable second act compared to the generation that preceded them, 1915-1944; in economics, politics, history, poetry, the novel, art – wherever you look. As George Miller – a baby boomer by the narrowest of margins! – has remarked, Australia is asleep, and the sleep is dreamless.

Salvation

The situation is so baroquely dysfunctional, it is not difficult to enumerate changes that would be a force for good (see Banks 2018).

The abolition of TESQA ... The dismantling of Australian megacampuses into their constituent faculties, so that each becomes a stand-alone university ... The sanctioning of genuine competition between existing universities by entrant institutions (chapters 12 and 13). The increasing of undergraduate fees – matched by increases in the Higher Education Contribution Scheme – to align the price of university enrolment more closely to its cost to society. ... The abolition of all academic titles in all peer to peer academic engagement; as academic journals did long ago ... Certainly, the abolition of 'courtesy' titles to former politicians, which are an insult to those who have earned the title of professor honestly: can an army be imagined enduring the conferring of the title of 'general' on someone who had never been a soldier?

But all such remedies are gratuitous as long as the patient declines to take the medicine. The problem of reform is plagued by an acute endogeneity of policy. The ruin of the Australian university is not the result of the asphyxiation of thought by custom – there has been plenty of thought; it is just completely ignored. Neither is the result a triumph of expedience over doctrine; doctrine – foolish doctrine – has often shouldered make-do. (What could be more inexpedient than the shotgun marriages of the Dawkins era?). Neither is it victory of confined interest over general interest; the present system is exploitative, but the exploiters are many; and many of the exploited are unborn.

References

Aspromourgos, Tony, 'The Managerialist University: an Economic Interpretation', *Australian Universities Review*, 54(2), 2012.

Banks, Gary, 'Public Policy and the Universities: Resolving the "Tensions",' The Australia and New Zealand School of Government, 2018.

Bhattacharjee, Yudhijit, 'The Mind of a Con Man', *New York Times*, 26 April 2013.

Birrell, Bob, 'Australia's Higher Education Overseas Student Industry: in a Precarious State', *Research Report*, The Australian Population Research Institute, 2018.

Coady, T., *Why Universities Matter: A Conversation about Values, Means and Directions*, St Leonards, NSW, Allen & Unwin, 2000.

Crowley, Frank (ed.), *Degrees Galore: Australia's Academic Teller Machines* 2nd ed. with supplements, Port Macquarie, NSW, 1998.

Hill, R., *Whackademia: An Insider's Account of the Troubled University*, New South, Sydney, 2012.

Huizinga, Johan, *The Waning of the Middle Ages*, E. Arnold, London, 1955.

Karmel, Tom and David Carroll, *Has the Graduate Employment Market been Swamped?*, National Institute of Labour Studies, 2016.

Kirkendall, Andrew J., *Class Mates: Male Student Culture and the Making of a Political Nineteenth-Century Brazil*, Nebraska Press, Lincoln, 2002,

Meyers, D., 2012, *Australian Universities: A Portrait of Decline*, at: http://www.australianuniversities.id.au/Australian_Universities-_Portrait_of_Decline.pdf

Norton, Andrew and Ittima Cherastidtham, *Mapping Australian Higher Education 2018*, Grattan Institute, 2018.

Overbye, Dennis, 'Are They a) Geniuses or b) Jokers?; French Physicists' Cosmic Theory Creates a Big Bang of Its Own", *The New York Times*, 9 November 2002.

2
The Administration of Australian Universities

A National Scandal?

or

Amiss in Funderland?

James Allan

Winston Churchill absolutely loved the prose style of the great historian, Edward Gibbon. He not only attempted to mimic much of the Gibbon's style, he absolutely devoured Gibbon's *The History of the Decline and Fall of the Roman Empire*.[1] Now, I would hope that most of the university students reading this chapter might have heard of Edward Gibbon. Or, failing that, I do hope that they at least know about Winston Churchill – Winston being both my pick and Charles Krauthammer's for the greatest person of the 20th century (Krauthammer, 2013, 22-24).

But this chapter should not be mistaken for a general knowledge quiz for current university students – aka 'learning partners' or 'cognitive apprentices' if there are any Deputy Vice-Chancellors of teaching and learning reading this book. No, I mention Edward Gibbon because in the course of his magisterial *Decline and Fall* Gibbon coins a wonderful phrase. He writes of the 'favourites of fortune' (Gibbon, 55). Gibbon is surveying Ancient Rome and is referring to those lucky

---

1 As detailed in Winston Churchill, *My Early Life: A Roving Commission* (1944, 120). Winston Churchill also had a great ability to use humour as a political weapon – a more obscure Churchillian quip I very much like occurred when the great man was First Lord of the Admiralty and Sir Dudley Pound was First Sea Lord. Sir Dudley sent his boss, Winston, a lengthy memo outlining some scheme or other and all Churchill did was mark 'Penny wise' on the top and send it back.

few for whom Lady Luck seems overwhelmingly to be on their side; not the myriad slaves, nor the many poor, nor the vast preponderance of women, but those well off few with freedom and wealth – the 'favourites of fortune'.

Before I begin my critique of some of the failings of the Australian university system, I would like to take a moment to make it clear, explicitly, that in all relevant senses, in today's Australian university galaxy, I am one of what Edward Gibbon would refer to as the 'favourites of fortune'. I have never once been criticised, questioned or disciplined by my university, the University of Queensland, for writing publicly about the failings of our university system, or for anything else I have written, including my right-of-centre political writings in newspapers, weeklies and monthlies. Not once. Nor have I been censured for saying that top university administrators in this country are massively overpaid – I believe I once said that a moderately numerate year 11 student could do the job almost as well as most of today's Australian Vice-Chancellors given that both salaries and government funding and fees are pretty much locked-in, and that the year 11 student might be less keen on one-size-fits-all centralisation, politically correct jargon, and stifling bureaucratisation. So why pay our Australian Vice-Chancellors upwards of four times what the Prime Minister makes or double what the President of Harvard University commands?

On top of that total scope to speak freely – for which I am incredibly grateful – I am also paid very well by my university, for doing a job that is far more pleasant and interesting and (let's be honest) easier than the big city litigator lawyer job I had for a few years in Toronto and London. My law school colleagues, who say they work incredibly hard, almost without exception have never had a job practising law at a big firm or at the Bar. In that sense it is plain, my friends, that we have it good.

It is also the case that I happen to work in what is arguably the most right-wing law school in Australia, which for someone with my views[2]

---

2 For a taste of which, read any of my nearly weekly columns in *The Spectator Australia*.

is certainly exceptionally lucky. (Though, of course, what it means in practice to work 'at one of Australia's most right-wing law schools' is that something nearing perhaps 20% of my legal academic colleagues vote for the centre-right Liberal Party, or did so because with a couple of recent retirements it is probably today closer to 15%. So the fact that one in six of my colleagues votes 'Right' rather than for the left-wing Labor Party or for the Greens sufficed to make my law school – what has been described by the crazier fringe as – 'a raving right-wing law school'.) But be clear, at my law school we have a critical mass of Righties and, because of that, the whole law school gets along. I fear that it is not like that in many law schools in this country, including some G8 ones, where an observer would be hard-pressed to spot a single, solitary Brexit supporter, Trump fan, Abbott praiser, small government adherent or openly right-wing voter. Sure, there might be a circumspect tax law professor or the like here or there who votes for the Liberals in the secrecy of the ballot box, he or she opting not to advertise that fact, but that would be about it. So, again, I am lucky about where I work and the fact there are others there with openly non-left-wing views; I am a real 'favourite of fortune' on this front as well.

Nor did I go through the regular academic doctorate pipeline and conditioning production lines of Oxbridge, Harvard, Yale, ANU etcetera etcetera. That may in part explain my unorthodox views – unorthodox by today's Anglosphere law school standards when it comes to my views on constitutional interpretation (Allan 2000 and Allan 2017), bills of rights (Allan 2011 and Allan 2014), overpowerful judges (Allan 2006 and Allan 2015), federalism (Allan and Aroney 2008), Brexit (Allan 2018), Trump, politics and, well, just about everything. In fact I was working at the Bar in London – well, lunching at Middle Temple back in 1989 – when, literally, I was invited over dessert by a Brit I had just met an hour earlier to work at a brand new law school being opened in Hong Kong that he was going to head up. I had really never thought about an academic career before that and, truth be told, my wife and I were not wholly sure just where on the map Hong Kong was. We went as a two year lark, discovered this wonderful pre-handover Somerset Maughamesque world, stayed for four years and I never went back to the practice of law, choosing instead to move to the wonderful University of Otago law school at the bottom of New Zealand in the mid-1990s. But my point is that, for my first ever law school job, it was a wonderful academic world in Hong Kong in the early 1990s with next to no university bureaucracy, no political correctness, really intelligent colleagues from all around the world and a great staff club. While there my wife was running the Canadian Chamber of Commerce and so, solely out of interest, I opted to do a PhD on the side on David Hume's moral and legal theory with a soon to retire Northern Irish philosopher as my sole supervisor. No paperwork. No mileposts. No confirmation bumpf. No forms to fill out. No idiotic one page posters to present. No massive postgraduate students' bureaucracy. Just a monthly meeting with a really smart guy, and boy could he write well.

That turned out to make me a 'favourite of fortune' not just because I enjoyed immensely reading David Hume and J.L. Mackie and others, and rediscovered my moral and legal philosophy, but because it insulated me from criticism when I now say that demanding doctorates in law is often dumb, or at least a silly, silly requirement in any sane cost-benefit world. You see, if you have a PhD yourself, you are immune to the obvious response. Meanwhile the faculties of law at a Harvard or a Chicago or anywhere in the US or Canada (much of Britain, too) is still chock full of law professors without doctorates.[3]

Law is a professional degree. Only in a country with a one-size-fits-all, centralism-run-mad university model, where the university bureaucracy shoves the science model down the throats of other parts of the university, does this unbending focus on demanding a doctorate make any sense at all. The country of which I speak is, of course, Australia. The attitude here is consistent with the Aussie public's

---

3 The need to have a PhD in law is spreading to Canada and elsewhere. This is part of the wider phenomenon of credentialism – here involving the mass production of quite often pointless doctorates that in turn leads to more and more academic jobs being reserved for those who have these credentials, however otherwise unnecessary or worthless.

general hostility to federalism[4]. And, consistently with that anti-federalist Australian mindset, our university administrators in this country and the proliferating DVCs, PVCs, Deans, Associate Deans, and research and teaching gurus are all adamant that you cannot leave the law schools to decide for themselves how to operate. No, you need an unbending uniformity of approach and unthinking, box-ticking bureaucratic centralism of the sort that imposes the science model on all other parts of the university. That means you simply must hire only people with PhDs, or ones with a doctorate in the immediate pipeline. What does Harvard Law School know anyway? And to illustrate further how ridiculous this mindset is – one I hasten to repeat that is less immediately noticeable at top Canadian law schools, or US ones, or British ones – the administrators at my university simply cannot understand that at a top G8 Australian law school like the University of Queensland our best students by far are our LL.B. students, the ones we get straight out of high school to do their first degree and who scored in the top one% in the State in high school. These are really bright students. (They may have pretty awful writing skills, next to zero knowledge of grammar and be jaundiced about the oppressive left-wing, politically correct nature of the school curriculum, but they are smart.)

And, when they finish at our law school, they go on to clerk with High Court of Australia judges and lesser God judges; they go to top law firms in this country and overseas; they get Rhodes Scholarships; some of the misguided ones go to work with UN agencies and the International Criminal Court; they go to the Bar; they might do graduate work at Harvard, Oxford, Cambridge or Yale. What the really smart ones never, ever do, however, is a Masters of Law at the University of Queensland, or anywhere else in Australia. And they do *not* go on to do doctorates in Australia either. Why would they? It would be silly. To advise them to do so would be negligent verging on unethical. So in law at a good Australian law school the calibre, intelligence, and

---

4 Do not get me started on how the High Court of Australia has perverted and undermined federalism these last 100 years to the point where we are alone in the federalist world in having States with no income tax power as well as living with the world's worst Vertical Fiscal Imbalance.

employability of the students varies inversely with whether it is a first, second or third degree. Put bluntly, the LL.B. students are smarter than the Masters students who are in turn usually smarter than the doctoral students. Yet the university administrators simply cannot, or will not, understand this. They think doing an Australian PhD is some sort of prize for a top law student, or at least they have institutional incentives to pretend they think this. Hence they treat the law school like part of the natural sciences. Heaven forbid that you have different models for different parts of a university. I mean, that sort of decentralised notion would put many of them out of a job! Heck, it would lead to a Switzerland-like model for the university rather than a former East Germany-style one-size-fits-all, top-down model and, Lord knows, they don't want that!

So, out of pure luck and boredom and waiting around for my wife in Hong Kong, I finished a doctorate, only a quarter of it to do with law at all, and now I am wholly immune when I point out – accurately in my view – that having a blanket rule requiring a PhD for law professors is just plain stupid. As I said, I am a 'favourite of fortune'.

And did I mention that I was recruited or head-hunted to come to a named chair in Australia? So I have never had to apply for a promotion in this country – and thus no mandatory health and safety inductions, or diversity seminars, or 'what leadership means to me' talks, or genuflections about 'unconscious bias', or compilations of teaching portfolios, reflective journals and national teaching citations, or application paperwork that is so voluminous and laden with embarrassing self-puffery ('greatest teacher ever' claims one former student; 'an unsurpassed original mind' states the recently retired professor from the back of nowhere university; 'gets more grants than a Nobel laureate' intones an ex-ARC grand chieftain, etc. etc.) and other bumpf that a vast forest had to be felled to provide the paper for this one vomit-inducing part of the promotion application.

And that is to omit mentioning the need in this country, the extremely dubious need, to be successful in getting grants in order to have any chance of being promoted (Allan 2016 and Allan 2014).

Suffice it here to say that I have never received or sought a grant of any sort. Talk about a 'favourite of fortune'! But the fact is that in law you can function quite well without these sources of grant money, as you are engaged in reading and thinking and arguing and being paid for all of that already. Leave aside the desire to fly in colleagues from overseas for a conference, say, and more often than not no grant monies are needed unless you are doing social science type projects, which in law often means bad social science research (not infrequently infused with dollops of so-called 'qualitative research'). It is here that a good deal of a law school's grant-seeking falls. And, remember, forcing academics who want promotion to seek grants requires a huge university bureaucratic machine to help seek those very grants, together with that bureaucracy's concomitant need to take a cut from each successful grant to pay the salaries of those staffing the grant-applying machine.

In medicine and the hard sciences the costs of all this applying-for-grants hullabaloo might be outweighed by the benefits. But in law, the humanities, and business? Well, it is not that difficult to be sceptical. And it is also true that, in social science type areas, those who submit winning or successful grant proposals overwhelmingly do so as regards topics or areas or from vantages and perspectives that just happen to be of the politically correct, left-wing variety. You can guess how many Australian legal academics whose proposed research favoured stopping the boats or which disliked bills of rights or which wanted to look at the benefits of limiting immigration or which was on the side of traditional marriage notions or which came down on the side of a no-holds-barred John Stuart Mill type approach to some free speech issue would win, indeed do win, Australian Research Council grants. The answer no doubt rhymes with the fifth Roman Emperor, the pyromaniac.

And all of that is to overlook the fact always overlooked by university administrators that grants are inputs; they are not outputs. The grant money is used, or is supposed to be used, to produce some publication or piece of research in a top journal. Yet Australian universities, when it comes to promotion and much else, judge academics largely on the basis of the inputs they receive – on whether they are good at getting grants – rather than solely on the basis of outputs, namely on what they have produced (which may or may not require a grant). Think about that for a moment, and how truly bizarre it is. Certainly you would not choose your car manufacturer or financial advisor on the basis of which one received the most government input monies or subsidies or grants from the state. And yet that is precisely the basis on which the vast preponderance of academics in this country are judged when it comes to promotions[5] and yearly appraisals and, indeed, it is also at the heart of how university departments are evaluated and scored in the government's highly bureaucratic, expensive and time-consuming to comply with Excellence in Research Australia ('ERA') process.

At any rate, I am certainly a 'favourite of fortune' on this, too, in that I have never had to apply for grants and never, in Australia, had to seek promotion.

All that said, I am well aware that I have been extremely lucky on all these fronts where others have not been. Many politically right-of-centre academics (and, yes, if you hang out with David Attenborough for long enough you will spot a few of them out there in the wilds of Australian academia) have to work almost wholly surrounded by lefties. And all junior, starting-out-academics have to apply for promotions. And the scope they have to speak, for many of them, is

---

5 It is beyond doubt that if two Australia-based academics, X and Y, produced precisely the same number of publications in the exact same top quality peer-reviewed journals and X did so without a single dollar of grant money – so without any taxpayer subsidies – while Y required huge amounts of grant money, or taxpayer subsidies, to produce his, that it is Y the grant-getter that would be feted and promoted by the university. X (the cost taxpayers nothing extra academic) might well even find that if this lack of grant-getting continued that she would lose her job. In that sense Australian universities operate in an Alice in Wonderland world. A sceptic might then point out that in a world in which faculties and deans are unwilling to rank and assess people's publications – to say this one in this journal is better than that one in that journal – that grant funding provides a sort of 'objective' marker insofar as winning $400,000 in grants is undeniably a bigger number than winning $30,000. For another Australian's critique of this obsession with grants, see Goldsworthy(2008).

far less than what I have. Want to guess how their promotion would go if they spoke out against affirmative action and the whole 'diversity' orthodoxy? And these junior academics likewise simply cannot just ignore inane bureaucratic requests or commands, as I have been known to do on a goodly number of occasions. Nor can they avoid filling out myriad of pages of idiotic bumpf for each year's 'performance review' – the getting of grants, as I have said, being a key aspect of such reviews.

So I am one of Gibbon's 'favourites of fortune'. I know that I am. I am immensely grateful to have been so lucky. As Napoleon said when picking his generals, 'it's better to be lucky than good', and you could not describe me more aptly than that: 'Lucky Jim'. And I also recognise that with the trends in university life being what they are, those starting out in the academic game today with anything remotely like my political or constitutional law or free speech views have almost zero chance of being as lucky as I have been. Certainly I would not wish to see my own children become academics in Australia.

But enough about me. I want now to list for you just some of the more specific problems with Australian universities. I have already hinted at the astounding level of managerialism and bureaucratic over-reach in just about all Australian universities. What you see are top heavy and noticeably overpaid university administrations – over 60% of employees at all Australian universities are administrators and bureaucrats (Department of Education and Training 2017), not researchers and teachers, and yet there are basically no secretaries around to enter marks or file papers or put exams into alphabetical order after marking or anything that remotely corresponds with a basic understanding of comparative advantage. No, a proliferation of administrators in Australian universities have jobs that fall largely into the category of what has been described as 'bullshit jobs' (Graeber 2018). If they went on strike no one would notice; indeed, the organisation would probably run more effectively. They are not really needed, these 'diversity divas' and 'how to teach gurus'. And yet, in Australian universities, administrators significantly outnumber those in the class and those actually producing peer-reviewed research. Moreover, these university bureaucrats love uniformity; they impose one-size-fits-all regimes on all parts of the university (because they simply cannot leave law schools or philosophy departments to decide for themselves what is best for law or philosophy, down to the nit-picking minutiae of how many assessments you absolutely must give, or whether you can opt to have an optional assessment in your course; no, you need some recently hired DVC brought in from a former teachers' college to issue uniform diktats for all parts of the university). Uniformity is king in Australian universities. Or, given that this DVC may well be in charge of 'diversity', let us say that 'uniformity is queen' and let us say it while cordoning off some computer lab that will be out of bounds for anyone who is not indigenous.[6]

As an aside, notice, too, that in the bizarre world of 'university diversity' that 'diversity' boils down to struggling to impose a 1:1 correlation between two or three features you find in the world at large and what these social engineers want you to find in the same ratio amongst university academics and, to a lesser extent, within the student body – most obviously *(a)* the statistically 'right' ratio of the type of reproductive organs on campus, or *(b)* the 'right' ratio of skin pigmentation specimens, or *(c)* the 'right' ratio of whether, plausibly or implausibly, students and professors can claim to be a descendant of a person who arrived here tens of thousands of years ago. You never, ever, ever see 'diversity divas' trying to get a statistical match within the university and the wider Australian public as regards political and economic outlooks. Never. Even though in general terms over time fifty per cent of Australians vote for right-of-centre parties it is nevertheless the case that right-of-centre conservatives in our universities are exceptionally rare. As I said, I have run through this in a different publication, but let me here give readers a taste

---

6 *Prior v Queensland University of Technology & Ors* [2016] FCCA 2853. Three QUT students were asked to leave a computer lab reserved for indigenous students by an administrative officer; the officer sued the students for racial discrimination after they complained in social media posts about having to leave the lab.

of the lack of conservatives in universities. In US Ivy League law schools, because donations to political parties are public information there, law professors who give to the left-of-centre Democrat Party outnumber Republican ones by more than 6:1 (McGinnis et al 2005), and it is worse at non-Ivy League law schools. (And that was before President Trump was elected and the ratio probably got even worse.) After fourteen years working here in a top Australian law school, and being the editor of a peer review law journal, and hence with a pretty good knowledge of this country's legal academics, I would say that the ratio is worse here in Australia. The ratio of conservative to progressive or non-conservative law professors is smaller in Australia than in the US.

Or just go and read Jonathan Haidt on how many academics in psychology in the US identify as right-of-centre conservatives. It is under one percent (Heterodox Academy 2016). Haidt is himself 'of the Left' but says this sort of imbalance is a disaster for students and for universities. Do any readers want to bet that here in Australia in women's studies departments or indigenous studies departments or, heck, even in most universities' sociology and politics departments, the percentage of Righties is very much better than it is with psychologists in the US?

But let me return for a moment to the astounding level of top-heavy, top-down and over-cooked managerialism in Australian universities. Now, someone might well say in reply to this charge of insanely too much managerialism and bureaucratic over-reach that, in fact, you actually need this bureaucratic managerialism in our universities to make things better. Collegiality in running tertiary education institutions was not working, goes this line of response. In other words, or so goes this claim, you need to break a few eggs to make an omelette. But this is precisely the sort of argument put forward by all one-size-fits-all centralists. There is no better answer to it than the one George Orwell mordantly threw back at the defenders of the Soviet system who relied on that sort of apologist's claim: Asked in response to this 'need to break a few eggs' assertion, Orwell replied, 'Okay, but where's the omelette?'(Orwell 1945). Or, to add a Jerry Maguire twist, 'Show me the omelette! Show me the omelette!'.[7]

Let me finish this chapter with a list that reiterates some of the main problems in our Australian universities, then adds to it:

1. I have mentioned the obsession with grant-getting and the bizarre world of treating inputs (money to do research) as though they were outputs – analogously to choosing which car or appliance to buy based on which company got the most government grants or subsidies. This also raises a raft of serious questions about the incentive structure in Australian universities as well as ones about the partisan nature of social-science grants from the ARC and others – namely, if it is harder for those on the centre-right to win such grants, as I most certainly believe, and these inputs play a crucial role in promotions and yearly performance reviews, is this a form of indirect discrimination against academics on the centre right[8] as well as being a disincentive for such people to work in our universities?

2. I have also mentioned the over-bureaucratic and massively managerialist nature of our universities. Issues concomitant to that include the stupidly high salaries paid to our VCs[9] and the strong likelihood that if each Australian university had to publish the top 20 salaries of all its employees together with what they did, my bet is that there

---

[7] Remember, we are talking cost-benefit analysis, *not* what you often see in Australian universities, namely 'benefit analysis' that counts any purported benefit however distant on the horizon and then ignores or sloughs off on others all the costs, and I mean *all* of them.

[8] See, for example, Phillips 2016. Phillips weighs various explanations by looking at citation and publication rates of law professors at the top 16 law schools in the US. After subjecting the data to regression analysis, propensity score matching and reweighting, nearest neighbour matching and coarsened exact matching, Phillips concludes that the clear explanation for the lack of conservatives was discrimination – not conservatives' greater greed, lesser brainpower or lack of interest in such jobs (see also French 2016).

[9] Australia's 38 public university vice-chancellors were paid an average $890,000 in 2016, and 12 earned more than $1 million (Lyons and Hill 2018). These levels of remuneration certainly create an incentive to take these university managerial jobs and then not to rock the boat while one attempts to work one's way up the managerial ladder to the million dollar plus Vice-Chancellor nirvana.

would not be a single, solitary name in any of those lists of an actively teaching and researching professor. VCs, DVCs, PVCs, deans, heads, to a Who's Who of administrators is where these top monetary rewards flow in Australia.

3. Here let me refer back to my earlier claim about the lack of balance in our universities. Throughout the Arts and Social Sciences, and, indeed, in Law and Business Schools, it is clear to me that it would benefit students to be exposed to occasional views broadly from the political right-of-centre; students already are well-supplied with those from the left-of-centre, indeed students sometimes seem to hear only these latter left-of-centre views. Just take a moment to think about on which side of the following debates most university professors' views would fall. On the side of protecting against hate speech or on that of more vigorously supporting free speech? On the side of wanting, nay demanding, a national bills of rights, or on that which thinks these instruments too greatly intrude on democratic decision-making? On the side of Britain remaining in the European Union or on the side that prefers leaving? On the side of thinking that Australia's stopping the boats bringing to this country those claiming to be political refugees is a bad or immoral action, or on the side that thinks any democratic nation state is entitled to, and in Australia's circumstances should, do whatever is required to stop the boats? On the side of big government Keynesianism or on the side of smaller government that cuts spending and reduces taxes? On the side that believes Gillian Triggs, the former President of the Human Rights Commission, did a splendid job, or on the side that believes she did a horrendous job that allowed this HRC government agency significantly to over-reach its mandate? On the side of international law however much it might appear to undercut democratic decision-making at the level of the nation state, or on that of nation state decisions made via the democratic branches of government? On the side that did not want Donald Trump or Tony Abbott to win, or on the side that did? Be honest now. Is it not the case that you agree with me that on each and every one of those debates I mooted the preponderance of Australian academics, in many of them

the vast preponderance, would be with the former option listed, not the latter? And doesn't that lack of exposing students to a spectrum of views give grounds for claiming that there has been a failure of leadership from the managerial class in our universities?

4. Here are some further problems infesting the Australian university sector, stated in broad terms. (A) There is too much mandated reporting by universities back to Canberra, with all the attendant and perverse funding incentives that comes with it; (B) University administrations are far too inclined to cave in to politically correct nonsense (just think of the fate of the three Queensland University of Technology students outlined in footnote 6); (C) What is expected of university students in Australia is low, and certainly the expectations placed on law students here versus the demands put on them in Canada, the US and the UK – all of which I know firsthand – are lower here. In large part this is because so many students in Australia are working, and often working virtually full-time, while purporting to be full-time students. No law student at any good US or Canadian law school works full-time, or ever tells a professor he or she cannot do something because of work commitments. So this is the tyranny of low expectations; (D) The 'Rory Sutherland insight', named after the Vice-Chairman of Ogilvy Group UK who writes fortnightly for the UK's edition of *The Spectator*. I quote Sutherland: 'It is a simple principle of business that, however badly your decision turns out, you will never be fired for acting as though [your new initiative will be a wonderful boon], even though its predictive value lies somewhere between water divining and palmistry' (Sutherland 2017). Sutherland's larger point is that those who impose these things never themselves pay the costs. And that claim, broadly understood, clearly applies to the senior management levels of all Australian universities. They never face the bad consequences that flow from mandates such as forcing all lectures to be recorded, or encouraging grade inflation, or forcing more and more people to apply for grants, or forcing departments to hire only those with doctorates, or imposing an alphabet soup of postmodernist jargon and acronyms into the thinking about teaching, or

allowing parts of the university to resemble quasi-religious left-wing seminaries, the list goes on and on while meantime no one is ever accountable when these initiatives and failures make things worse.

5. Lastly, let me list the deficiencies with Australian universities that can be understood through the lens of the notion of competition. If you are like me, you will believe that competition is overwhelmingly a force for good, and not just in terms of productivity and the needed incentives that drive better performance. Indeed, competition is why democracies that have federal systems outperform unitary states – Australia having federalism in name only due to the centralising tendencies of our High Court and the fact we now have virtually no competitive federalism, only worthless 'co-operative' federalism. At any rate, take this concept of competition and notice in the following examples how fundamentally lacking it is throughout the Australian university sector, and I mean real competition, not some bogus pretend sort.

(a) In my native Canada, and in the US and in the UK and even in New Zealand, lots and lots and lots of undergraduate students choose to move away from home for university. So in Canada there is competition between Queen's University and McGill University and the University of Toronto and Western Ontario and the University of British Columbia, and lots more, to attract the very best high school students. That competition is even fiercer in the US, and it is patently there in Britain and New Zealand. It occurs for all students. It forces universities to offer something better to get the better students.

In Australia, the vast preponderance of students stay at home and commute back and forth from home to university. So the competition between universities is massively enervated, and more so where there is only one G8 university in the city. The level of competition for top undergraduate students between, say, Sydney and Melbourne universities, or between those two and the University of Queensland or the University of Western Australia, is barely noticeable. All of them would be better as providers of an undergraduate education (something rarely related to any of the world rankings of universities) if there were this competition between them. The same goes for all of the laments and complaints a good many graduated university students in this country have about their university experience; that for many it was pretty awful. Those lucky enough to spend a semester at a university in Canada, the US or the UK know this to be true almost immediately on arrival overseas.

(b) What about the research assessment exercise in this country, the so-called ERA or 'Excellence in Research Australia'? Let me be blunt. The data produced by this process – one that costs tens of millions of dollars not to mention how much of the supposed 'free time' of academics it eats up – is not much better than meaningless. Allan's Law about Australian universities is that meaningless data is for them always better than no data at all but, even conceding that, the way the ERA process works in Australia is shameful. In New Zealand, in their similar PBRF research assessment exercise, a committee of the great and the good in each discipline takes the four self-nominated best publications over the last five or six years of each academic, purports to read them all, and then gives each academic a personal score of A, B, C or R. These correspond with numbers. To get a department's score everyone in that department is counted and you just add up the individual scores and divide by the number in the department.

Yes, this New Zealand approach is pretty arbitrary. Yes, it involves a big dollop of judgment by the committee of the great and good in your discipline. But it looks miles and miles better than the bureaucratic process used here in Australia – and I say that as one of the assessors in the first ERA assessment round. So let me just remind you that, in the Australian ERA, individual academics are not, I repeat not, assessed in the sense of individually scored. No competition there. And the publication pieces that come to the assessors from some department do not all get read, not even close. Assessors pick a small fraction of what is presented to read. And no individual academic gets a score, as I said. And, this being Australia, the grants that a department pulls in count for far, far too much. And then it goes to another higher-up committee. Perhaps the members sitting on this higher-up one then drink a homeopathic brew, wave a wand, apply some sort of ineffable 'holistic' analysis, and somehow your department gets a grade of 3, 4 or 5 star, a sort of ordinal ranking. Or perhaps they somehow else come up with that grade. But given that individuals are not scored or graded, and that not every academic needs to have submitted research to the committees, and you can see that however it is that the scores are determined they will have a hard time being defended against claims they are unreliable, too subjective or even close to meaningless. Indeed, the results correspond fairly well with what you would get if you just asked a cross-section of academics in these specific fields to grade different universities – though that would be 30 or 40 million dollars cheaper.

At least, in the US and Canada, this ranking of universities and university departments is done by private magazines. They do it to sell copies to wannabe students. Yes, the magazines use arbitrary and highly gameable methods and criteria. Yes, what you get more or less corresponds with what most academics would have guessed. But, then again, that process is free to the taxpayer; in terms of your average academic's time, it takes up a minute fraction of what this Australian ERA process does. Yet in my view it is at least as reliable as our Australian process, though in terms of generating jobs and employment it cannot be denied that such private magazine options do not lead to the creation of a sizable Commonwealth government bureaucracy or a host of such ERA bureaucracies within all the universities.

So I suppose we can concede that Australia's ERA process does indeed foster a sort of competition. But it is a competition to succeed at being good at the ERA bureaucratic process itself. Meanwhile, for academics who want a job overseas, well, they only want to know what you have published and where.

(c) Here is the last gravamen I will note in this chapter. I will pass over the seeming competition between universities to be ever more politically correct. And I will pass over some of the degrees on offer in universities in Australia and, indeed, around the Anglosphere, which are frankly money-wastingly worthless – hijacked by post-modernist and mind-warping drivel that makes you wonder (and I quote the British journalist, James Delingpole) 'what kind of employer in his right mind (or her right mind, come to that) would be insane enough to take on a graduate with an intellectually worthless degree indicative of shrill resentment, bolshiness and weaponised resentment?'(Delingpole 2017). Perhaps if students had to pay more of their degree costs themselves, as they should have to do, then these sort of valueless degree offerings would wither – and let me be clear that I am a big fan of old-fashioned Arts subjects such as philosophy, classics and economics when taught properly.

At any rate, I will skip over the explosion of political correctness on campus and the proliferation of seemingly worthless degrees and, instead, finish by saying a brief word about teaching awards. These have the appearance of being part of a competition that rewards those who are good in the classroom. Alas, what they often reward are people who are prepared to compile dossiers of jargon-filled verbiage. (And, lest you be interested, here are just a few examples of the current jargon: 'student-centredness', 'blended and technology enhanced delivery methods', 'authentic assessment', 'life-long learning', 'constructive alignment', 'evidence-based reflective practices', 'enhanced learning outcomes' and 'cognitive apprentices'.)

Put bluntly, more than a few teaching awards reward people who throw that sort of linguistic rubbish around, who normally have to self-nominate to be considered, who are judged solely on the papers they submit, and who regurgitate the words 'innovative' and 'self-reflective' with stunning regularity. More than a few of the winners of these awards would struggle to stand up in front of 350 students and do a better than competent job. So here again there is competition, but it is competition to be good at applying for teaching awards, not at teaching itself. (And, for what it is worth, my view on how to pick the good university teachers is that you ask students what they think – but not current students who clearly want to be spoonfed and be given easy top grades; no, instead you ask students who have been graduated for four or five years and who can look back and assess their past lecturers with some knowledge of how well they were in fact prepared and taught.)

Here ends what this 'favourite of fortune' happens to think are the main problems with Australian universities.

References

Allan, James, 'Constitutional Interpretation v. Statutory Interpretation: Understanding the Attractions of "Original Intent" ', 2000, 6, 109-126, *Legal Theory*.

Allan, James, 'Statutory Bills of Rights: You Read Words In, You Read Words Out, You Take Parliament's Clear Intention and You Shake It All About – Doin' the Sankey Hanky Panky' in Campbell, T., K. Ewing and A. Tomkins, (eds) *The Legal Protection of Human Rights: Sceptical Essays,* Oxford University Press, 2011.

Allan, James, 'Portia, Bassanio or Dick the Butcher? Constraining Judges in the Twenty-First Century', 2006, 17, 1-26, *King's College Law Journal*.

Allan, James, 'Why Australian Universities are not Good Enough', *Quadrant*, March 2014.

Allan, James *Democracy in Decline,* McGill-Queen's University Press, 2014a.

Allan, James, 'The Activist Judge – Vanity of Vanities' in L. Coutinho and S. Smith (eds), *Judicial Activism: An Interdisciplinary Approach to the American and European Experiences*, Springer, 2015.

Allan, James (ed.), *Making Australia Right: Where to from Here?*, Connor Court, Australia, 2016.

Allan, James, 'One of My Favourite Judges: Constitutional Interpretation, Democracy and Antonin Scalia', 2017, 6, 25-40, *British Journal of American Legal Studies*.

Allan, James, 'Democracy, Liberalism and Brexit', 2018, 39, 879-904, *Cardozo Law Review*.

Allan, James and Nicholas Aroney, 'An Uncommon Court: How the High Court of Australia has undermined Australian Federalism', 2008, 30, 245-294, *Sydney Law Review*.

Churchill, Winston S., *My Early Life: A Roving Commission,* Bloomsbury, 194.

Delingpole, James, 'Do Penises Cause Climate Change: Discuss' *The Spectator,* 3 June 2017.

Department of Education and Training, *Selected Higher Education Statistics – 2017 Staff Data,* 8 December 2017.

French, David, 'The Real Cost of Academic Discrimination against Conservatives', *National Review Online,* 17 May 2016.

Goldsworthy, J., 'Research Grant Mania', *Australian Universities,* 2008, 50(2), 17-24.

Graeber, David, *Bullshit Jobs: A Theory,* Simon & Schuster, 2018.

Heterodox Academy, 'New Study Indicates Existence of Eight Conservative Social Psychologists', *Heterodox Academy,* 17 January 2016.

Krauthammer, Charles, *Things That Matter: Three Decades of Passions, Pastimes and Politics,* Penguin, 2013.

Lyons, Kristen and Richard Hill, 'Million-dollar Vice-chancellor Salaries Highlight what's Wrong with our Universities', *The Conversation,* 5 February 2018.

McGinnis, John L., Matthew Schwartz and Benjamin Tisdell, 'The Patterns and Implications of Political Contributions by Elite Law School Faculty', 93 *Georgetown Law Journal,* 2005.

Orwell, George, 'Catastrophic Gradualism', *Commonwealth Review,* November 1945.

Phillips, James, 'Why Are There so few Conservatives and Libertarians in Legal Academia? An Empirical Exploration of Three Hypotheses', 2016, 39, 153-206, *Harvard Journal of Law & Public Policy.*

Sutherland, Rory, 'Even the Most Successful Companies Can be Wrecked by Idiots with MBAs', *The Spectator,* 6 May 2017.

3
You Can't Say That

Steven Schwartz

> If liberty means anything at all, it means the right to tell people what they do not want to hear.
>
> – George Orwell, Preface to *Animal Farm*

For your safety, dear reader, I will begin with a trigger warning. This chapter deals with the holy trinity of campus politics: race, gender, and identity. If you feel threatened by these subjects, if they make you feel uncomfortable, then close this book, go to your 'safe space', and listen to some soothing music. This chapter is not for you. On the other hand, if you want to understand the current state of speech on campus, then join me on a Willy Wonka tour of universities. Like Charlie in the Chocolate Factory, you will be amused, amazed, and even appalled by what you learn.

To put our tour into context, let's begin with a little history.

I believe in free speech, but ...

On April Fool's Day, 1943, John Anderson, Professor of Philosophy at the University of Sydney, attended a meeting of educators. He shared the platform with an Anglican bishop and two Catholic scholars. Anderson, an unabashed stirrer, took the opportunity to speak out against religion in schools. 'Religious doctrines are a direct attack and assault on a child's common sense,' he said. 'If a child is forced to swallow doctrines of a religious nature, it will undermine his understanding of things in general.'

Anderson's remarks caused a media sensation, and the New South Wales Legislative Assembly spent an entire session debating his blasphemies. The independent member for Mosman, a former Presbyterian minister, named D. P. Macdonald, extolled the right to free speech but he made an exception for those with the temerity to criticise religion. (When it comes to free speech, there is always a 'but.') Macdonald moved a motion of condemnation: 'Professor Anderson's statements are a travesty of the Christian religion, and are calculated to undermine the principles of the constitution of the Christian state.' The Leader of the Country Party supported the motion and demanded that Sydney University fire Anderson and pay his fare to 'somewhere out of Australia' (*Canberra Times* 1943). The motion of condemnation was agreed without a single member of the Assembly speaking in Anderson's support. The Legislative Council, the Parliament's second chamber, passed a motion asking the Senate of the University of Sydney to 'define the limits' universities should place on the discussion of controversial matters.

Anderson, who had already been condemned by the University Senate for saying that war memorials sanctify war, was unrepentant. He organised a rally and told an overflowing audience of enthusiastic students that 'University lecturers should be allowed to be as blasphemous, obscene, and seditious as they like.' He mobilised students, sympathetic colleagues, and members of the press to fight on his behalf and the position was saved. He went on to serve the University of Sydney for nearly a quarter century, making outstanding contributions to philosophy (Horne 1946). Other academics were not so lucky; giving voice to unpopular ideas killed their careers (Finkin 2009).

There are two vital points to take away from Anderson's experience. First, like Mr Macdonald, the MP, everyone champions freedom of expression in the abstract, but few can resist calling for the censorship of speech they do not like. Second, in the 1940s students were eager to *defend* free speech, even when it was 'blasphemous, obscene, and seditious.'

During the 75 years since the NSW Parliament condemned Anderson, confrontations – between those who wish to silence speakers and the defenders of free speech – have occurred many times at universities, and not only in Australia. One notorious case involved George Lincoln Rockwell, the leader of the American Nazi Party. An unabashed fascist who campaigned against civil rights, he claimed the Holocaust was a hoax and fomented as much mischief as he could. In 1966 Rockwell was invited by students to deliver a public lecture at Brown, an Ivy League University (Rosenfeld 2016). Politicians and community leaders fiercely opposed the invitation to Rockwell. If ever there was a person who deserved to be shunned, surely it was this despicable fascist. But the students held their ground, and the talk went ahead.

Rockwell, a former student at Brown, performed as expected — mixing racism and anti-Semitism with repugnant remarks about gay men. Some students heckled, but no attempt was made to silence him. Another American Nazi Party official, Ralph Forbes, spoke at the University of California, Berkeley. That event also passed without incident.

From our current vantage point, it is difficult to imagine Nazis speaking at any university. But it was the 1960s; civil rights and anti-war protests were at their zenith. Universities responded by banning outsiders from speaking on campus. Beginning at the University of California, Berkeley, the Free Speech Movement arose to fight campus censorship, and at least some campus leaders sided with the students (Freeman 2004). Responding to those who criticised universities for giving platforms to unsavoury people, Clark Kerr, president of the University of California, explained, 'The university is not engaged in making ideas safe for students. It is engaged in making students safe for ideas' (Berdahl 2004).

Now, let's fast-forward fifty years to the present. The right to speak on campus is as contentious as ever, but the protagonists have reversed roles. Instead of trying to silence controversial speakers, politicians, journalists, and community leaders lament university censorship while students are becoming increasingly intolerant. Convinced of their fragility, today's students believe that exposure to challenging ideas can be harmful, even traumatic. Some demand 'safe spaces' where they can avoid exposure to ideas that make them uncomfortable, and many universities comply. They have turned Clark Kerr upside down. Rather than expose students to challenging ideas, universities are determined to 'protect' them. Disraeli's institutions of light, liberty, and learning, are gradually turning into repressive Orwellian dystopias (Disraeli 1873).

Everyone is a fascist

Academics make up only a minority of the staff employed in Australian universities. The majority, 57% to be exact, consists of bureaucrats and platoons of service professionals – mental health counsellors, student-life deans, diversity officers – all employed to meet the needs of today's fragile students (Department of Education and Training 2017). Still, whatever they do never seems to be enough. Designating some university spaces as 'safe' implies the rest of the university is not safe. Students who fail to get to a safe space in time might still be exposed to challenging ideas. To protect students, a 2017 poll conducted by the Knight Foundation found that 37% of university students believe it acceptable to shout down speakers and 10% think that using violence against speakers is sometimes acceptable (Knight Foundation 2017). Another poll of 800 students commissioned by Yale University found 51% of respondents favoured codes to regulate speech on campus. Almost two-thirds wanted academics to issue trigger warnings before presenting potentially disturbing materials to students (Buckley Free Speech Survey 2015).

A determined provocateur might contrive to give the speech police the slip. Should this happen, the Brookings Institution reports that 50% of university students believe it is acceptable to disrupt speakers by shouting, and 19% go so far as to condone use of violence to silence those whose views they find objectionable (Brookings Institution 2017).

Polls such as these are not perfect (*Guardian* 2017), but their consistency suggests a profound change in attitude over the last 50 years. It is safe to say that George Lincoln Rockwell would not be invited to speak at a university today. No great loss, you might think. Who needs to hear from a fascist? The problem is that the term, 'fascist', has evolved to include all speakers who find themselves on the wrong side of campus politics. Michael Schill, president of the University of Oregon, found this out when he was shouted down by megaphone-carrying students. They called him a fascist for defending free speech on campus (*New York Times* 2017). (Alas, the modern university campus is an irony-free zone.)

Feminists such as Christina Hoff Sommers and Ayaan Hirsi Ali have also been labelled fascists as has the psychologist and journalist Bettina Arndt (Weiss 2018). The language that students use to vilify these women soars into the stratosphere of hyperbole. For example, a group of law students claimed that Christina Hoff Sommers' belief that the public school system favours girls over boys constitutes an act of 'aggression and violence,' which can 'harm' university students. Laura Kipnis, a professor of film studies, who wrote an article saying that universities are conducting too many sexual misconduct investigations, became the subject of a misconduct investigation when students claimed her comments created a 'hostile environment' (Weiss 2018). (Note, the idea that words are violent and cause harm is a common rationale for limiting speech on campus.)

Bettina Arndt's heresy was to disagree with the conclusions of a 2017 report produced by the Australian Human Rights Commission. The report claimed that 21% of Australian university students experienced sexual harassment in a university setting (Australian Human Rights Commission 2017). Arndt pointed out that the Commission's definition of harassment included unwanted compliments, leering, staring, and bad jokes. The number of respondents who reported being assaulted was 1.6% (and some of those incidents did not occur on campus but on public transport while travelling to and from university). According to the Australian Bureau of Statistics, the incidence of sexual assault on campus is lower than the rate of sexual assault in the general community, and the number has been declining for years (Australian Bureau of Statistics 2017).

Students at Melbourne's La Trobe University invited Arndt to voice her views at a campus lecture. University administrators refused permission, claiming Arndt's ideas did not 'align with the values of the university and the campaign they've been running against sexual violence on campus' (Arndt 2018). It seems that La Trobe University would prefer students, and the public, believe its campus was unsafe than let Arndt speak. The University relented when its attempt to censor her became public; still, no one on campus ever heard her talk because she was shouted down by protestors as security guards stood idly by. Despite requiring her sponsors to pay for security, Arndt's next speech, at the University of Sydney, met a similar fate. The riot police were needed to protect her and the audience from aggressive protestors.

In some notorious cases, protestors resorted to violence to silence 'fascist' speakers. Demonstrators physically attacked sociologist Charles Murray when he tried to speak to a group of students (Beinart, 2017). An academic accompanying him wound up in hospital. Underlining the irony-free nature of the campus politics, the topic of Murray's talk was the evil of social division.

In the 1940s, John Anderson urged students to fight hard for free speech 'without restrictions.' Today, students are fighting hard to achieve just the opposite. And once the censorship genie escapes from the bottle, there is no telling who might be targeted. Even grammar is political. To see just how silly campus politics can get, let us visit the battlefields where the pronoun wars are being fought.

The pronouns wars

Edinburgh University provides pronoun badges for freshers so they can choose what they wish to be called: 'he', 'she,' 'they,' etc (Turner 2018). At least Edinburgh gives students a choice; the University of Sydney Department of Gender Studies is not so generous. It insists that students replace singular pronouns such as 'he' and 'she' with plural ones (Foster 2018). Thus, if *a* Sydney University student wishes to get full marks on an essay, *they* must write ungrammatically. Sounds amusing, but consider what happened to a graduate student named Lindsay Shepherd when she tried to get a group of undergraduates to think about the politics of pronouns.

To stimulate a discussion, Shepherd, a teaching assistant in the communications department at Canada's Wilfrid Laurier University, showed her class of first-year students a short video clip featuring the famous University of Toronto professor, Jordan Peterson. In the clip, which had previously been broadcast nationally by the CBC (Canada's public broadcaster), Peterson debates another academic on the use of gender-neutral pronouns such as 'ze' and 'zis' (don't ask).

Because she did not want to bias the discussion or inhibit the expression of different points-of-view, Shepherd did not take a side in the debate. For remaining neutral, she was subject to a harrowing inquisition led by the manager of her university's 'gendered and sexual violence prevention and support office.'

According to this wannabe Torquemada, the subject of gender-neutral pronouns is not debatable and, by showing video clips without offering a preliminary (biased) view of her own, Shepherd created an 'unsafe' learning environment and may have even 'broken the law.' Shepherd tried to defend herself by arguing that a university should be open to diverse viewpoints, but her inquisitor disagreed. According to the sexual violence and prevention officer, playing a Jordan Peterson clip while remaining neutral 'is like neutrally playing a speech by Hitler.'

Unknown to her tormentor, Shepherd surreptitiously recorded her interrogation and uploaded it to the internet. Listening to the young teaching assistant sob as she tried to deal with her inquisitors unleashed a tsunami of media criticism of Wilfrid Laurier University. Ultimately, the president of the university was forced to offer Shepherd an apology.

Once pronouns become political, everyone is fair game. Consider, for example, the fate that befell a student at Wellesley, a women's college. The student, who applied to the college as a female, announced that she now identifies as a 'masculine-of-centre genderqueer' (Padawer 2014). (I know what you are wondering, dear reader, but I am sorry, I cannot help you. Try Google.)

The 'masculine-of-centre genderqueer,' adopted the name Timothy, and asked to be referred to by male pronouns. Much to his chagrin, the college informed Timothy that he was no longer eligible to be the college's coordinator of multicultural affairs because he was now a white male and therefore insufficiently diverse to serve as a diversity officer.

I wish we could linger longer in the topsy-turvy battleground of the pronoun wars, but I am afraid we have more stops to make on our tour. So, hop aboard as we pay a visit to the desolate land of the easily offended.

What's your grievance?

The Queensland University of Technology (QUT) maintains a segregated computer lab open only to indigenous students. (Somewhere in heaven, Nelson Mandela and Martin Luther King are shaking their heads in dismay.) When non-indigenous students were turned away from the indigenous computer lab – even though it was empty – they turned to social media to point out the irony of trying to foster inclusion through segregation (Forrester et al, 2016). A staff member who worked in the computer laboratory lodged a complaint about the students' remarks with the Australian Human Rights Commission. She alleged that the students' remarks were offensive, humiliating, and insulting. What followed was a harrowing ordeal, which finally ended up in court. Although the students were eventually cleared, their names remain associated with an allegation of racism – a high price to pay for trying to use an empty computer laboratory.

In the land of grievance, hyper-vigilant university officials spend their time searching for offence. Beverly Kopper, Chancellor of the

University of Wisconsin at Whitewater, thought she found one. She issued a strong statement to all university staff and students:

> Last night a disturbing racist post that was made to social media was brought to my attention.... This post was hurtful and destructive to our campus community. While social media can certainly bring about positive change, it can also be a place that deeply hurts and harms others (Kingkade 2016).

Kopper went on to announce that the Vice-Chancellor for Student Affairs would start work on the development of an action plan. Also, a series of events were planned across campus:

> ... to capture the student voice and develop a collective response to these issues.... You have my promise that these steps are only the starting points and together, we will determine actions that will ultimately create a long-term cultural change.

The reason for her alarm – the 'racist post' to which Kopper referred – was a picture that two female students had posted to social media supposedly showing themselves in blackface. There was only one problem; the students were *not* in blackface. They were having a mud facial. They thought they looked funny and decided to share a selfie. For this, the Chancellor branded them racist, a charge guaranteed to make them pariahs. As one commentator pointed out, the girls were not guilty of racial discrimination; the University was guilty of facial discrimination (Steyn 2016).

What was the Chancellor's response to learning that the photo was entirely innocent? She said that the action plan, complete with public meetings, working groups, and committees, would proceed. The Chancellor magnanimously agreed that the two students would not be disciplined but criticised them for 'failing to think about the implications' of their behaviour. It seems the students should have anticipated that their Chancellor (without first investigating) would over-react and find offence where none was intended.

In a rare case of cosmic justice, Chancellor Kopper is now receiving a taste of her own medicine. Her husband, Pete Hill, has been banned from campus after an independent investigation concluded that he sexually harassed female employees (Fox6 2018). One woman says Hill squeezed her knee under a table. Another says Hill leaned in 'for what she thought was going to be a kiss on the mouth.' She turned, landing it on her cheek. In a third incident, a woman says Hill gave her a full-body frontal hug she thought lasted too long. According to an investigator's report, Hill '… did not express any remorse or take any responsibility for inappropriate treatment of a female colleague.'

'I'm shocked,' said one student. 'You think something like that wouldn't really happen,' said another. In response, Kopper released an open letter asking the campus community to understand the 'challenging and unique set of circumstances' she faces 'as a wife, as a woman, and as your Chancellor.' Too bad she did not show a similar concern for the two students who just wanted to show off their funny facial.

Leaving the Koppers to their well-deserved fates, our tour will next visit the most idiotic of all campus obsessions – the search for 'microaggressions.'

Tragedy gives way to farce

Microaggressions are comments or actions which people find insulting when no insult is intended. For example, starting a sentence with the phrase, 'as you know', is offensive because it assumes people know things when they may not (Timpf 2018). Once you get started in the business of identifying microaggressions, the possibilities are endless. For example, the phrase, 'in the blink of an eye', is insulting to the visually handicapped. (There are no metaphors in the land of the microaggressions.) The comment, 'it was a crazy time', is an ablist slur against the mentally disabled.

Janet Napolitano, President of the University of California, the sanctimonious queen of microaggressions, wishes to eliminate them from campus. Her list includes: 'America is a land of opportunity' (a form of coded, covert racism that creates a toxic campus culture). She also warned staff not to say that 'the most qualified person should get the job' or 'there is only one race, the human race.' Even small talk is dangerous; she wants staff to refrain from asking students 'where are you from?' According to Napolitano, banning these microaggressions will 'improve campus climate' (Wold 2015).

As Marx would have predicted, attempts to control speech, once tragic, have now deteriorated into high farce. Geeky students at a California college threw a science fiction party; decorations included pictures of spaceships and creatures from other planets. The refreshments included a variety of Mexican foods. A student complained that serving burritos at the party was offensive because it suggested a connection between Mexican asylum seekers and aliens from outer space. University administrators immediately offered an abject apology for the 'cultural insensitivity' that caused 'harm' to the campus community and 'negatively impacted' students. The college now requires 'cultural competence training' for anyone who wants to serve food (KPIX 2015). But, as we will learn as our tour continues, such training would never be able to anticipate every conceivable (mostly manufactured) offence.

Multiculturalism means maintaining boundaries

In 1994, the Australian art critic, Robert Hughes, published a prescient book, *The Culture of Complaint* (Hughes 1994). Hughes worried that society had become obsessed with the 'recognition, praise and, when necessary, the manufacture of victims.' A quarter of a century later, this obsession has not waned. Instead, it has found a home in a perverse version of multiculturalism.

Multiculturalism, as initially proposed, was a cornerstone of the modern university. One of the benefits of attending a university was the opportunity to study with students from all around the world. Exposure to the arts, cuisines, and customs of other cultures encouraged mutual understanding. As a sign of multicultural respect, students would sample foreign foods, watch foreign films and wear exotic clothing such as a sari or a kimono, or arrange their hair into dreadlocks. Not any more. In a well-known 2016 incident at Yale University, a respected academic wound up leaving the university for suggesting that students should be allowed to dress up in 'ethnic' costumes for their Halloween party. Multiculturalism is no longer about seeing past cultural borders. It is about erecting walls around a set of cultural enclaves — the same attitude that produces a segregated computer laboratory.

In the modern university, exclusion is not limited to race; the genders are also being segregated. In England, the University of Sheffield has created halls of residence only for LGBT students (Mintz 2018). Also in England, an Oxford University debate on abortion was cancelled because female students objected to men participating (Stanley 2014).

Regrettably, the trend toward cultural enclaves is leaking out of universities and infecting the community at large. For example, the valuable Horne Prize for essay writing is offered yearly by the *Saturday Paper.* The prize is named for Donald Horne, an Australian writer and editor whose social commentary continues to be cited years after his death. Horne was particularly well known for his thoughts on Australian identity. This year (2018), the paper's editor decided not to accept 'essays by non-Indigenous writers about the experiences of First Nations Australians' or 'essays about the LGBTQI community written by people without direct experience of this community,' or 'any other writing that purports to represent the experiences of those in any minority community of which the writer is not a member.' Horne would be spinning in his grave. The editor was forced to reverse his decision when several high-profile prize judges resigned rather than enforce the guidelines – a rare victory for traditional conceptions of multiculturalism (Marr 2018).

Cultural enclaves harm precisely those whom it claims to help. Self-esteem can never arise from segregation and 'inclusion'; it comes from accomplishing something worthwhile. Politically correct posturing serves to make people prisoners of their own victim mentality. It's not your group identity that matters, but what you do with the skills you have.

Curiously, despite the concern with respecting every gender, religion, and belief, there remains one set of ideas that is so beyond the pale it is deemed unworthy of respect, and that is Western civilisation, the next stop on our tour.

Hey hey, ho ho, Western civ has got to go

What's in a name? Among the reasons offered by the leaders of the Australian National University for rejecting a multimillion-dollar gift to the study of the humanities was a dispute about the name of the proposed course. The Ramsay Centre for Western Civilisation wanted to call the course, 'Western Civilisation' while the ANU preferred 'Western Civilisation Studies' (Karp 2018).

If this reminds you of John Cleese trying to explain the difference between the Judean People's Front and the People's Front of Judea in *Life of Brian,* then you are old enough to remember that we have been here before. In 1988, civil rights campaigner, Jesse Jackson, led Stanford students chanting, 'Hey, hey, ho, ho, Western civ has got to go!' Stanford dropped the course, and other universities followed suit. Except for a few diehards that still teach the 'Great Books' (Chicago, St John's, Columbia), courses in Western civilisation have mostly faded away. As a result, humanities academics live in perpetual fear of being tossed overboard as leaky finances force universities to jettison disciplines to stay afloat. So, on that blissful dawn, when the Paul Ramsay Foundation announced that it would use part of its $3.3 billion endowment to revive the humanities in Australia, universities rushed to register their interest.

The foundation established the Ramsay Centre for Western Civilisation and chose John Howard – a former prime minister from the conservative side of politics – to chair its board. The Centre created an 'indicative curriculum' that begins with Homer and ends with Foucault, making stops at Dante, Shakespeare, Marx and a broad smorgasbord of worthy books, musical works and fine art along the way. The Centre proposed that all subjects be taught in small tutorials so that students and academics could discuss their readings in depth; it offered to provide generous scholarships for students and stipends for academics to make such small group teaching possible.

It did not take long for disquiet to emerge. ANU Student Association president, Eleanor Kay, feared that Western Civilisation was 'a rhetorical tool to continue the racist prioritisation of Western history over other cultures' (Groch 2018). Kay did not explain how thinking deeply about Marx and Foucault, not to mention Bartolomé de las Casas, the 16th-century campaigner against colonialism (who is also on the Centre's reading list) could make someone a racist. It is possible that she has not had the opportunity to study these texts – which is the whole point of the Ramsay Centre's initiative.

Global politics, university style

In this section, our Willy Wonka tour takes turns from Western civilisation to look in the direction of Eastern civilisation. We begin with a look at the University of Newcastle in NSW, where Chinese international students claimed to be insulted by a lecturer who suggested that Taiwan might be an independent country (Riordan 2017). Mindful of the high fees international students pay, the offending lecturer was quickly re-educated and sent forth to make a grovelling apology to the students for his transgression.

Down the road, a University of Sydney lecturer faced the same fate for showing international students a map that depicted territories claimed by China as part of India. In his apology, the lecturer promised to buy a new map (Riordan 2017).

Moving to Melbourne, a company, called Journey West Media, booked a venue at Victoria University to screen a film critical of Chinese government-backed 'Confucius Institutes' (Ferguson 2018). There are nearly 500 such institutes around the world, including one at Victoria University. When the University learned the topic of the film, it cancelled the screening, claiming that the theatre was double booked and that there were no alternative venues anywhere at the University. Neither of these excuses turned out to be true; the theatre was empty on the proposed night – and so were several others on campus. It seems that Victoria University engaged in censorship by deception so as not to annoy the financial backers of its Confucius Centre (the Chinese Government) and its fee-paying international students.

Although our tour could go on, you now have a reasonable idea of the state of free speech on campus. The next section examines how we got here and what could be done about it.

How did we get here and what can we do about it?

Two books with similar titles, both published in 2018, attempt to explain how we contrived to come to a place where serving Mexican food at a college party is not only culturally insensitive but also traumatic.

In *The Splintering of the American Mind*, William Egginton blames social and economic inequality, which has caused the national identity to fragment into smaller and smaller groups. Americans, he says, have lost their 'fellow feeling' (Egginton 2018). His prescription is a well-rounded education in the liberal arts. The liberal arts are all about liberty; they give meaning, purpose, and value to education. Who could argue? But, given the dismissive attitude toward Western civilisation on many campuses, it seems unlikely that many students will embrace the liberal education which Egginton recommends.

In *The Coddling of the American Mind* (2018), Greg Lukianoff and Jonathan Haidt blame the problem on a generation of students who have been cosseted since childhood. Adult-supervised activity (piano lessons, organised sports, play dates) crowded out free play and kept children from developing the arts of association, particularly the ability to compromise for the greater good. This 'emotionally stunted' generation is obsessed with 'safety' and unwilling to engage with people or ideas that make them uncomfortable.

Universities cannot be expected to make up for a lifetime of pampering. Besides, there is a statute of limitations on blaming one's parents for one's faults and, surely, by university age, we should expect students to grow up. One way that we can help them is to refuse to see danger where none exists. Serving Mexican food at a party does not cause trauma; saying that schools favour females is not an act of violence; and discussing pronouns does not produce a toxic climate on campus. Echoing George Orwell, Robert French, former Chief Justice of the High Court, described so-called 'offensive or hurtful' speech as the price we pay for liberty (Merritt 2018).

Expressing alarm at the censorious environment on our campuses, Ed Santow, an Australian Human Rights Commissioner, is encouraging universities to develop codes of conduct that protect robust debate (Koziol 2018). The Federal Minister for Education, Dan Tehan, agrees, expressing support for 'The Chicago Statement,' (Vivanco 2016), which commits universities to unfettered 'debate and deliberation' even when 'the ideas put forth are thought by some or even by most members of the University community to be offensive, unwise, immoral, or wrong-headed' (Koziol 2018). The Chicago Statement also forbids anyone from interfering with the freedom of others to 'express views they reject or even loathe.' (That is, no shouting down speakers as happened to Bettina Arndt.) Thirty-five American universities have adopted the Chicago Statement, but no Australian university has done so.

Justice French, now a university Chancellor, believes that expanding the meaning of words such as violence and trauma to include speech provides a spurious excuse for censorship. He says that universities risk eroding their public standing and may face legislative intervention if they fail to defend free speech. French's prediction is not just hypothetical. Based on model legislation drawn up by the Goldwater Institute (2017), the American states of Arizona and North Carolina have legislated free speech codes for their universities and so has the Wisconsin Board of Regents (Butcher 2018; Leef 2018). These legislative 'cures' are, in some ways, worse than the problem they were introduced to solve; indeed, they can lead to suppression of legitimate protest. It would be far better for universities to mount a robust defence of free speech than to wait for governments to intervene. Australian universities would significantly advance the cause of liberty by taking the following five actions:

- adopt the Chicago Statement or issue a statement of their own affirming the value of free speech despite its potential to hurt someone's feelings;
- forbid administrators from disinviting speakers whose views are opposed by some groups on campus;
- discipline students or staff members who try to silence speakers, particularly repeat offenders;
- remain *institutionally* neutral on matters of public policy; and
- do not use security charges as a censorship tool by levying such charges on all speakers, not just on those who find themselves on the unpopular side of campus politics.

It is fitting that our tour ends where it began, with John Anderson. After being condemned by the NSW Parliament, Anderson addressed students. His words are worth repeating: 'There is no absolute right of free speech,' he said. 'It exists only so far as people are prepared to maintain it and fight for it.' For the sake of their souls, universities owe it to the public to join the fray.

References

Arndt, Bettina, 'Young Women are Quite Safe at University, and Should be Told that', *The Australian*, 2 August 2018.

Australian Bureau of Statistics, 'ABS Survey Shows Decline in Rates of Violence', Australian Bureau of Statistics, Canberra, 8 November 2017.

Australian Human Rights Commission, *Change the Course: National Report on Sexual Assault and Sexual Harassment at Australian Universities*, Australian Human Rights Commission, 2017.

Beinart, Peter, 'A violent attack on free speech at Middlebury', *The Atlantic*, 6 March 2017.

Berdahl, Robert M., *Clark Kerr Memorial*, Berkeley, 2004.

Brookings Institution, *Views among College Students Regarding the First Amendment: Results from a New Survey*, Brookings Institution, Washington D.C., 2017.

Buckley Free Speech Survey 2015, William F. Buckley Jr Program, Yale University, New Haven, 2015.

Butcher, Jonathan, 'Arizona Passes Law to Protect Free Speech on Campus', *Daily Signal*, 27 April 2018.

Canberra Times, 'Philosophy tutor criticised by State Parliament', *The Canberra Times*, 7 April 1943.

Department of Education and Training, *Higher Education Statistics*, Department of Education and Training, Canberra, 2017.

Disraeli, Benjamin, 'A University Should be a Place of Light, Liberty and Learning', speech delivered to the House of Commons, London, 1873.

Egginton, William, *The Splintering of the American Mind*, Bloomsbury, 2018.

Ferguson, Richard, 'University Cancels Screening of anti-Confucius Institute Film', *The Australian*, 24 September 2018.

Finkin, Matthew W. and Post, Robert C., *For the Common Good: Principles of American Academic Freedom*, New Haven: Yale University Press, 2009.

Forrester, Joshua, Zimmerman, Augusto, and Finlay, Lorraine, 'QUT discrimination case exposes Human Rights Commission failings', *The Conversation*, 7 November 2016.

Foster, Ally, 'Gender-specific Words Australian University Students Can't Use', news.com.au, 19 June 2018.

Freeman, Jo., 'The Berkeley Free Speech Movement', in *Encyclopedia of American Social Movements*, Immanuel Ness (ed.), New York, M.E. Sharpe, 2004, 1178-1182.

Fox6, 'Husband of UW-Whitewater Chancellor Accused of Sexual Harassment, Banned from Campus', Fox6, 14 September 2018.

Goldwater Institute, 'Restoring Free Speech on Campus', *Goldwater Institute*, 2017.

Groch, Sherryn, 'Political Agenda: ANU Academics Sound Alarm on "Radically Conservative" New Degree', *Sydney Morning Herald*, 7 May 2018.

Guardian, ' "Junk Science": Experts Cast Doubt on Widely Cited College Free Speech Survey', *The Guardian* (Australia), 22 September 2017.

Horne, Donald, 'University's Stubborn No-man', *The Daily Telegraph* (Sydney), 14 September 1946.

Hughes, Robert, *Control of Complaint: A Passionate Look into the Ailing Heart of America*, Oxford University Press, New York, 1994.

Karp, Paul, 'ANU accuses Ramsay Centre of wanting "effective veto" over Western civilisation degree', *The Guardian*, 16 June 2018.

Kingkade, Tyler, 'UW-Whitewater Chancellor Reprimands Students After Mistaking Skincare Product for Blackface', *HuffPost,* 20 February 2016.

Knight Foundation, *Free Expression on Campus*, Knight Foundation, 2017.

Koziol, Michael, 'You Protest, You Pay: Education Minister's Bid to Bolster Free Speech at Universities', *Sydney Morning Herald,* 22 September 2018.

Koziol, Michael, 'University Free Speech Rules "Definitely Worth Considering", says Human Rights Commissioner', *Sydney Morning Herald*, 27 September 2018.

KPIX, 'UC Santa Cruz Apologizes for Mexican Food Served At "Alien"-Themed Event', 5 KPIX, 9 April 2015.

Leef, George, 'Despite North Carolina's Campus-Free Speech Act, UNC Continues to have Problems', *National Review*. 27 August 2018.

Lukianoff, Greg and Haidt, Jonathan, *The Coddling of the American Mind*, Penguin, 2018.

Marr, David, 'Why I Refused to Judge the Horne Prize over a Restrictive Rule Change', *The Guardian* (Australia), 24 September 2018.

Merritt, Chris, 'Unis Urged: Freedom of Speech More Important than People's Feelings', *The Australian*, 18 September 2018.

Mintz, Luke, 'Universities Warned of 'Creeping Segregation' as Sheffield Launches LGBT-only Student Halls', *The Telegraph* (London), 30 June 2018.

New York Times, 'The Misguided Student Campaign against "Fascism"', *New York Times*, 23 October 2017.

Padawer, Ruth, 'When Women Become Men at Wellesley', *New York Times*, 15 October 2014.

Riordan, Primrose, 'Uni Lecturer Targeted over "Separate" Taiwan. Wrong Map Ignites University Fury', *The Australian*, 24 August 2017.

Rosenfeld, Gavriel D., 'When an Actual Nazi Spoke at an American College Campus', *Forward*, 28 November 2016.

Stanley, Tim, 'Oxford Students Shut Down Abortion Debate. Free Speech is Under Assault on Campus', *The Telegraph* (London), 19 November 2014.

Steyn, Mark, 'Punching Back Twice as Hard', *Steynonline,* 21 October 2016.

Timpf, Katherine, 'The Phrase 'As You Know' Declared a Microaggression', *National Review*, 19 July 2018.

Turner, Camilla, 'Edinburgh University Student Union Officials to Hand out Pronoun Badges at Freshers' Week', *The Telegraph* (UK), 25 August 2018.

Vivanco, Leonor and & Rhodes, Dawn, 'U. of C. Tells Incoming Freshmen it Does not Support "Trigger Warnings" or "Safe Spaces" ', *Chicago Tribune*, 26 August 2016.

Weiss, Bari, 'We're All Fascists Now', *New York Times*, 7 March 2018.

Wold, Nathan, '10 Most Absurd Things Banned on Politically Correct College Campuses', *ListVerse*, 25 August 2015.

4

Law Schools in Australia and the 'Free Speech' Turmoil

Michael Sexton

Law schools occupy an important place in Australian universities. In addition to providing the members of the practising legal profession, the courts, they produce the judges of all Australian courts, a significant number of members of parliament, civil servants and members of the corporate sector. Lawyers have tended to dominate many bodies comprised of statutory appointments, such as human rights commissions, ombudsmen and industrial tribunals. In the role of former judges or senior practitioners, they have had a considerable impact on public policy by presiding over royal commissions and other forms of inquiry, as exemplified by the conduct of the banking royal commission by former High Court judge, Kenneth Hayne.

The explosion of law schools over the last half century

When I arrived at Melbourne University Law School in 1965, there were eight law schools in Australia – one in each of the State capitals, one at the Australian National University that had been established in 1960, and one at Monash University in the south-eastern Melbourne suburb of Clayton that had been established in 1963. A little over 50 years later there are 41 law schools in the country with approximately 40,000 students enrolled in their courses (Coper 2016).

On a per capita basis this number represents approximately three times as many accredited law schools as in the United States and Canada and twice as many as in the United Kingdom. In 2015 the total number of Australian law graduates was a little over 7,500 in number (Council of Australian Law Deans 2016). Between 1988 and 1992 law student numbers increased by 60% in comparison with 50% in business and health and 34% in disciplines generally (McInnies and Marginson 1994).

What can explain this explosion in the pursuit of legal studies? In part, the answer lies in the Dawkins changes to the tertiary education system that resulted in an increase in higher education students from 393,000 in 1987 to 650,000 in 1997 (Sharpham and Harman 1997). As part of these changes the Higher Education Contributions Scheme (HECS) was introduced which provided in effect an interest free loan to most Australian resident students to cover the bulk of their course costs. The scheme envisages the repayment of the loan after the student has graduated and reached a certain income level in employment. The reality is that much of this money will never be repaid and amounts to a transfer of funds to students in the tertiary sector.

But, as the figures above indicate, this is not the whole story. In the 1970s several universities established legal studies departments that almost inevitably were transformed into fully-fledged law schools in the 1980s and 1990s. In addition, law has become a generalist degree in the way that a Bachelor of Arts once was and obviously still is, to some extent. This is reflected in the fact that just over 45% of 2013 law graduates went into private legal practice, although some of those who were employed in the public sector or in industry and commerce would have been practising law as well (Graduate Careers Australia, 2014, Supplementary Table A1). All of this indicates, however, that there has been a boom in law schools and law students over recent decades.

The ethos of Australian law schools

In 1982, Laurence Maher and myself published a book on the role of lawyers in Australia – *The Legal Mystique*. We made the following comment about legal education:

> Australian law schools have, overall, accepted a role

of supplying lawyers to the legal profession. Many law teachers have accordingly adopted the myth of neutrality and put forward the law as it stands, without any comment as to how it developed, what effect it is having on society or where it might be going next. It is an approach that teaches skills but makes no mention of the goals to which they might be directed. This is not to suggest teachers should espouse one set of goals to the exclusion of others. But the choice should be evident (Sexton and Maher 1982, 12).

This was really a complaint that the law was presented in law schools in something of a vacuum, without reference to its social, economic and political context. In the area of tort law, to take one example, cases involving claims of negligence were often presented as simply a series of judicial decisions without any suggestion that these questions of allocation of loss could be more rationally dealt with by private insurance or legislative schemes of compensation. There was also amongst many law teachers a visible admiration for what seemed to be the most conventionally successful sectors of the legal profession – the commercial Bar and the large commercial firms. Justice Harlan Stone of the US Supreme Court, who had himself worked in two Wall Street law firms, noted the dangers of this view in 1934:

> Steadily the best skill and capacity of the profession has been drawn into the exacting and highly specialised service of business and finance. At its best the changed system has brought to the command of the business world loyalty and a superb proficiency and technical skill. At its worst it has made the learned profession of an earlier day the obsequious servant of business, and tainted it with the morals and manners of the market place in its most antisocial manifestations (Stone 1934, 7).

Nearly four decades on, there have been significant changes in legal education and these comments do not have the same application, although a place in one of the – now mega-sized – law firms still represents a glittering prize for those law students who graduate towards the top of their class, even more so with the mergers that have taken place between a number of Australian firms and their international counterparts, so providing scope for employment in London, New York and other major world cities.

But, overall, a new and rather different ethos is now reflected in the views of many law teachers and law students. This is what can broadly be described as an internationalist view of the role of law in the modern world. This view places great weight on what is described as international law and the various international organisations that rely on it, most particularly the United Nations and its agencies, high commissioners and special rapporteurs. On this approach, Australia's regime of border control is often said to be contrary to international law, as if conventions or customs at the international level could override the domestic law of a country without having been adopted by way of legislation in that country. This essentially denies the concept of national sovereignty which was at the heart of the plebiscite over Brexit in the United Kingdom. The UK had, of course, voluntarily agreed to cede a significant portion of its sovereign powers to the European Union but Brexit represented an attempt to retake those functions.

Another integral component of the prevailing ethos in law schools is the focus on what are described as human rights. These are highly generalised values, contained in international covenants or domestic bills of rights, and so very different from the traditional concepts taught in law schools. But, in recent decades, what are now known as human rights lawyers have become an increasingly common group at both the global and national levels. So it is said that one of the reasons why Australia's border control regime is contrary to international law is that it violates the human rights of those seeking to enter Australia from overseas but not as part of the normal immigration or refugee programs. There have been established, within both Melbourne and UNSW Law Schools, centres that provide programs and carry out research into the specific subject of refugees.

There is strong support in academic legal circles – and in legal professional bodies – for a bill of rights in Australia at the State, territorial and federal levels. Such statutes already exist in Victoria and the ACT and legislation to this effect has been introduced into the Queensland Parliament[1]. In similar fashion to the way a preference for international law detracts from national sovereignty, a bill of rights detracts from parliamentary sovereignty by transferring a range of political, social and economic questions from the jurisdiction of the legislature to that of courts comprised of unelected judicial officers.

Those in favour of bills of rights do not, however, consider this to be a meaningful criticism of this kind of legislation. On the contrary, they consider that judges are better qualified than parliamentarians to deal with these kinds of issues, not least because they do not have to take account of the prejudices of an uninformed electorate. It is true that, under the Victorian and ACT charters of rights, courts are not able to declare legislation invalid on the basis that it is inconsistent with the charter. A formal declaration of inconsistency, nevertheless, obviously exerts considerable pressure on the government that has enacted the legislation in question.

Many proponents of bills of rights want their provisions to deal not only with such traditional issues as freedom of assembly and freedom of speech – which are already the subject of extensive existing legislation and so arguably do not need further protection – but also what are described as social and economic rights, such as education, housing and health care. These might be thought to be budgetary decisions – the allocation of scarce resources – by an elected government and hardly questions for litigation in the courts. But they are seriously put forward by promoters of bills of rights as entitlements that can be guaranteed by legislation and effectively enforced by actions in the courts.

In an earlier time law schools – and lawyers generally – were often strong defenders of freedom of speech. It was a former law school

---

[1] *Charter of Human Rights and Responsibilities Act 2006* (Vict); *Human Rights Act 2004* (ACT); *Human Rights Bill 2018* (Qld).

teacher, Justice Oliver Wendell Holmes, who said in 1919 in the course of his judgment in *Abrams v United States*:

> ... I think that we should be eternally vigilant against attempts to check the expressions of opinions that we loathe and believe to be fraught with death, unless they so imminently threaten immediate interference with the lawful and pressing purposes of the law that an immediate check is required to save the country ...[2]

In these more politically correct times, however, little has been heard from law schools in the debate over recent years about section 18C of the federal *Racial Discrimination Act 1975* which, amongst other things, makes publications unlawful if they offend or insult various groups within the community. There are similar provisions in anti-discrimination legislation in the States and territories. It is true that all these statutes provide a defence to a complaint of unlawful conduct but this usually requires the defendant to establish that the conduct took place in good faith and/or in the public interest – both highly subjective notions in the eyes of the tribunal or court considering the case. Moreover, even if a complaint is ultimately dismissed, this is likely to be after lengthy and expensive legal proceedings that the defendant has been forced to undergo.

Freedom of speech in Australian universities

If it can be said that Australian law schools are not in the forefront of opposition to legislation that impinges on robust public debate in this country, it is also true to say that they now exist in a general university environment that places little value on freedom of speech in universities themselves. It might be thought that the search for truth would be at the heart of any university. But these institutions, originally in the United States but more recently in Australia, have seen a sustained attack on this value. It is true that freedom of speech is not an unqualified value. It has always been subject to a range of

---

2 250 US 616 (1919) at 630.

restrictions under the legal system, including the law of defamation, which is designed to protect individual reputation; the law of contempt, which is designed to protect the administration of justice; and laws dealing with issues of national security. But what has happened in recent years on a number of occasions in Australian universities is that student groups have objected to persons with whose views they disagree being allowed to speak on campus and, if those persons have come to speak anyway, their meetings have been disrupted by attempts to stop them being heard. The response of the universities in question to this kind of anti-social conduct has usually been lacklustre, with campus security staff simply observing these events and taking no action against those harassing the speakers.

Another example of this phenomenon is the use of 'trigger warnings' in course materials or classes to warn students that some of them might be offended by references to, for example, certain historical events. Again, this began in some American universities but there have been increasing instances of this tolerance of hyper-sensitivity on the part of Australian academics in recent times. It represents a direct attack on the search for truth because it is designed to prevent students even becoming aware of another side to a political, social or economic question.

One factor that may have contributed to this climate of intolerance in Australian universities is the greatly increased incidence of students, including law students, working while pursuing their degrees, theoretically part-time work but in many cases occupying a significant proportion of their time. This obviously limits their ability to take part in activities on campus, including not only sporting and social activities but also political debates. This often leaves the field clear for the small group of dedicated activists who are able to dominate speaking events on campus. During my own time in law school, in the second half of the 1960s, it was rare for students to have outside employment and so most tended to spend a great deal more time on campus than is the case with today's students. Sydney University Law School was at that time an exception to this model because students worked in law firms during most of the period they were completing their studies, although this system was later phased out in favour of full-time attendance on campus. Yet many law students now are spending considerable amounts of time in off-campus employment in the same way as once occurred in the case of Sydney Law School except that the employment is not in a law firm.

Is there a role for vocational courses in universities?

There is a question as to whether vocational studies, such as law, medicine and business, should be located in universities or in separate tertiary institutions. The same question can even be asked in relation to degrees in physics and chemistry, despite the notion of scientific research that underlies this field of study. It is this kind of speculation that has resulted in the existence of a series of liberal arts colleges in the US where students focus on the study of literature, philosophy and history. This is in some ways an adoption of John Henry Newman's view that a university was a place for teaching universal knowledge. No doubt it is far too late to exclude existing professional courses from Australian universities but Newman's ideas remind us that even those kinds of studies need to be conducted in their broad social context and to allow a full exchange of opinions.

The rise of the doctoral qualification

There have been no figures collected on this subject but anecdotal evidence suggests that a doctorate in legal studies has become, if not a requirement, at least a considerable advantage in gaining appointment to academic posts in Australian law schools. There has been some limited research on this development in the US and this suggests that a doctorate has become a more common qualification in the case of appointments to law faculties and, more particularly so, in the case of the top-ranking law schools (see LoPucki 2016 and McCrary et al 2016).

It must be doubted whether this is a useful development. Until relatively recently doctoral dissertations in law were rare both in

Australia and in the US, no doubt because the scope for original research is obviously less than in many areas of scientific experimentation. This is not to say that they have not been, on occasions, significant contributions to legal scholarship that have been awarded doctoral status, for example, H. V. Evatt's doctorate in law, conferred in 1924 by the University of Sydney.[3] But a doctorate was never considered in either the US or Australia to be a necessary or even desirable qualification for appointment as a law school teacher. Even Master's degrees were far from common and some of the most celebrated teachers in American law schools, like Archibald Cox at Harvard Law School, survived with the simple degree of LL.B. The publication of articles in law reviews has always been one relevant criterion for appointment to an academic post but what seems to be an increasing emphasis on the possession of a doctoral degree may well constitute an unnecessary emphasis on a formal qualification and one that may have no particular correlation with teaching ability.

Conclusion

Australian law schools do not operate in a vacuum separate from the universities in which they are situated and the surrounding society. So they are functioning in an environment where most of the public institutions in Australia, including universities, and many large corporations subscribe to an agenda of political correctness that is actively hostile to rigorous public debate on many social, economic and political questions. It would no doubt be unrealistic to expect law schools to stand out sharply in opposition to this milieu, but instances of dissenting opinions in law schools appear to have been relatively rare over recent years. Law schools – and universities generally – in Australia might do well to heed the injunction of Hanna Holborn Gray, President of the University of Chicago from 1978 to 1993:

> . . . education should not be intended to make people comfortable, it is meant to make them think. Universities should be expected to provide the conditions within

---
3 This dissertation was published 63 years later under the title, *The Royal Prerogative*.

which hard thought and therefore strong disagreement, independent judgment, and the questioning of stubborn assumptions, can flourish in an environment of the greatest freedom.

References

Coper, M., 'Does Australia Have Too Many Law Schools?', *Australian Law Journal*, 2016, 90.

Council of Australian Law Deans, 'Data Regarding Law School Graduate Numbers and Outcomes', 2016.

Graduate Careers Australia, *Graduate Destinations Report 2014*, 2014.

LoPucki, L., 'Dawn of the Discipline-Based Law Faculty', *Journal of Legal Education*, 2016, 65.

McCrary, J., J. Milligran and J. Phillips, 'The Ph.D. Rises in American Law Schools: 1960-2011: What Does It Mean for Legal Education?', *Journal of Legal Education*, 65, 2016.

McInnies, C. and S. Marginson, *Australian Law Schools after the 1987 Pearce Report*, Government Printing Office, Canberra, 1994.

Sexton, M. and L. Maher, *The Legal Mystique: The Role of Lawyers in Australian Society*, Angus & Robertson, Sydney, 1982.

Sharpham, J. and G Harman (eds), *Australia's Future University*, University of New England Press, Armidale, 1997.

Stone, H., 'The Public Influence of the Bar', *Harvard Law Review*, 1934, 17.

5

From Realism to Surrealism

The Study of International Relations and the
Closing of the Australian Mind

David Martin Jones

Before the millennium, the study of international relations (IR) constituted a minor field in the politics discipline in Australia. Most undergraduate courses included an international relations or foreign policy component, but the discipline's mainstream was comparative politics, Australian politics and public administration. Political thought occupied a curious place, eking out a half-life somewhere between the history, philosophy and politics departments.[1] Unlike political thought, Australian IR, however secondary, enjoyed a certain cachet. It had produced a number of significant scholars and scholar diplomats who helped define the new field after 1919, and more particularly after 1945. Hedley Bull and Robert O'Neill achieved international reputations. During the Cold War period scholars of various political persuasions like Peter Boyce, J.D.B. Miller, Tom Millar, Owen Harries, Harry Gelber and Coral Bell evolved a distinctively realist approach to Australian foreign policy, the region and the world.[2] Even those who found inspiration in Whitlam's foreign policy 'watershed' after 1972, and Keating's subsequent 'engagement' with Asia in the 1980s, still worked within a framework that understood the paramount

---

1 One Australian political scientist told me, when I arrived at the fatal shore in 1995, that political theory was 'a bit airy fairy, mate'. Not, however, any more, once it evolved, after the millennium, into the fashionable revelation that is 'international relations theory'.
2 For a summary of this realist disposition, see Owen Harries, 'A Tribute to Coral Bell', *The Spectator*, 6 October, 2012.

significance of the national interest, however construed, in an uncertain world.

Returning to the Australian campus in the second decade of the new millennium, the shades of Australia's IR scholars of times past would be struck by the shift from realism to surrealism, and the dominance of something called 'international relations theory' in a discipline that once emphasised diplomatic history, war, and treaties. They would also be surprised at the manner in which International Relations and its younger and radically pacifist cousin, peace studies, now dominates the political science discipline both in terms of personnel and student numbers. In 2016, 75% of the undergraduate intake of the University of Queensland's School of Political Science and International Studies enrolled in IR. The figures are similar throughout Australia and the UK. What accounts for its recent appeal?

The appeal, in part, is IR's current concern, not with how state and non-state actors do operate in the world as it is, but with how they ought to act. Embedding utopianism, idealism, justice and post-colonial guilt tripping evidently appeals to the student of the snowflake generation rather more than a historically nuanced appreciation of modern statecraft, or the use of state force and fraud in international politics to achieve interests and ends. A scholar of Harries' or Boyce's vintage would, one suspects, struggle to recognise the courses taught in modern university international relations programs. They certainly would not consider them having much to do with the subject they once studied.

A brief examination of undergraduate course offerings at some of Australia's highest ranked institutions tells the tale of where the study of international relations locates its priorities. At Melbourne, undergraduates study topics ranging, from terrorism; nuclear proliferation; human rights; humanitarian intervention; 'trade liberalisation and its critics; global inequality; climate change; and the refugee crisis'. The purpose, it seems, of choosing these otherwise random subjects is 'to demonstrate the relevance of competing theories of international politics, including realism, liberalism and critical theories (such as Marxism and feminism)'. Down the road at Monash students explore the relationships between international structures, processes and political institutions including states, non-government organisations (NGOs), social movements, and international organisations such as the United Nations and its specialised agencies, the World Trade Organisation, NATO, and the European Union. Meanwhile, at Adelaide University, environmental citizenship features strongly, appealing to students 'concerned with issues of environmental sustainability, social justice and citizenship in the 21st century'. When not contemplating the environment, students might engage with 'global governance and justice' and 'global citizenship'. At Flinders, undergraduates 'explore Australia's role in the world community', but they may 'also study international organisations and regimes like the United Nations, NATO, ASEAN, the ANZUS alliance and the Kyoto Accord'. Sydney University introduces its freshpersons to 'the big issues'.

These include, for no evident reason, terrorism, war in Syria, climate change, nuclear proliferation, and the global refugee and global financial crises. Students also examine 'politics and international ethics using critical and interdisciplinary perspectives'. Meanwhile ANU, the nation's highest ranked university, also focuses on theory and the different ways 'theorists have attempted to ... understand different aspects of international relations'. It introduces 'students to the nature and purpose of theory as well as the major theoretical concepts employed by IR scholars and policymakers before exploring in more detail different theoretical approaches to: power politics ... anarchy and interdependence ... decision making ..., perceived threats, and relationships of inclusion and exclusion (critical theory and feminism).' The 'possibilities for global co-operation around major issues such as transnational conflict, international political economy, global environmental management, and human and social rights' also occupy the undergraduate curriculum. Meanwhile, at Queensland, undergraduates find themselves exposed to 'Global Security in World Politics', 'International Equality and

Development', 'Humanitarianism and World Politics' and 'Gender and Global Politics'.

What time travelling academics from the recent past would find particularly surprising is the preoccupation with 'ethics' and its importance to 'critical' understandings of global justice, human rights, environmental and global citizenship, gender and 'inclusivity'. When not obsessing over ethics our academic would be surprised to learn that transnational and regional arrangements like ASEAN, the EU and the UN now dominate the curriculum at the expense of state behaviour or the recent history of great and not so great powers.

If our time travellers paused to listen in at a postgraduate seminar series, they would find themselves treated to doctoral candidates musing upon, inter alia: 'Anarchism Critical Theory and Emancipation: towards the realisation of an ideal speech situation'; 'Recognition theory and indigenous self-representation: the place of indigenous identity; Paranoid Politics Conspiracy thinking and International Relations;' 'Imagining (In) security: recovering an agential dimension'; or 'Fear No More: emotions and world politics'.

Concerned by the emoting, emancipating and imagining, our increasingly perplexed visitors from the late twentieth century might be tempted to seek enlightenment by attending the staff seminar series presented by nationally and internationally recognised scholars in the discipline.

However, a cursory examination of a leading Australian School of Politics and International Studies postgraduate seminar series (2017-18, (University of Queensland)) would only perhaps add an additional layer of obscurity upon what passes for 'cutting edge' and Australian and European state-funded research of international relations. Thus Meera Subaratnam asks, 'Is International Relations theory white'? While Anthea Roberts enquires, 'Is international law international?' The questions are purely rhetorical. As Dr Subaratnam explains, 'white subject positions permeate the core of influential contemporary International Relations theories'. Indeed, whiteness as 'a set of historically specific hierarchies of entitlement ... produce (sic) particular kinds of subject positions in the world'. Subaratnam, a visiting scholar from London University's School of Oriental and Asian Studies, not entirely surprisingly, also chairs the University of London's Academic Senate's *Decolonising the University* working group.

In a similar vein, Anthea Roberts (ANU) finds that 'Western actors, materials, and approaches in general, and Anglo-American ones in particular' determine the 'international'. These patterns, however, are 'set for disruption'. As the world moves 'past an era of Western dominance', Roberts encourages her readers 'to seek to see the world through the eyes of others'. Embracing this perspective, Andrew Phillips discovers the neglected 'Asian roots of the modern world'. In the process, Phillips resists the distorting Eurocentric view that claims modernity might have had something to do with the industrial revolution in England, the European Enlightenment and the democratic revolutions in the United States and France.

In a similarly optically challenging endeavour Professor Roland Bleiker 'looks inside the Korean DMZ' in order to rethink 'Security Through Visual Autoethnography'. Somewhat self-indulgently, Bleiker uses his holiday snaps to engage in something called 'the politics of visuality'. Via the visuality paradigm, Bleiker identifies two otherwise neglected obstacles to the resolution of the Korean conflict: firstly, 'a form of militarised masculinity that transcends ideological and political boundaries' and, secondly, 'the inability to understand the conflict in neutral ways and the ensuing implications for how North Korea is seen and approached politically'. David Duriesmith, in the same series, is also preoccupied with masculinity and violence through a somewhat prurient but comprehensive examination of the 'masculinities of Indonesian jihadis'. Bleiker's generously funded *Visual Politics Program* also hosts a variety of 'exciting' workshops and roundtables on the theme of 'How Images Matter in World Politics'. The participants know images matter, but, somewhat problematically, we learn that 'they are not sure why.' No doubt, generously taxpayer funded roundtables on 'How Artists Address Our Nuclear History,' and panel discussions on 'Emotional geography, memory and the personal' will help to illuminate the visuality paradigm.

In an ethical, but still critical, mode, Professor Maja Zehfuss (University of Manchester) offers seminars and master classes on the ethics of war, 'not to show how ethical war can be fought, but to challenge the ethical view of war'. More particularly, Zehfuss challenges the view that Western war since 1939 might have been waged 'for the good' treating war instead 'as a politics of ethics' which is, she does not seem to realise, a contradiction. Professor Giorgio Shani (ICU, Tokyo) adds to the obscurity with an examination of 'human security as ontological security: a post-secular approach'. Shani would no doubt find much in common with Griffith University's Samir Suliman and his colleagues who explore 'security from the outside'. Security, Suliman avers, 'remains aligned to both normative and analytical frameworks that foreclose a comprehensive understanding of the political constitution of security and insecurity, in global, and especially ecological, terms'. By contrast, critical security would play a more 'productive role in the knowledge landscape of an as-yet-unknown future through widening its disciplinary connections with the humanities and other creative scholarship', leading to 'reimagining the politics of security in the Anthropocene'.

Not to miss out on this reimagining, Professor Peter Sewell (Sussex) explains how a green political critique will bring about 'a more realistic, just and sustainable global society'. Elsewhere, Adjunct Professor 'Aunty' Mary Graham recounts her role at the UN committee for eliminating racial discrimination in Australia, and the workshops to embed into the department's teaching indigenous understandings drawn from her own Waka Waka community. One of the school's ARC fellows offers a way forward in embedding local knowledges with a version of her internationally peer reviewed publication on 'Sexual violence and hybrid peacebuilding: how does silence "speak" '?

How indeed!

Postgraduate and seminar series exhibiting a similar range of theoretical, post colonial, post human, feminist, environmental and ethical concerns might be found advertised on any week in any of the great eight campuses. International relations, in other words, has become home to an idealist and ethicist post Cold War ideology of Kantian derivation posing as 'theory'.

Normativism's not so long short march through the institutions

The leading luminaries holding various chairs in the nation's research-focused, large-grant-getting schools helps in part to explain why this ideology has achieved such influence. For example, the new director of the ANU Coral Bell School of Asia Pacific Affairs is Professor Toni Erskine. She is an international relations theorist, specialising in 'the ethics of war', editor of the latest (2016) edition of *International Relations Theory Today*, co-editor of the recent, but highly academically ranked, journal, *International Theory*. Yet, for a director of a prestigious school, she is author of surprisingly few books. Not surprisingly the one she did publish addresses *Embedded Cosmopolitanism: Duties to Strangers and Enemies in a World of 'Dislocated Communities'*. Curiously, for a school devoted to Australia's role in the Asia Pacific, she has never worked or studied in Asia.

This lacuna, however, does not matter for theorists and ethicists of international relations possessing the correct, cosmopolitan and critical ideological tools. In this context, Sydney University benefits from the expertise of another international relations theorist, Professor Colin Wight, editor-in-chief of another recent, academically rated, but little read, journal, *The European Journal of International Relations*. Wight's publications indicate a preoccupation with *Rethinking Terrorism, Dogmatic Anti-Dogmatism* and the evidently 'fragmented culture of international relations theory'. He no doubt finds interaction with the holder of the Michael Hintze Chair of International Relations, James Der Derian. Der Derian applies the nihilistic relativism of French deconstruction of a Foucauldian and Derridian provenance to international relations and offers an anti-diplomatic reading of the 'genealogy' of Western diplomacy. His pathbreaking *International/ Intertextual Politics: Postmodern Readings of World Politics* sets the deconstructive tone for the 1990s. At Melbourne University Senior Executive Provost, Professor Adrian Little, moved from critical studies of Irish politics to pontificate on 'Fear, hope and disappearance in the politics of reconciliation and conflict', *The Politics of Radical Democracy* and 'invisibility and the politics of reconciliation'. Meanwhile, at the University of Queensland, new pro-Vice-Chancellor, Tim Dunne, rose rapidly, from his appointment at the university's UN-approved Centre for the Responsibility to Protect, to the Dean of Humanities, to the commanding heights of the University bureaucracy. He is, he claims, 'internationally recognised for his work on human rights protection and foreign policy-making in a changing world order'. Whilst advancing human rights, diversity and his career, Tim co-edits books on *Human Rights in World Politics* (1999) and *Terror in Our Time* (2012). He works closely with colleagues in the School of Political Science and International Studies to produce 'significant' edited volumes: *The Oxford Handbook of the Responsibility to Protect* (2016), co-edited with Alex Bellamy, and the oxymoronic, *The Globalization of International Society* (2017), co-edited with Christian Reus-Smith, another 'internationally recognised' critical and constructivist theorist.

Managing the leading IR departments across Australia means that the university appointment committees they dominate select only candidates whose work reflects their idealist and progressive world view. Interestingly, their commitment to global norms and social justice does not prevent what amounts to an academic cult controlling and corrupting academic processes of appointment and research grants in order to advance and impose a cultic orthodoxy.

Fixing appointments; manipulating the distribution of large state grants; establishing new 'critical theory' journals that are then ranked highly, but arbitrarily, for promotion and appointment purposes; stacking editorial boards with those who adhere to the correct agenda; and overseeing university or academically ranked book series like the

Cambridge University International Studies Series or Polity Press: these are just a few of the techniques they deploy to identify and promote themselves and their epigone as the leading international relations scholars on the planet.

Appointments throughout Australia now reflect the social justice principles and discursive ethics at the core of the new normativism. Diversity is encouraged in terms of quotas for excluded minorities, but there is no tolerance of diversity for alternative views to the ruling ethical theoretical orthodoxy. It is not insignificant, one suspects, that all the leading players in IR theory can trace their origins to the rather obscure Department of International Relations at the University of Aberystwyth and its more prestigious but equally theoretically driven cousin, the School of International Relations at the London School of Economics. It was from a beachhead established at these institutions in the 1980s, and through student IR journals like *Millennium*, that radical democrats and post-modernists like Anthony Giddens, Steve Smith, Ken Booth David Held and others launched the movement for emancipatory ethics, international theory, global democracy and global justice.

There is, then, something rotten in the study of international relations on the Australian campus. It reflects a wider problem that has haunted the social science and Western liberal democracy since the end of the Cold War. It is the problem of the new liberal or progressive normativism and the ethical ideology posturing as theory that accompanies it. It is at its most perverse in the social sciences and, in particular, in the study of international relations and its *soi disant* critical theorising.

At the core of this project is an understanding that the wealthiest liberal democratic states on the planet at the end of the Cold War were somehow responsible for all the world's problems. Consequently, the campus left, empowered by its access to universal norms of global justice, had the duty both to expose the colonial guilt of the West and establish the campus as the forcing house for a new transnationalism devoted to human rights, emancipation and global justice. How did this remarkable process of ideological capture inimical to traditional values of scholarship and an assault on the Western practice of liberal democratic government occur?

The End of History and the Kantian Moment

In order to reveal the process, it is necessary to examine the way the Cold War ended and how a new normative political philosophy, sometimes termed new liberalism or progressivism, emerged after 1990 from the murky archipelago of the modern university and inform a rationalist third way of governance devoted to multiculturalism at home and social justice abroad.

The problem begins with the idea first promulgated by Francis Fukuyama that history had ended in 1991, and only one ideology prevailed, namely liberal democracy and its commitment to open markets and representative government. As Fukuyama and those who followed this increasingly influential viewpoint in media, business and politics recognised, it required new policies adjusted to the processes of globalisation to address both the wealth creating but socially divisive consequences of globalisation, open markets and open borders. The answer required a new ideology adjusted to what Tony Blair termed 'modernisation' and the third way project. In this context, it should be noted that the Australian campus functions as part of a transnational network devoted to an emancipatory agenda of a normative left and radical democratic devising that first captured the study of international relations in the UK, before transferring a number of its key apparatchiks to the command and control of the Australian universities. The former colony proved wide open for such post-colonial critical colonisation.

The borderless world that globalisation opened up, in fact, offered the opportunity for a new class of radical and progressive thinkers to apply normative, utopian, reflective and critical 'theories' to the conduct of what was now termed, 'world politics'. What did this mean for the progressive project and its assumption of an emancipatory global order instantiating world peace and cosmopolitan citizenship?

Neither Marxism, neo-realism or liberal institutionalism anticipated the way the Soviet Union collapsed. This failure permitted a new preoccupation, not with conventional ideology which had, of course, 'ended,' but with 'theory' or, more precisely, 'theories' of a left and idealist provenance (Lebow and Risse-Kappen 1995) which took their rational and communicative lead from the new cosmopolitan and communitarian liberalism advanced by contemporary political philosophers at the end of the Cold War.

The leading thinkers in this approach to social and eventually global justice that came to dominate political thinking at the end of the Cold War, Jurgen Habermas and John Rawls, had, by the 1990s, already anticipated that their conceptions of ethical transformation and justice as fairness transcended the increasingly redundant nation state. Thus, they now updated and filled in, for contemporary liberal consumption, what Kant's philosophical sketch of a perpetual peace had anticipated in 1784.

By the early 1990s, developments in political theory that reflected a growing normative commitment to the return of grand theory founded upon abstract principles of social justice had swept North American and Anglospheric campuses (see Skinner 1985). It deployed an unhistorical and abstract individualism in the service of a legalist or jurisprudential paradigm of political philosophy. The task of this normative philosophy was conceived as 'one of deriving the ideal constitution-assumed, at least in principle to be everywhere the same' (Gray 1995, 6).

The new transnational normativism traced its development from Immanuel Kant's eschatological hope for universal and perpetual peace, founded on a *foedus pacificum* or league of peace between a confederation of constitutional regimes (Kant [1784] 1970). Central to this understanding is a teleology that assumes a progressive global movement towards a reasonable, rule governed, international order founded on universally agreed norms, rather than the dictates of state interest, culture, power, or pelf.

This hope informed Francis Fukuyama's influential post Cold War treatise, *The End of History and the Last Man*. Fukuyama assumed that ideology ended with the collapse of the Soviet Union. The triumph of open societies and market states meant liberal democracy represented the only sustainable political and economic model for a developing or developed state (Fukuyama 1992). However, although it was the limited, and liberal, market state that created the richest societies on earth, as globalisation evolved, radical democrats, social progressives and normative philosophers questioned the burgeoning inequalities it apparently created. Remarkably, despite the success of the market state, the need to modernise democracy to meet the demands of globalisation, as Tony Blair termed it, required, it seems, a more just, regionally and globally inclusive third way (Friedman 2000, 234). In its most philosophically coherent post Cold War formulation, John Rawls maintained, in *The Law of Peoples* (1999), that any hope we have of reaching this benign historical terminus, or what Rawls considers a 'realistic utopia', rests 'on their being reasonable liberal and constitutional (and decent) regimes sufficiently established and effective to yield a viable Society of Peoples' (Rawls 2002, 30). By such a society, Rawls understood, 'those peoples who follow the ideals and principles of the Law of Peoples in their mutual relations' (Rawls 2002, 3).

In Rawls' scheme the prospect for both global and, more specifically, regional peace and progress requires the projection of a law of peoples, or, more precisely, a norm of justice as fairness into the international order.

As Rawls explained it, recalibrating the international or regional order means 'we must formulate the powers of sovereignty in light of a reasonable Law of Peoples and deny to states the traditional rights to … unrestricted autonomy' (Rawls 2002, 27).

This perspective accorded with a dramatic shift in how 'many would like international law to be understood'. Since 1945, international law had become stricter. It limited a democratic 'state's right to wage war to instances of self defense ... and it also tends to restrict a state's right to internal sovereignty. The role of human rights connects most obviously with the latter change as part of the effort to provide a suitable definition and limit on a government's internal sovereignty' (Rawls 2002, 27).

From the evolving left the apparently successful democratic states of North America and Western Europe suffered from a debilitating moral and political deficit, namely its preoccupation with power and national interest, inimicable to global inclusivity.[3] Whilst Rawls looked to international legal regimes to oversee a just society of peoples, Habermas and his followers envisaged those informed by an awareness gained in uncoerced deliberation through protest groups or in the rapidly expanding numbers of international non-governmental organisations promoting global norms and unmasking the rapacious egoism at the core of contemporary Western political practice. Those who took this ethical perspective seriously were not states, but those emerging social movements, like Greenpeace, Amnesty, or Human Rights Watch, who resisted the Western state and its systems of control to promote values locally and globally that are inclusive of the other, environmentally conscious and aware of the emerging extrapolated networks that offered the basis of a global domestic policy and a 'reconfigured' political power drawing upon the resources of a 'globalised lifeworld' (Habermas 1996, 14).

'There is', Habermas opined sanctimoniously, 'no constitutional state without radical democracy' (Habermas 1996). But radical democracy, like Rawls' law of peoples, required the withering away of the state. Indeed, 'the social and ecological reconstruction of industrial capitalism' required the puncturing of the illusion that such matters can be treated 'from our nationally limited perspectives'.

Radical democracy transcends the nation state and, like Rawls' normative philosophy, considered international legal regimes and

---

[3] Those who advocate some redistributive or post-national condition would include Jurgen Habermas, Thomas Pogge, David Held and Charles Beitz.

multilateral and supranational institutions as the building blocks of an emerging world society. International law and the norms arrived at in internationally inclusive committees extend unproblematically from state to globe as the nation state loses its world historical significance.

Given the lead provided by Habermas and Rawls, it was not surprising that a new generation of academic entrepreneurs saw the study of international relations, as it stood at the end of the Cold War, wide open for radical and progressive critique and the promotion of a developing ideology for the ethical emancipation of world politics.

Post-Cold War international relations 'theory'

The entrepreneurs who opened this exciting new ethical field began their not so long march through academe at the otherwise obscure University of Wales, Aberystwyth. In their highly influential edited volume that shaped the academic study of *International Relations Theory Today* (1995),[4] Steve Smith and Ken Booth announced, ominously, from their Department of International Relations overlooking Cardigan Bay, that 'international politics cannot be a discipline unto itself'. Its 'global perspective' meant it should 'become the subject of all subjects in the social sciences'(Booth and Smith 1995, xii). This endeavour evidently required theory, or, in fact, a bewildering variety of new and 'post positivist' theories, to understand, or, to use the argot of the time, deconstruct and discursively construct this global perspective.

The new international relations theory program reflected and reinforced the left, normativist and transnational mood of the 1990s. It not only redefined the field of study but, over time, excluded any understandings that did not fit with its global, 'emancipatory', ethical and political agenda. Ironically, it sought to turn its version of global justice into a new, post-ideological ideology calibrated to its own grand theoretical agenda. It exposed global politics to a new range of

---
4 Director of the ANU Coral Bell School, Toni Erskine, edits the current (2016) edition.

theoretical possibilities that were no longer rational nor explanatory but, to use the distinctive vocabulary of the new theory, 'critical' and 'constitutive'.

In other words, an ethical approach to international relations promotes an increasingly radical and, what a number of its proponents termed, an 'emancipatory' program for advancing international norms and a global public sphere. This was most particularly evident in the field of critical terror studies that Booth and Smith launched and which presented Islamism, not as an illiberal ideology, but as a form of emancipation and global resistance. Thus, in the first edition of the (now highly ranked for promotion purposes) journal, *Critical Studies on Terrorism* (2008), UNSW ADFA Associate Professor Anthony Burke contended that a critically self-conscious 'normativism' requires the analyst, not only to 'critique' the 'strategic languages of the West,' but also to 'take in' the 'side of the Other' or, more particularly, 'engage' 'with the highly developed forms of thinking' that provide groups like al Qaeda 'with legitimising foundations and a world view of some profundity'.[5]

This new theorising derived and expanded its idealist project from the work already undertaken in normative political philosophy which it now projected onto a global canvas with increasingly negative consequences for the outmoded nation state and the traditional practice of democracy, diplomacy and statecraft. Constitutive and critical 'theory' as opposed to the empirically falsifiable variety, stretched conceptually and promiscuously to embrace a wide variety of left enthusiasms. Sir Steve Smith, whose former colleagues at the University of Wales, Aberystwyth, now dominate the higher echelons

---

5 Burke continues that critical thinking additionally demands a capacity not only to empathise with the 'other,' but also to recognise that both Bin Laden in his *Messages to the West* and Sayyid Qutb in his Muslim Brotherhood manifesto, *Milestones,* not only offer 'well observed' criticisms of Western decadence, but also their ideas 'converge with elements of critical theory' (page 45). This is not surprising given that both Islamist and critical theorist share an analogous contempt for Western democracy, the market, and the international order it inhabits and whose structures it has done much to establish.

of Australian International Relations departments, did much to identify and promulgate them. Smith and his colleague, Ken Booth, averred theory to be no longer empirical or 'positivist', but critical and 'reflexive'. The traditional empirical approach to international relations represented, for Smith and his followers, 'a narrow and particularly political reading of international theory'. Where, Smith wondered, rhetorically, 'is class, ethnicity, or gender in this self-image? Where are the concerns of developing countries to be found in this canon?' The dominant paradigms represented 'a Western/ white/male conservative view of international relations theory' (Smith 1995, 17).

But not if the Smithian model could help it. Post positive theory was to be emancipatory rather than explanatory (Smith 1995, 12). This new, abstract and ideological, rather than theoretical, position reflected debates elsewhere in the social sciences that, in a mood of post modern self-indulgence, permitted alternative theories, or what Smith termed 'self images' of the discipline. Smith identified ten such 'self images' which led him to conclude that theory, instead of being falsifiable, served only as a somewhat arbitrary 'simplifying device that allows you to decide which facts matter and which do not'. The new idealists promoted 'one of the most quoted lines of contemporary International Relations theory', namely that 'theory is always *for* someone and *for* some purpose' (Cox 1981, cited in Bayliss and Smith 2001).

Armed with this Gramscian and deconstructive slogan, the new IR theory began its ideological march through the institutions to achieve its rightful status as the 'master social science discipline'. Its post positivist images of IR theory would reveal, as the seminar series we have discussed earlier indicates, the 'silences, identities and discontinuities submerged within the dominant discourses of international theory' (Booth and Smith 1995, 31).

However, before emancipation and justice could emerge, the Cold War edifices of international relations required deconstruction. A radical scepticism, seeking to deconstruct not only the prevailing scientific understanding that described the world, but their reflection of a dominant and oppressive Western Cold War international practice of knowledge and power, swept away an outmoded rational view of international relations premised on systems, rational choice and behaviourist social science. The new IR theorists, following the nihilistic assault that Lacan, Derrida and Foucault had launched upon liberal humanist epistemology in the 1980s, extended and applied it to exposing the regularities and normalising behaviour that the West practised internationally. Political theory and international theory, it was now assumed, 'presumed each other' and this entailed that the deconstruction of the former also applied to the latter. Those of a deconstructive disposition, like David Campbell, a product of ANU and Johns Hopkins, and James Der Derian, applied radical scepticism to the post Cold War world order and the US's place as its indispensable power. In this deconstructive enterprise, James Der Derian read international relations 'intertextually' (Derian 1992). In a similar vein, David Campbell exposed the discourse of 'danger' at the core US foreign policy and the manner it secured and assured the identity of those on the inside of the liberal world order through the association of threat with those on the outside (Campbell 1992).

These identities discursively imposed by the West thus constituted socially constructed modes of oppression. As feminist theorists pointed out, these identities were framed in gender terms, where effeminacy, as J. Ann Tickner pointed out, applied to the non-Western 'other'. It was no accident that communists were 'pink' (Tickner 1995, 192).

Feminist, like post structural theorists and Habermasian cosmopolitans, naturally 'questioned the boundaries that have locked traditional security analysis into its statist framework' (Tickner 1995, 193). Such radical doubt about conventional liberal democratic claims concerning international order cleared the ground for new dogmatic assertion, revelation and radical critique – in other words, all the ingredients for a new ideological style of thought premised on values rather than material factors like interests. Deconstruction of the international order at the end of the Cold War established the basis for ethical revelation on a global scale and the progressive theories necessary to address, redress and emancipate the post historical global order. Ethical idealism now acquired, at least in theory, high value status in understanding and transforming international relations.

World Community, its justice and its emancipation, increasingly became the dominant preoccupation for a new brand of global democratic theorist/advocates. The key question for the new global liberalism, at the start of the new century, was, Tim Dunne asserted, somewhat incoherently, 'whether it can reinvent itself as a non-universalising, non-Westernising political idea, which preserves the traditional liberal value of human solidarity without undermining cultural diversity' (Dunne 2001, 179). As with normative philosophy more generally, this reinvention perversely overlooked the distinct and contingent historical conditions that facilitated the evolution of a liberal order in the West.

From a more radical perspective, more critical cosmopolitan democratic theories of global citizenship advanced by David Held and Andrew Linklater took their inspiration from Habermas and sought greater forms of emancipatory 'post sovereign governance' which denied that 'the interests of insiders ... took precedence over outsiders'.

Habermas had predicted in 1989 that 'the hollowing out of the sovereignty of the nation state will continue, and requires us to develop capacities for political action on a supranational basis' (Habermas 1996, 168). Indeed, the global tensions generated by 'power pragmatic' nation states like the US would only be overcome if 'large continent wide actors like the EU ... and ASEAN develop into empowered actors capable of reaching transnational agreements ... taking over responsibility for an ever more closely tied transnational network of organisations, conferences and practices'. Only with these types of global players able to form a counterbalance to the liberal democratic state 'would the UN find a base for the implementation of high-minded programs and policies' (Borodori 2003, 40).

Following this agenda cosmopolitanism would extend political community beyond borders to universalise and realise 'a cosmopolitan ethic' (Linklater 1975, 257). This emancipation not only required the transformation of global society, it also envisaged 'the organisation of diversity to achieve rational and humane governance'– utopian realism to create the future required continental or 'global functional organisations to deal with poverty and environmental harm'. The new theorists of world politics regarded 'the individual state' as 'helpless' to address these global problems. 'Reinventing the future', Ken Booth asserted, required the UN Charter to be rewritten to acknowledge the victims of 'traditional theories about world politics and the structures that sustain' them (Booth and Smith 1995, 315).

In a similar but equally influential vein, Alexander Wendt sought to bring together the various normative concerns of the new international relations theory and synthesise them into a grand *Social Theory of International Relations* (1999).

Wendt maintained that constitutive or critical theory showed that 'social kinds like the international system' are processes, rather than things, and 'ideas authored by human beings'. Wendt's idealist sociology recognised that international life depends on what states do 'that anarchy is what states make of it – and that IR should therefore focus on showing how states create that culture and so might transform it'. To give this idealism historical content, Wendt offered a constructivist teleology of how the modern state system evolved. Somewhat eurocentrically, it showed that, since 1945, a Kantian culture of political inclusivity where political authority is internationalised and perceived from a more feminist and relational view of conduct, where 'inter state rivalry' was less gendered, 'less intense and collective action more likely' had appeared.

Projecting Australian political scientist Robert Goodin's normative rationalism into the global sphere, Wendt maintains there can be no turning back from the new 'higher international culture' taking shape. The 'endogenous dynamic' that the Wendtian constructivist edifice reveals is that 'the history of international politics will be unidirectional, [and] if there are any structural changes they will be historically progressive' (Wendt 1999, 312).

Wendt's constructivism, Rawls' society of peoples and Habermas' cosmopolitanism all assume a progress towards a rational, ethical organisation of the globe that Kant first sketched. Global order and global society, the new normativist theorists of International Relations assume, requires the progressive withering away of the nation state and its replacement with transnational and regional authorities. Projecting universal norms into a global community, notable only for its deep cultural pluralism, like the normative political philosophy from which it derived, it dismissed ethnic, religious or nationalist attachments as ultimately redundant. Habermas, Rawls, Wendt and their followers contended, somewhat melodramatically, that the alternative to their 'realistic utopianism', would 'force us to turn away in revulsion' (Kant [1784] 1970, 55) and make us 'wonder whether it is worthwhile for human beings to live on earth' (Rawls 2002, lxii).

New and critical normativism triumphant

This normative and idealist evolution in political philosophy and international relations theory seemed in the 1990s of merely parochial, academic concern. John Gray dismissed it as the conventional wisdom of 'the liberal establishment in North American and British Universities'. The new liberals and their Habermasian interlocutors were, it was argued, reduced 'to talking with each other, and to no one else about topics of interest to no one else, least of all in the political democracies they are supposed to be addressing'. This 'murky academic archipelago' appeared in the 1990s both 'marginal', 'foolish', 'Monty Pythonesque' and manifestly politically irrelevant (Lilla 2001; Barry 2001; Gray 1995).

How wrong was this assessment. By the new millennium this ideological understanding, formed on the Western campus, came to exercise enduring influence over Western liberal progressive politics and public and international policy. Anthony Giddens, perhaps, represented the model for linking progressive theory to public policy, and establishing its otherwise marginal concerns at the core of public and foreign policy. Giddens, in the course of a stellar career through the academic firmament, from the relative obscurity of Hull University to Cambridge, the London School of Economics and the House of Lords, became the emblematic model of the new progressive, academic bureaucrat *persona* wielding public influence.

Those entrepreneurial theorists who trod the bureaucratic academic path that Lord Giddens broke, like Sir Steve Smith, Vice-Chancellor of Essex University and Chair of the Russell Group, or Richard Higgott, former Vice-Chancellor of Murdoch University (2011-14), saw the promotion of a progressive world view not only as a means of silencing those who expressed scepticism regarding the progressive third way agenda, but also of giving a 'voice to the voiceless', promoting cosmopolitan democracy and global justice. Ironically, this leftist thinking and the ideology it promoted was at the expense of the nation states that provided the progressive scholar bureaucracy with their chairs, perquisites and access to very large grants. It helped if, like Giddens and his LSE colleague, David Held, you had your own academically recognised, Cambridge printing press, Polity, to advance the world view.[6]

Thus, despite the fact that the Anglo-Saxon, libertarian, market state unleashed globalisation's economic potential, by the late 1990s, liberal normative thought held that the free market required tempering by 'solidarity in social relations'. The new way with its flexible amalgam of market economics and progressive policy particularly admired enhanced regionalism and global regimes rather than the instrumental, limited, 'withering' nation state.

A *bien pensant* post-Cold War progressive transnational consensus thus emerged in the course of the 1990s. It came to dominate government and political thinking in Europe, Australia and the United

---

6 In 1984 Tony Giddens, together with David Held and John B. Thomson, founded Polity Press in Cambridge where they all taught in 1984. It rapidly established itself as a leading social science publisher. Meanwhile, Sir Steve Smith is editor in chief of the Cambridge University Press Studies in International Relations Series and a number of similarly like-minded theorists like Andrew Linklater and Chris Brown sit on the board.

States for a quarter of a century. It assumed that history ended and the world turned according to a teleological timetable towards a socially just, human rights based, borderless world where globalised economic dynamism would unleash 'creativity and innovation'.

The last phrase appeared in the European manifesto, *Europe: The Third Way-Die Neute Mitte*, that British Prime Minister Tony Blair and German Chancellor Gerhard Schroder issued in 1999. This global, progressive vision went 'beyond left and right'. It also went beyond the nation state.

Hubristic is the epithet that springs to mind to describe the imposition of a leftist rule, or norm-based order that transcended conventional Western party political lines and their traditional vehicle, the nation state. US Democrats such as Bill Clinton, Tony Blair's New Labour, Schroder's SDP and, in Australia, John Howard's Liberal coalition government, all promoted, by various means, global democratic integration, as did their twenty-first century Republican, Conservative and Social Democratic successors: George W. Bush and Barack Obama in America, David Cameron in the United Kingdom, Angela Merkel in Germany and Kevin Rudd and Malcolm Turnbull in Australia.

As Tony Blair's favourite theorist, Anthony Giddens, prognosticated in 1998, that, given developed states were 'without enemies', and large-scale war was 'unlikely, it was no longer utopian to connect issues of national and global governance'. On this basis, the key political issue was how, as Giddens' Polity Press co-founder, David Held, and his Australian followership contended, to embed utopia creating sustainable 'economic improvement' in global markets while not sacrificing the basic cohesion of developed and developing societies. An evolving elite in the mainstream media, business, finance, and government, as well as academe, where liberals of various hues combined with a species of cultural Marxism and 'radical democracy', disseminated a progressive worldview for a borderless twenty-first century world.

It viewed 'cosmopolitan pluralism' and 'democratising democracy' as means of 'responding structurally to globalisation' (Giddens 1998, 67). Cosmopolitan democracy, as identified in the new normative philosophy and emancipatory international relations theory, unlike the traditional political variety, welcomed the diminution and fragmentation of state sovereignty and the replacement of the nation, with an oxymoronic 'cosmopolitan nation in a cosmopolitan democracy operating on a global scale'. It offered the progressive prospect of 'the movement of governance to a world level and diffusion downward to the local level'.

Global democracy could only be 'sustained by ensuring the accountability of all interrelated and connected power systems'. In the new progressivism, the people, like themselves, 'enjoy multiple citizenships ... They would be citizens of their immediate political communities and of the wider regional and global networks which impacted upon their lives'. This borderless cosmopolitan polity would somehow reflect and embrace the 'diverse forms of power and authority that operate within and across borders'.

As Ralf Dahrendorf observed at the time, there was already something 'slightly contrived almost elitist about a concept' which attracted attention through 'evangelistic methods of communication'. Third way thought, Dahrendorf contended, deflected all criticism by an amalgam of spin, diffidence and dogmatism that reflected its cool, but now increasingly uncool, global elitism (Dahrendorf 1999).

Although this process has been in train since at least the early 1990s, only now and in the wake of the populist explosion across the West has it come to the belated attention of a Western commentariat just how ideologically and utopia-fixated the study of politics in general, and international politics in particular, has become.

As Giddens and others showed, the third way thinking enabled radicals of various hues to promote their critical views on campus and advocate them as public policy. In the humanities and social sciences they took hold, and it is difficult now to find a course in the humanities or social sciences that is not infected with this particular plague. But it is in the study of international relations where the plague reached epidemic proportions and has affected, not for the better, the discipline of political science.

How liberal fascism ends

H.G. Wells, a dead white male, not much studied on campus these days, was, in his day, the most energetic intellectual advocate of totalitarianism on the early 20th century British left. He told the Oxford Union in 1932: 'I am asking for a Liberal Fascisti for enlightened Nazis. The world is sick of parliamentary democracy. The Fascist party is Italy. The Communist is Russia. The Fascists of liberalism must carry out a parallel ambition on a far grander scale' (cited in Goldberg 2008, 27).

It took six decades, and the collapse of both Fascism and Communism – Wells drew no distinction between them – for his vision to come to fruition. Its forcing house was the university campus and its idealist commitment to global justice and world community which became an enduring academic preoccupation, especially after 2001.

Although Wells had advocated liberal *fascisti* at the Oxford Union, only at the end of the Second World War did he see its potential to evolve into an all consuming vision for the future organisation of the world. The university campus served as the engine for the dissemination of this ideology at the end of ideology and, in the process, has not only contributed to the meltdown of the campus but to what many now consider the suicide of the West (Goldberg 2017).

References

Barry, Brian, *Culture and Equality: an Egalitarian Critique of Multiculturalism*, Cambridge, Polity, 2001.

Bayliss, John and Steve Smith (eds), *The Globalization of World Politics. An Introduction to International Relations*, Oxford University Press, Oxford, 2001.

Booth, Ken & Steve Smith (eds), *International Relations Theory Today*, Polity Press, Cambridge, 1995.

Borodori Giovanna, *Philosophy in a Time of Terror. Dialogues with Jurgen Habermas and Jacques Derrida*, University of Chicago Press, Chicago, 2003.

Burke, A., *Critical Studies on Terrorism*, May 2008, 1(1).

Campbell, David, *Writing Security United States Foreign Policy and the Politics of Identity*, Minneapolis, University of Minnesota Press, 1992.

Cox, Robert, 'Social Forces, States and World Orders: Beyond International Relations Theory', *Journal of International Studies*,10(2), 1981.

Dahrendorf, Ralf, 'The third way and liberty, an authoritarian streak in Europe's new charter', *Foreign Affairs*, 78(5), 1999.

Derian, James Der, *Anti-Diplomacy: Spies, Terror, Speed and War*, Oxford, Blackwell, 1992.

Dunne, Tim, 'Liberalism', in John Bayliss and Steve Smith (eds), *The Globalization of World Politics: An Introduction to International Relations*, Oxford, Oxford University Press, 2001.

Friedman, Thomas, *The Lexus and the Olive Tree*, Harper Collins, London, 2000.

Fukuyama, Francis *The End of History and the Last Man*, Penguin, London, 1992.

Giddens, Anthony, *The Third Way: The Renewal of Social Democracy*, Polity Press, Cambridge, 1998.

Goldberg, Jonah, *Liberal Fascism: the Secret History of the American Left from Mussolini to the Politics of Meaning*, Doubleday, New York, 2008, 27.

Goldberg, Jonah, *The Suicide of the West,* Doubleday, New York, 2017.

Goodin, Robert and Phillip Pettit (eds), *The Cambridge Companion to Political Philosophy*, Blackwell, Oxford, 1993.

Gray, John, *Enlightenment's Wake*, Routledge, London, 1995.

Habermas, Jurgen, *Between Facts and Norms,* Polity Press, Cambridge, 1996.

Habermas, Jurgen*, Berlin Republic: Writings on Germany,* Polity Press, Cambridge, 1998.

Harries, Owen, 'A Tribute to Coral Bell', *The Spectator,* 6 October 2012.

Kant, Immanuel, 'Perpetual Peace' in H. Reiss (ed.), *Kant's Political Writings,* Cambridge University Press, Cambridge, [1784] 1970.

Kant, Immanuel, 'Idea for a Universal History' in H. Reiss (ed.), *Kant's Political Writings*, Cambridge University Press, Cambridge, [1784] 1970.

Lebow, Richard Ned & Thomas Risse-Kappen (eds), *International Relations Theory and the End of the Cold War*, Columbia University Press, New York, 1995.

Lilla, Mark, 'The Reckless Mind Intellectuals in Politics', *New York Review of Books*, New York, 2001.

Linklater, Andrew, 'Neo Realism in Theory and Practice', in Booth and Smith (eds), *International Relations Theory Today*, Polity Press, Cambridge, 1995.

Mendietta, Eduardo, 'America and the World: A Conversation with Jurgen Habermas', www.logosjournal.com/habermas_america.htm 2004.

Rawls, John, *Political Liberalism*, Columbia University Press, New York, 1993.

Rawls, John, *The Law of Peoples,* Harvard University Press, London, 2002.

Skinner, Quentin, 'Introduction' in Skinner (ed.), *The Return of Grand Theory in the Human Sciences*, Cambridge University Press, Cambridge, 1985.

Smith, Steve, 'The Self-Images of a Discipline: A Genealogy of International Relations Theory', in Booth and Smith (eds), *International Relations Theory Today*, Polity Press, Cambridge, 1995.

Tickner, J. Ann, 'Revisioning Society' in Booth and Smith (eds), *International Relations Theory Today*, Polity Press, Cambridge, 1995.

Wendt, Alexander, *Social Theory of International Politics*, Cambridge Studies in International Relations, Cambridge University Press, Cambridge, 1999.

6
'And Gladly Teach'[1]
The Destruction of the University Teaching Culture on the Contemporary Australian Campus

Barry Spurr

When you consider the salient characteristics of the genuine and worthwhile teaching and learning experience of a distinctively 'university' kind, you can clearly perceive what a scandalous falling-away there has been from this ideal in the modern Australian university. A forty-year teaching career which began in 1974 as a Teaching Fellow and culminated in my appointment in 2011 as Australia's first Professor of Poetry is the background and experience I bring to the description and assessment of this phenomenon. What was, in fact, a long decline began to be most sharply evident from about 1990, when the impact of the campus revolutions of a generation before started to make its influence very apparent.

A university education: you know it when you see it

Any explanation of this lamentable situation must take into account the principles and practices that were once regarded as essential to the formation of the university-educated man or woman. Writing in *The Spectator*, Declan Mansfield has given a succinct summary of the characteristic outcomes of that education:

> ... a broadness of mind, an openness to the world, an understanding of what underpins the study of history or philosophy or art; it's knowing that some questions have

---

[1] Of 'a Clerk from Oxford', Geoffrey Chaucer writes (in the General Prologue to *The Canterbury Tales*) that 'gladly would he learn and gladly teach' (l. 310).

many answers and the obvious answer may not be the right one. It's giving an opponent the benefit of the doubt when they make a valid argument — and knowing when someone is talking nonsense. Education is hard to define but you know it when you see it. You also know it when you don't see it. What it is not, though, is knowing how to *do* something. It's knowing how to *think* (Mansfield 2018).

At the core of a university education should be the principle of freedom of expression. In 'Of the Liberty of Thought and Discussion', John Stuart Mill explains the reasoning behind this ideal:

> If all mankind minus one, were of one opinion, and only one person were of the contrary opinion, mankind would be no more justified in silencing that one person, than he, if he had the power, would be justified in silencing mankind.... But the peculiar evil of silencing the expression of an opinion is, that it is robbing the human race; posterity as well as the existing generation; those who dissent from the opinion, still more than those who hold it. If the opinion is right, they are deprived of the opportunity of exchanging error for truth: if wrong, they lose, what is almost as great a benefit, the clearer perception and livelier impression of truth, produced by its collision with error.

More recently, George Steiner, in his 'Universitas' Lecture in 2013, described this principle as being of the essence of a university true to its mission:

> A true university serves neither political purposes nor social programmes, necessarily partisan and transitory. Above all, it rebukes censorship and correctness of any kind.... And it should honour anarchic provocation.

Students who come to the university with their minds made up will not be ready to take from that valuable education what it most beneficially has to offer. And academics who are themselves determined to bring students into lock-stepped conformity with their ideological convictions are similarly depriving those students of what a university education at its best is meant to achieve – effectively sabotaging education with instruction and indoctrination, instead of opening and broadening students' minds to all possibilities of thought and opinion, of claim and counter-claim, and encouraging them carefully and intelligently to weigh and assess any and every hypothesis.[2]

The last place one would once have expected to find such rigidity – and whose very name contradicts such a mental straitjacket – was the university. The last place, one would have supposed, where 'safety first' would be the mantra governing (and, thereby, fatally inhibiting) the expression of ideas – lest anyone should be disturbed or offended by an opinion contrary to their own, or to a new idea, or to an awkward thought, or to a challenging of the 'correct' notions of the *Zeitgeist* – was the university. Writing of his undergraduate experience at Oxford in the 1960s, David Combie recalled:

> None of us ever expected (or wanted) University to be a 'safe place'. It was scary and challenging – *that's what we were there for*. We were often shocked by the views of others but always tried to establish the genesis and rationale behind those views (Combie 2015-6, 149).[3]

As Richard Dawkins has pithily observed, in 'Don't be so offensive':

> a university is not a 'safe space'. If you need a safe space, leave, go home, hug your teddy & suck your thumb until ready for university (cited in *The Economist* 2016).

The true university as an intellectual test

Formerly, university study was students' introduction to an adult world of rigorous debate and robust discussion, the gold standard *rite*

---

2 Bertrand Russell ([1935] 2004, 133,) warning of 'modern homogeneity', spoke of the dangers of 'uniformity in matters of thought and opinion'.
3 My emphasis.

de passage to intellectual maturity. Not so today. Universities invite *parents* to Orientation Week, their vice-chancellors addressing such gatherings with repeated references to the 'children' (yes, 'children') who have come into their care, and how they will be looked after by the university. This deplorable mindset would degrade these young adults' experience of higher education into a crèche, where no-one should be mentally discomforted. A wit succinctly summed up the position recently:

1944: 18 year olds storm the beaches of Normandy, facing almost certain death.

2016: 18 year olds need a safe place where words will not hurt their feelings.

Novelist Richard Flanagan, commenting on the exclusion of former NSW Premier Bob Carr and Germaine Greer from the 2018 Brisbane Writers Festival because their views might offend somebody, has said that it 'takes courage to listen to different ideas'. *Corragio*! Matters have come to a strange pass, indeed, where you are deemed courageous if you are prepared to be exposed to an opinion that diverges from your own. But bravery is certainly required if you would dare to propose and express a counter-cultural argument at such events, committing thereby a Thoughtcrime (in Orwellian terminology). 'Who would have thought', Flanagan asks, 'it would have been writers' festivals that would now act against such freedom?'

Exactly the same rhetorical question can be posed of today's universities. In August, 2018, Bettina Arndt, a well-credentialled psychologist, author and social commentator, was scheduled to give an address at La Trobe University, in which it was anticipated that she would critique an Australian Human Rights Commission report that 'alleged sexual harassment was endemic to Australian campuses', offering a scrutiny of the presented facts and her analysis of them, encouraging discussion and debate – a process, once, that was the heart and soul of the mission of a university. 'Administrators' banned her attendance. In response to this, Arndt commented: 'I think it is appalling that universities, our centres of higher learning, are conspiring with feminists to lie about the research, frighten young women and demonise male students'. What is astonishing about this is that Arndt was astonished. On the contrary, it was exactly what one would expect of the contemporary Australian university: toe the party line, or you will be silenced. A *Daily Telegraph* headline coined a new word, in the context of the Arndt brouhaha, that deserves wide currency:

> 'How a monoversity tried to shut up Bettina Arndt.'[4]

In the free-thought-stultifying environment that universities have become, where, instead of being exposed to and tussling with potentially dangerous ideas, students need to be protected from them by Nanny Vice-Chancellors, the highest accolade for a lecturer is not that he or she is intellectually demanding or confronting, but 'supportive', like a truss.

Recalling the Cambridge English Tripos in the 1930s, distinguished Shakespearean scholar, Professor Muriel Bradbrook, noted that 'there was a general feeling that a student ought to have his wits stretched. We were not very charitable to fools' (cited in Haffenden 2005, 176). The same phrase was used in this year's obituary for Professor Eric Stanley, the Rawlinson and Bosworth Professor of Anglo-Saxon at Oxford from 1977 to 1991:

> Stanley did not suffer fools. A student who neglected his studies might be told that 'your indifference to your own success is exceeded only by mine'. But the more assiduous ... came back after an hour or so filled with knowledge, a sceptical attitude to cherished theories, and an extensive list of references (*Telegraph*, 2018).

'Supportive' in the modern sense? No way.

---

4 In the face of criticism of their actions, La Trobe reversed its decision, but issued this statement: 'The university has said it will cover the cost of any counselling required if students who attend the talk are upset by its content'.

In my memoir of my own experience of Australian university life, currently in preparation, I recount my first day in English I at Sydney University, in 1970. As a fresher, and with the university term swinging into action, I began attending classes – lectures and tutorials – in English, Philosophy and Ancient History. My first lecture in English, in the cavernous Wallace Theatre, was a momentous occasion. It was scheduled to be on William Blake's poetry, his *Songs of Innocence and Experience*. I had never heard of either the poet or these works or, indeed, of any of his poetry – even 'Jerusalem' was unknown to me then. We had never sung it at school or church. As I took my seat, surrounded by hundreds of others and (having come from Canberra) knowing nobody, I wondered how I would fare among these men and women, so many of whom seemed far more confident than I, and most of whom seemed to be in happy groups of friends or in the process of making them. Then a hush fell on the theatre, as a statuesque middle-aged woman, with a flowing black gown, over a yellow and white dress, mounted the podium and made her way to the lectern. She gave no greeting (there was no 'Hi, I'm Leonie and I want to support you', with contact details), but opened her book of Blake's poems and began to read in a beautifully modulated voice from the beginning of 'The Marriage of Heaven and Hell':

> The Prophets Isaiah and Ezekiel dined with me, and I asked them how they dared so roundly to assert, that God spoke to them; and whether they did not think at the time, that they would be misunderstood, & so be the cause of imposition. Isaiah answer'd, I saw no God, nor heard any, in a finite organical perception; but my senses discover'd the infinite in every thing, and as I was then persuaded, & remain confirm'd; that the voice of honest indignation is the voice of God, I cared not for consequences but wrote.

I sat there stunned. Perhaps others were stunned too, but I cared not a jot for them. I was, as the phrase goes, blown away. Then, Leonie Kramer (later, Dame Leonie), Professor of Australian Literature, began to unfold the mysteries of Blake's thought and how it was conveyed in both his prophetic books, such as this, and in the much simpler (although not simple) lyrics of the Songs, set for our study.

This was what I had come to university for, and I was not disappointed. No concession was made to ignorance or subliteracy. I did not feel 'safe' – far from it, and it would have been the last thing I would have wanted to be, nor would it have been in any way good for me, let alone my intellectual development (which, *mirabile dictu*, was the reason I came to the university in the first place). I was being properly challenged and confronted; taken out of my too-comfortable comfort zone of school success; made (most importantly) patently aware of my almost total and profound ignorance, and introduced to a great poet, and stirred, thereby, to do something about my gross inadequacy. I was being initiated (through the dignified deportment, elegant articulation and brilliance of this lecturer, who understood that a lecture should be a polished performance, and who was an adult speaking respectfully to other adults, but without any faux-egalitarianism that would have been ludicrous under the circumstances) into what, once, was regarded as the university culture. That is, a grown-up world (not a nursery misconducted by nurturing nannies for fragile victims, ripe for indoctrination) that brought appropriate seriousness and high learning to complex intellectual concepts for the attention and stimulation of students capable of absorbing such material.

To the extent that such university teachers of the 'old school' were supportive, their support consisted not in cossetting students, ensuring that they were feeling comfortable and reassured, let alone 'safe'. They promptly and directly called out laziness, sloppy thinking, careless expression and – most importantly – un-argued and ignorant assertion. The contemporary tedious (and, needless to say, entirely humourless and utterly predictable) trotting-out of approved responses to texts, historical periods and other phenomena in lockstep with race, gender and class orthodoxy (for example) would have astonished as much as it would have dismayed them.

The implications of the modern universities' walking-on-eggshells culture, where the catalogue of taboo subjects is ever-increasing in a stifling environment of censorship, for a vigorous and rigorous teaching and learning experience are as obvious as they are devastating. In such a domain of circumscribed thought, one is always second-guessing what one is about to say, in case someone might be upset or be turned into some sort of victim by the mere expression of an opinion or idea, even by a witticism or an ironic aside, and not feel 'affirmed' or 'included', as the list of the potentially offended continues to ramify. So either complicity or silence becomes the preferred option. This wariness of offence being taken, even when none was intended, now prevails in the society at large, as we have allowed ourselves to submit to the perpetual surveillance of the Thought Gestapo; but that it should have permeated the academy is shocking to anyone who believes in freedom of thought and expression and the university as the forum for teaching and learning where all ideas and opinions, however eccentric or anarchic (as Steiner puts it), may be respectfully tested and where careless thought and platitudinous, sub-standard expressions of it need to be called out.

These constraints on the common pursuit of truth (the essential business of a university) are most evident in the Humanities faculties, historically and traditionally seen to be at the core of university life. Challenge dominant campus ideologies and you will suffer the consequences. As numerous academics have found, who have spoken out-of-turn on such matters, even in whimsy or in private, the punishments can be dire – career- and life-destroying. The shaming brigades patrol the Australian university campus, roaming about, in the words of Scripture, seeking whom they may devour.[5]

A notorious example of this phenomenon was the case of Professor Sir Tim Hunt, Nobel Laureate, of University College, London, who made a mildly humorous self-deprecating reference to women in laboratories at a luncheon address to female scientists at the World Conference of Science Journalists in South Korea in 2015:

> It's strange that such a chauvinist monster like me has been

---

5 1 Peter 5:8.

asked to speak to women scientists. Let me tell you about my trouble with girls. Three things happen when they are in the lab: you fall in love with them, they fall in love with you, and when you criticise them they cry. Perhaps we should make separate labs for boys and girls? Now, seriously, I'm impressed by the economic development of Korea. And women scientists played, without doubt an important role in it. Science needs women, and you should do science, despite all the obstacles, and despite monsters like me.[6]

For this jokey interlude, he was subjected to a global shaming as 'sexist' on a scale that would have been surprising had he been a convicted child molester or serial murderer. He had, in fact, broken no law and had harmed nobody. Within 48 hours, he was forced to resign from his professorial appointment and from the Royal Society (of which, of course, as a world-renowned scientist, he was a Fellow). The most shocking aspect of this lynching frenzy was that Hunt received no support from his university (which told him that he must either resign or be sacked) or his cowed and cowardly colleagues there, who – to affirm their politically-correct credentials – either remained silent or joined the baying crowd of his accusers. If anyone has any doubts about what has happened to universities in recent times, a consideration of the case of Sir Tim Hunt should dispel any lingering uncertainty.

The vital minority

Next, in the destruction of the campus culture of teaching and learning, is the issue of the growth and proliferation of Australian universities over the last half century, driven by the ludicrous aspiration that everybody should go to university, deriving, in turn, from the preposterous idea that everyone is equally suited to university study. Declan Mansfield notes:

---

6 See under 'Personal': https://en.wikipedia.org/wiki/Tim_Hunt (accessed 11 October 2018).

The idea of equality is the root cause of the problem. Our educational establishment has not understood this lesson. It has tried, through social engineering, to overturn the idea that there are innate cognitive differences between people. In other words, self-esteem trumps ability. One way this has been achieved is by changing vocational courses into tertiary courses. The results have been disastrous. Encouragement is good. But overstating someone's abilities is as evil as understating them (Mansfield 2018).

'Everybody has won and all must have prizes', as Lewis Carroll's Dodo has it, in Alice's topsy-turvy world, producing (Mansfield continues)

> a generation of graduates who have studied subjects that should never be taught at university level…. By teaching vocational subjects at university we've lowered the standards of tertiary education without lowering the idea of what a degree represents…. Instead of an educated elite we have a mass of delusional people who falsely believe they are educated.

In the real world, education is for the educable (that is, virtually everyone, up to a certain point); but higher education is for the highly educable, always a small minority of the population.

The source of this ill-conceived ideologically-driven project, which has had a devastating roll-on effect on the quality of university teaching and learning, was the conviction – which, for example, drove the New South Wales Wyndham scheme of the early 1960s – that it would be to everyone's advantage, including the nation's, if all pupils stayed on at school for twelve years to matriculation level. In the previous decade, university places in Britain, for example, 'were available for only about five per cent of the relevant age group in the population'(Lodge 2015, 124) – which was probably about right, in terms of ability and aptitude for university study, and much the same figure would have applied in Australia. Nobody stopped to think that by urging everyone on to the matriculation year at the end of high school and then on further to higher education, proclaiming the progressive doctrine that this was raising the opportunities of education for everyone and producing a Clever Country, that what in fact would happen, has palpably occurred: the standards have had to be lowered, at all levels, so everybody can be included and graduated.

By the end of the twentieth century, students who could scarcely read and write, and for whom ordinary arithmetical processes were utterly beyond their reach, were going on to 'you-nee', as if it were an automatic, inevitable process in their life's journey. And this was in the context of a demonstrably worsening level of attainment in such as the 2018 NAPLAN results, reported as the 'worst ever' in the field of writing:

> This year, a staggering 16.5% of Year 9 students across Australia were below benchmark in writing.... Not only are the numbers of low-performing students increasing, but the inverse is occurring for our high-achieving students: their numbers decrease as they move through school (Adiniou 2017).

And on to university. Students with ATARS between 0 and 20 (it was reported in September, 2018) were being admitted to teaching degrees by universities, which tried to suppress this scandalous information.[7]

Ad nauseam, educationalists and politicians gleefully refer to the vast increase of undergraduate numbers, as if they amounted to a notable triumph, without ever pausing to consider the destruction of the quality of school and university education in this process of fauxegalitarianism and the disposal of a meritocracy. No consideration was ever given, either, to another of its damaging consequences: how those who are intellectually able to profit from what was once regarded

---

[7] Had this been in medicine, there would have been a national outcry. But as it was 'only' for teaching and merely concerned education, there was scarcely a ripple of protest.

as matriculation-standard work at school, had to be held back so everybody could keep up (including, in many cases, the teachers themselves). Then, at university, those brainy enough to be worthy of it continued to be grossly disadvantaged by having to submit to the watered-down curricula that were dished up and to risible assessment processes and debased standards (of student participation and discussion, for example, in so-called seminars) so that nobody would be the victim of the dreaded elitism or feel excluded – for which, read the requirement of a decent standard of quality of work, performance and commitment at the genuinely tertiary level.

The nadir of the Wyndham scheme was reached in July 2016, when the NSW Minister for Education, Adrian Piccoli, appeared on television to announce that 'basic literacy and numeracy tests' would be introduced and mandated for all students aspiring to gain the HSC qualification. 'Basic literacy and numeracy'!

In 2017, it was reported – in 'shock-horror' mode – that one in three university students dropped out before completing their degree, and at some of the nation's universities, less than 50% of enrolled students went on to graduation. When you consider that fewer than four out of five students at universities today should be there in the first place, that one of three should be dropping out is utterly unremarkable – indeed, it was a surprising figure for the opposite reason to what the reports were suggesting: namely, that so *few* are drop-outs.

Accompanying these dismal statistics are reports of the sharp decline in the number of students signing up for disciplines which have been most damaged by the trends in education at large and which have been destroying the universities for more than a generation. In his study of the discipline of Modern History, Keith Windschuttle (in the aptly-titled, *The Killing of History: How Literary Critics and Social Theorists are Murdering our Past*) compares the period when the subject was at its healthiest 'until the end of the 1960s', to 'its worst decline' of the twentieth century in the 1990s. He places the blame squarely at the feet of 'postmodern theory and identity group politics'. Unsurprisingly, with these influences in the ascendant, 'young people are abandoning [History] in droves... the reversal has become a rout'. In America, the proportion of high school students studying the subject has declined from two-thirds in the 1960s to less than 20% by the 1990s, even though these were the decades which witnessed 'a period of great increase in overall college enrolments and degrees awarded'. Necessarily accompanying this unprecedented fall-off in demand has been the shrinking of History departments, with even the 'once most prestigious being reduced by half' (Windschuttle 1996, 315-16).

The same, unsurprisingly, is happening in English and for the same reasons. As William Deresiewicz noted of US colleges some years ago, 'the number of students studying English literature appears to be in a steep, prolonged and apparently irreversible decline' (Deresiewicz 2008). As philosopher David Stove reflected a generation ago:

> So far as there still survives anything of value from the Western tradition of humanistic studies, it is in spite of most of the people in the universities who are the heirs of that tradition (Stove 1986).

But this astonishing calamity is, in fact, a blessing disguised as a disaster. The only hope for the revival of those humanistic disciplines (and, thereby, of the true idea of the university) is for them, in their present degraded form, to die out completely. And it is happening at speed. They are already corpses in decomposition. Then, reconstituted versions and the recovery of the disciplines and of the university at large may emerge from the ruins.

Students who do not study

Then, there is the issue of attendance – or, as it should more appropriately be termed, non-attendance – which is linked, principally, to matters of students' extra-mural employment and aided and abetted by the disastrous implementation of the mandated recording of lectures for supposed subsequent on-line access by students. No single innovation by university authorities in recent times has so devastated the quality of teaching and learning on campus. This widespread phenomenon is the most obvious sign of how the university teaching and learning environment has succumbed to the general meltdown of universities and of their quality and standards in our time. Before this policy took over, students attended university, several times a week in term. They went to lectures and seminars and tutorials – where they actually spoke to their teachers and fellow students and shared ideas, in person – and, in between those commitments, had time to join campus groups and societies, where they met further students, often with the valuable enrichment of encountering students in other and diverse disciplines and sharing and debating ideas with them, and, generally, enjoyed and derived much, intellectually and personally, from the experience of being full-time 'at university' over three or more years. In one fell and foul swoop, the recording of lectures has destroyed that rich and humane culture. The situation may now easily be envisaged where a student could do their whole degree without ever attending the campus at all, never meeting or interacting with a lecturer in person or another student, or simply bumping into someone with whom to have a conversation about a lecture they had just attended or a book they were reading. It is indicative of the perverse topsy-turvy looking-glass-land into which universities have transformed themselves that this disaster is touted as a wondrous triumph by vice-chancellors and their minions and of inestimable value to students.

The recording of lectures has enabled students to take on all-but-full-time jobs, as they fancy they can catch up with their university work after they have finished their money-earning employment. One Arts student I knew in recent years had no less than three jobs; one of them requiring his attendance for three full working days a week. Consequently, he chose his subjects (and his rare attendance at university that followed from the choice) on the basis of the days that the classes were timetabled. Any material that he missed was recorded on-line. By the end of his degree, he had come to rely on the recorded material almost entirely. An intelligent and outgoing young man, with the capacity to develop a range of interests and to have his narrow intellectual outlook broadened and deepened, he joined no university clubs or societies, made no contribution to campus life and simply rushed in and out of class to this or that work commitment. He was, in effect, a full-time student living (at best) a part-time student's life.

The principal justification for the recording of lectures and of students' consequent non-attendance on campus for the purpose of paid employment is that they are in a state of dire poverty and, so, whatever demands universities would make on them must accommodate their need to go to work while they are studying. Instructively, this consideration does not apply at the world's leading universities, such as Oxford and Cambridge, where, even if the possibility of those towns affording the student population sufficient part-time work existed, all students are expected to be – literally – full-time members of the university and physically present there. What an antiquated idea! A report issued in August 2018 claimed that many Australian university students were suffering severe financial hardship. This suggests – as do so many other elements of the dysfunctional campus today – that the entire system is crying out for a complete review and reform. The band-aid solution of making university study a second-rate, on-line experience – which would be unthinkable at the best universities – is no solution if teaching and learning at the highest standard is to be pursued.

While the quality of lecturing on campuses varies widely (as it always has, and even at the most prestigious institutions) from the brilliant to the risibly incompetent, and much of it is mediocre, the recording of lectures is not only going to worsen the bad elements of that situation, as without a visible audience to react to and engage – which any lecturer, worth his or her salt, is determined to achieve – the most obvious incentive to perform well is taken away; but, much worse, and scandalously so, with regard to excellence in teaching and learning on campus (which university bigwigs perpetually profess to be committed to) is the denial, by those very authorities, of the experience by students of the brilliant, memorable, passionate and inspiring – even life-changing – lecture performance, such as Leonie

Kramer's, described above. Nothing can replace that; certainly not an audio recording. Others' memories of wonderful university lecturers abound. Recollections of Charles Williams, poet, novelist and literary and theological scholar, who lectured in the English Faculty at Oxford during the Second World War, recall his genius for engaging, challenging and inspiring his student audience. C.S. Lewis (not prone to hyperbole) went to hear Williams, his colleague (and fellow Inkling) in the Faculty on several occasions when he lectured. Lewis noted that Williams delivered 'without a single note a perfectly coherent and impassioned meditation, variegated with quotations in his incantatory manner'. It was 'a most wonderful performance and impressed his audience very much' (Lindop 2015, 314). Routinely, Lewis observed, Williams's lecture audiences would leave the hall 'at the end of the hour, bubbling with suppressed amusement, puzzlement, and enthusiasm, and eager for debate, many felt keen to come back for more':

> It was a beautiful sight to see a whole room full of modern young men and women sitting in that absolute silence which cannot be faked, very puzzled, but spellbound… he forced them to lap it up and I think many, by the end, liked the taste more than they expected to (Lindop 2015, 319-20).

Williams's biographer notes that Williams 'never lowered his level to suit the audience, but it didn't matter. His sincerity and enthusiasm carried people along. His prodigious memory for poetry made his recitation fluent and hypnotic, and he spoke every word as if straight from the heart':

> He could command a room, hold attention, and transform the atmosphere (Lindop 2015, 90).

As any good lecturer will, and no recorded lecture ever could. Leaving one of these memorable occasions, Lewis declared:

> I have at last seen a university doing what it was founded to do (Lindop 2015, 320).

What 'beautiful sight' of the bubbling and babbling enthusiasm of young people, leaving together, eager for debate after a stimulating lecture and the collectively generated excitement at the prospect of the next lecture, could the recorded lecture replicate, as the student sits alone at home, listening to a disembodied voice on his or her computer? Or selectively tuning in to the recordings as they juggle that commitment with their increasingly demanding extra-mural work requirements. Like Matthew Arnold's crowned Philistine, Henry VIII, at the dissolution of the monasteries, today's vice-chancellors have emptied the lecture theatres and silenced the classrooms, recalling Shakespeare's 'bare ruin'd choirs, where late the sweet birds sang'.[8] This is a university being precisely what it was *not* founded to be.

The student as customer

Next, the idea that senior university administrators now have of themselves as akin to CEOs in the corporate world has spawned the debased conception of students as customers consuming goods and services. With such a mindset firmly in place, the degrading principles of the service economy – for example, that the customer is always right – follow inevitably. Again, the impact on teaching and learning could not be more devastating. Instead of students conceiving of themselves as participants and collaborators in learning – in what T.S. Eliot called 'the common pursuit of true judgement'[9] – they have now been reduced to passive recipients of a product which, furthermore, most be so tailored as to conform to their personal expectations of satisfaction (including the demand for recorded lectures). If the product is not to their liking or not perfectly adapted to their needs, prejudices and expectations, then they will wreak vengeance in such as student evaluations of courses and on their teachers (who are increasingly under pressure to teach 'to' those evaluations, to secure permanency or promotion) or simply not enrol in this or that course or degree

---

8 Sonnet LXXIII.
9 'The Function of Criticism', http://tseliot.com/prose/the-function-of-criticism (accessed 20 September 2018).

because of its 'bad' reputation for placing what were once regarded as appropriately stringent demands on tertiary students (in terms of attendance, preparatory reading and research, class participation, closed-book examinations and so forth). Thus, as in so many of the absurd aspects of university life now, the student tail wags the campus dog. David James, in 'Academics tangle with managerial oppressors', arguing that 'the imposition of what is termed "managerialism" or "marketisation" ' on universities has been a disaster, points out that

> students are not consumers, because the relationship between them and the teacher is the opposite of that between a consumer and a business provider. In a business transaction, value is determined by the consumer, the receiver: will they pay for the product or not? The business may be able to use various methods to influence the perception of value, but in the end the buyer decides.
>
> With education, it is the opposite. Value is necessarily determined by the provider, teacher. The teacher knows what needs to be learned and the student does not. To say that a student is a consumer is to misunderstand what a student is (James 2018).

Academics without an academy

In this litany of problems that have so damaged our universities, and particularly the quality of teaching and learning within them, the final one I would mention (in this by-no-means exhaustive list) is the issue of the increasing casualisation of academic staff. Colin Long describes the phenomenon as nothing less than 'a national disgrace':

> The universities' exploitation of casual and fixed-term staff is an affront to academia, undermining academic freedom (who will express difficult opinions or explore controversial research directions if there is nothing to protect one from having one's employment terminated?)

The extent of casualisation in the Australian university system is breathtaking, as Long notes:

> fully half of undergraduate teaching is performed by casual staff, many of whom need multiple jobs to survive ...

and at the University of Wollongong, for example, 71% of the staff are casual (Long 2018) . With the Damocles' sword of non-renewal of a casual teaching contract poised over staff members' heads, compliance with the party line in all matters can be assured, with the pursuit of what Long describes as 'difficult' and 'controversial' topics and approaches being very ill-advised. Additionally, what he does not mention is that the erosion of the concept of sustained appointment of an academic staff member means that the long-term development of a teacher's skills, nurtured through decades of experience, is thwarted; and, with that, the developing familiarity that a student might have with a particular scholar-teacher-mentor, beginning in undergraduate classes, that can lead to future research supervision and even post-doctoral collaboration, is endangered. Worst, and most damagingly of all, with this increasingly insecure model of the profession, who would want to embark on such a career in the first place? I know several very gifted junior scholars, with the potential to be great teachers who, even after having completed doctorates, abandoned any idea of a career in academe because of the insecurity – in addition to their astute apprehension about the toxic environment they would be entering under the censorious and intellectually stifling surveillance of the Thought Stasi stalking the Humanities departments in particular. As Long concludes:

> If universities don't change their employment practices soon, it will become harder to attract young, qualified people into the academic profession.

It is not only the employment practices that are deterring them. The whole system has been corrupted and degraded.

*****

The critique I have offered will attract the customary dismissive mantra of denunciation from the usual suspects – as elitist, white supremacist, conservative, and, if these fail to hit the mark, 'racist', today's all-purpose abusive discussion-silencer. But there are signs that, at long last, the community at large, and employers and, most importantly, prospective university students are approaching a full realisation of what has happened. Universities need to be recalled to their proper purpose and function as domains of teaching, learning and critical thinking for the intellectually gifted, rather than bloated propaganda units for mass social engineering. All we can hope is that this general awakening will be coming soon. It promises to be a rude one.

References

Adinou, Misty, 'NAPLAN Results Show It Isn't the Basics that are Missing in Australian Education', *The Conversation*, 2017.

Combie, David, 'Posing for the Camera: Life at the Hall in 1964', *St Edmund Hall Magazine*, 2015-16.

Daily Telegraph, 'Professor Eric Stanley, Scholar of Medieval English Literature', *The Daily Telegraph*, 5 August 2018.

Deresiewicz, William, 'Professing Literature in 2008. Why is the Intellectual Agenda of English Departments Being set by Teenagers?' *Nation*, 11 March 2008.

Economist, 'Don't Be So Offensive', *The Economist*, 4 June 2016.

Haffenden, John, *William Empson: Volume I: Among the Mandarins*, Oxford University Press, Oxford, 2005.

James, David, 'Academics Tangle with Managerial Oppressors', *Eureka Street*, 28(11), June 2018.

Lindop, Grevel, *Charles Williams: The Third Inkling*, Oxford University Press, Oxford, 2015.

Lodge, David, *Quite a Good Time to Be Born*, Vintage, London, 2015.

Long, Colin, 'Casualisation of University Workforce is a National Disgrace', *Sydney Morning Herald*, 3 August 2018.

Mansfield, Declan, 'Thinking Versus Doing', *The Spectator*, July 2018.

Russell, Bertrand, *In Praise of Idleness*, Routledge, London, 2004.

Stove, David, 'A Farewell to Arts: Marxism, Semiotics and Feminism', *Quadrant*, July-August 1986.

Windschuttle, Keith, *The Killing of History: How Literary Critics and Social Theorists are Murdering our Past*, Encounter Books, New York, 1996.

7

Teaching Quality in Australian Universities
Present Measures, Politics, and Possibilities

Gigi Foster[1]

When teaching academics recall their favourite university teachers, they typically stand out in our memory for reasons far beyond the academic content they taught. With hindsight, we see that great teachers changed the way we think about ourselves and the world, unlocked our potential to absorb new lessons with less effort, and prepared us for our later courses and life. Poor teachers made it more difficult to learn, by somehow getting in our way – perhaps through poor organisation, inadequate feedback, obfuscation of content, or negative attitudes about us, the content, or the job of teaching.

Now working as teachers ourselves, we are directly affected in our own careers by attempts to reduce the multi-faceted collection of largely intangible qualities that make a teacher good or bad into a single tangible measure or suite of measures, as these attempts lead to measures used in performance evaluation and management processes. Yet accurate and reliable measurement of teaching quality is a necessary input into good institutional policy-making. In an ideal world, one would track the quality of teaching in a way that is fair to teaching staff, and that also promotes better teaching and learning. Are Australian universities presently measuring teaching quality in a way that is able to achieve these twin objectives?

In this chapter I review Australian universities' usual methods of measuring teaching quality, discuss what those methods do and do not capture, and evaluate the extent to which our systems enable

---

[1] My thanks go to Jack Skelley for research assistance. All errors that remain are mine alone.

university teachers to use these measures to improve the quality of their teaching. In the latter part of the chapter I suggest enhancements to our present measures and to the ways they are used, and nominate the main barriers to implementing these changes.

The current state of play

Recent examinations of teaching evaluation systems in Australian universities, reviewed in detail by Alderman et al. (2012), conclude that these systems are 'poorly suited to the task of supporting outward-looking institutions that are seeking to benchmark with others and improve learning and teaching' (270). While these prior examinations have revealed significant variation across Australian institutions in the systems used to evaluate teaching, all 21 Australian institutions included in the QS Rankings' top 400 universities in the world[2] use reasonably similar means of measuring teaching quality at the coal face. Specifically, they all survey enrolled students towards the end of each teaching term to ask them course- and teacher-specific questions – usually in separate surveys, one evaluating the course[3] and the other(s) the teacher(s) of that course – that focus on broad learning goals and specific behaviours, similar to the questions in Svinicki and McKeachie (2011). These surveys typically include one question evaluating 'overall' quality of the course of the teacher, and conclude with open-ended questions asking respondents to nominate a strength and a weakness of the course or the teacher. Course and teacher evaluations are increasingly implemented online rather than via pencil and paper,[4] and this switch has been found to depress response rates

---

2 These are James Cook, La Trobe, Griffith, Tasmania, Deakin, South Australia, Curtin, RMIT, QUT, Macquarie, Wollongong, Newcastle, UTS, Adelaide, WA, Monash, Sydney, Queensland, UNSW, Melbourne, and the ANU; see httpspp.//www.topuniversities.com/university-rankings

3 Throughout this chapter, I use the term, 'course,' to refer to a particular unit of study offered in a particular term (such as 'Microeconomics 1, Term 1, 2019').

4 Hoffman (2003) estimates that online surveys were used at fewer than 10% of US universities at the turn of the century. There is no reliable analogous figure for the present day covering the whole sector, but many Australian universities' websites now indicate that they are using online evaluations.

by on average 23% (Nulty 2008; also discussed in Capa-Aydin 2016), several reasons for which are examined in Nulty (2008) and Guder and Malliaris (2013). Most Australian universities disclose neither the results nor the response rates of their surveys; what data are available indicate average response rates in the range of 20 to 40%.[5]

Questions about teaching quality asked of students at the top 20 universities in the US according to the QS 2018 rankings are similar to those asked in top Australian institutions, but there is a greater emphasis on student engagement.[6] Leading US universities routinely ask students to report how much time they spent studying for the course, how often they went to class, how much they participated, or similar estimates of own effort. Additional questions sometimes asked by these US universities but rarely appearing in Australian universities' student evaluation surveys aim to gauge students' level of interest in the subject matter before and after taking the course.

In addition to course- and teacher-specific surveys administered at individual universities, first-year Australian university students have been surveyed every five years since 1994 by the Melbourne Centre for the Study of Higher Education. Data from these Australian First Year Experience surveys indicates that first-year students' views about the quality of teaching in Australian universities have become significantly more positive over the past two decades (Baik et al 2015). In 1994, 66% of respondents agreed that the quality of teaching in their courses was generally good, rising to 78% in 2004 and 89% in 2014. In 2014, only 2% of the first-year students surveyed disagreed

---

[5] The University of Tasmania most recently reports a 34.1% mean response rate for semester 1 2016 (httppp.//www.utas.edu.au/__data/assets/pdf_file/0006/862215/2016-Sem1-Faculty-Comparative-Report.pdf), and Deakin University reports a 23% response rate for their Trimester 2 2018 survey (httpspp.//apps.deakin.edu.au/evaluate/results/summary-rep.php?schedule_select=1761&faculty_select=%25&school_select=%25&unit_select=%25&location_select=%25).

[6] These institutions are Brown, NYU, Carnegie Mellon, UCSD, UCLA, Northwestern, UC Berkeley, Michigan, Duke, U Penn, Columbia, Johns Hopkins, Yale, Cornell, Princeton, Chicago, CalTech, Harvard, Stanford, and MIT. Representative banks of question used on the student surveys at such institutions may be found by googling 'evaluations' and either 'teaching' or 'course', along with university's name.

with the proposition that the quality of teaching was generally good. Areas of teaching performance that appear to have fed this increase in satisfaction over time include the provision of feedback, enthusiasm, the quality of explanations provided, and making the subject interesting. However, this positive view apparently held by first-year students contrasts sharply with the picture of teaching quality painted by the Productivity Commission in 2017 based on its read of data from recent national surveys of students beyond the first year of study (Productivity Commission 2017, citing from QILT 2017).

The way in which national annual surveys of university students and recent graduates have been implemented in Australia has changed over the years. For the past few years, a random sample of all Australian university students has been asked to take part each year in the Student Evaluation Survey (SES), funded by the Commonwealth Department of Education and Training.[7] This survey replaced the University Experience Survey, initially rolled out in 2012 with funding from the then Department of Industry, Innovation, Science, Research and Tertiary Education, by the Australian Council on Educational Research (ACER). The SES, now run every August and coordinated by the Social Research Centre at the ANU, asks responding students to rate several things in aggregate about what they are experiencing at university, including teaching quality (as measured by specific behaviours and also in questions about content relevance and overall quality), learner engagement, learning resources, support for students, self-perceived skills development, and the educational experience overall. The Social Research Centre reports an aggregate rate of response to the 2017 SES of 36.2% (Challice 2018, 2).

Until 2015, recently-graduated university students also completed the Australian Graduate Survey about four months after graduation. Run by Graduate Careers Australia, this survey consisted of two parts, the Graduate Destination Survey (GDS) – recast from 2016 as the Graduate Outcomes Survey (GOS), which continues today under the

---

7 httpspp.//www.srcentre.com.au/our-research/student-experience-survey

management of the Social Research Centre – and the Course Experience Questionnaire (CEQ), now also administered by the Social Research Centre. Neither GDS nor GOS surveys ask detailed questions about teaching quality, though respondents are queried about their overall satisfaction with the university experience and with teaching quality. The CEQ contains more detailed questions, such as about students' self-rated skills and their assessment of certain teaching behaviours, as well as asking about their overall satisfaction with the program of study from which they recently graduated.

In its 2017 report, the Productivity Commission notes a wide degree of heterogeneity across institutions in the satisfaction with teaching quality reported in the 2016 GOS, together with a high (37%) average degree of reported dissatisfaction with the quality of teaching in the sector overall (QILT 2016). The Commission also delves into Appendix 8 of the SES 2016 report (QILT 2017) – a report whose headline teaching quality message is that 78% to 83% of students report a positive assessment of teaching quality, depending on the career stage of the student – to point to high student dissatisfaction with particular teacher behaviours and with self-assessed acquisition of particular skills. The Commission ascribes these problems mainly to the heavier focus on research performance than on teaching performance in the systems that reward academic staff.

Today's SES, like the CEQ, targets whole programs or suites of courses and teachers rather than individual courses or teachers. Hence, perhaps understandably, these tools have historically been used more for ranking university quality (for example, in the *Good Universities Guide*[8]) than as input into the virtuous cycle (Harvey 2011) as feedback about teaching quality that is used to motivate changes designed to improve teaching quality. There is no way to connect feedback on the SES to individual teachers or courses; at best, students' responses on the SES can be matched to the level of the program. As the SES does not directly identify good and bad teachers, heterogeneity in teaching quality within a given program – while it may be seen in SES response

---

8 httpspp.//www.gooduniversitiesguide.com.au

histograms at the program level – is difficult to address using this feedback tool.

What is captured by common measures of teaching quality?

Much classic education literature (exemplified by papers like Marsh 1984 and Ramsden 1991) promotes students' evaluation of teaching as a reliable and useful indicator of teaching quality in higher education. The authors of such classic papers do not intend to imply that teaching quality is unidimensional (e.g., 'Teaching effectiveness is multifaceted'; 'There is no single criterion of effective teaching' (Marsh 1984, 709); 'The existence of recurring differences in ratings between disciplines ... argues for the exercise of caution in interpreting differences among institutions' (Ramsden 1991, 145)).

However, when exposed to the realpolitik of Australian universities, the tacit nod contained in this literature to the notion of judging academics' teaching quality by simply asking current students their opinions of it creates a seductive enticement to university administrators who, for bureaucratic reasons unrelated to pedagogical concerns, are motivated to reduce teaching quality to a single simple score. Students' degree of agreement with a single statement, such as, 'Overall I was satisfied with the quality of the teaching in this course', or 'Overall I was satisfied with the quality of this person's teaching', provides a metric that appears on its face to be comparable across teachers and across time and to capture something analogous to customer satisfaction. The average response given by enrolled students on a Likert-type scale to a single question like this is commonly used at Australian universities as the primary indicator of the quality of teaching in a given course. The average response to such a question for a particular course is typically compared to the average response given by students enrolled in other courses offered at that university, and often shapes career development discussions and decisions about whether to promote academic staff.

Given the incentives facing modern universities' bureaucracies that I have discussed elsewhere (Foster 2011), this result might have been anticipated, though all too frequently the political implications of championing different approaches to measuring teaching quality have been ignored or discussed in only abstract terms by those academics who have deeply pondered and researched the nature of quality teaching. Yet there are some signs that this lack of political realism on the part of educational researchers, whether intentionally put on or reflective of true naivete, is beginning to change. As one indicator of this changing stance, papers published more recently in education and related fields have shown signs of a backlash against the use of teaching quality measures based solely on student feedback (e.g., Sulis et al. 2018; Hornstein 2017; Darwin 2016; Carrell and West 2010).

Apart from the uni-dimensionality inherent when only one question is used, what problems has this recent literature highlighted in using student satisfaction measures to gauge teaching quality? I review these problems here, while also offering broader comment on the consequences of Australian universities' use of student responses about their level of satisfaction with the teaching they have experienced in a course as the primary measure of the quality of teaching in that course.

One practical problem with using student evaluations to measure teaching quality relates to the incentives faced by the student evaluator. In many Australian universities, including those using online rather than paper-based evaluations, no negative consequences materialise for students who fail to submit evaluations of teaching. Moral suasion may assist in improving response rates on the margin, but without clear material incentives, an experienced observer of human behaviour would expect low response rates overall and the highest likelihood of response amongst those students who have the strongest personal reasons to respond. Strong personal incentives are most likely to be in place for students with strong feelings about a course – whether positive or negative – creating a situation where evaluations can be distributed bimodally and/or where the opinions of the vast majority of students in a course go unheard. Thus, problems of small sample size and unrepresentative sampling frequently constrain the interpretability of student evaluation data. This in turn ultimately constrains the ability of the teaching quality measurement system in fact to deliver sound measures of teaching quality and hence to stimulate actions to improve quality.

Another, less easily solved problem with using student evaluations of satisfaction with teaching as a measure of teaching quality is that student satisfaction is likely to be driven by factors other than the amount or quality of learning achieved in the course. Student learning is arguably a main driver of teachers' pedagogical choices such as delivery style, assessment design, and selection of readings, and it is also arguably a social objective of funding universities in the first place; we would like things to be learned by students. However, the recent meta-analysis conducted in Uttl et al. 2017, correcting for methodological flaws in many earlier studies – many related to the improper handling of small sample sizes – suggests soberingly that students' ratings of teachers are essentially *unrelated to how much is actually learned in a given course*, with student evaluations of teaching capable of explaining at most 1% of the variation in levels of student learning.

In a similar vein, Nasser-Abu Alhija [2017] finds that students associate good teaching most strongly with whether they perceive the assessment in a course to be good, and least strongly with their own long-term development as a student. The title of a recent post on the website of the American Association of University Professors recently proclaimed bluntly that 'student evaluations of teaching are not valid,'[9] and went on to provide a withering indictment of the use of teaching evaluations to measure teaching or learning quality. This implies that if teachers who receive feedback relating to student satisfaction subsequently change their decisions about delivery, assessment, or other aspects of a course in order to maximise student satisfaction in ensuing terms, these changes may have little or no impact on the amount of learning that their students achieve.

One problem with a heavy reliance on student evaluations as a measure of teaching quality results from our large numbers of international students and students from non-Western educational and

---

9 httpspp.//www.aaup.org/article/student-evaluations-teaching-are-not-valid

cultural backgrounds. Lack of fluency in the English language may impede some students' ability to answer accurately questions about the quality of teaching they have been exposed to. Students from other cultures may also have a different set of expectations than do Australian students about what constitutes good teaching. While these expectations are neither right nor wrong in an absolute sense, any increased heterogeneity of students' expectations of teaching today as compared with a generation ago due to the great increase in international students on Australian campuses (documented in Haugh 2015) would translate to more uncertainty today than in the past about what student evaluations of teaching are truly picking up. Ultimately, diversity in the internal criteria and benchmarks that students use when responding to the teaching evaluations that in turn weigh heavily in universities' deliberations and judgments about teaching quality suggests, again, the spectre of guiding teaching practice in Australia's universities using a measure that not only contains significant measurement error but of which the underlying driver is indeterminate.

Strikingly, the education literature reveals no robust evidence that the student evaluations Australian universities use to measure teaching quality are robustly tethered to the quality of teaching or learning achieved as conceptualised by the academic workers whose everyday job it is to teach well and inspire learning. No researcher known at time of writing has set out to explore whether a correlation exists between student evaluation measures (essentially, students' beliefs about the quality of teaching or learning) and teachers' beliefs about whether good teaching or learning has been achieved.

A variety of other problems plague the way student evaluations of teaching are collected and used in Australia. One area of particular concern is the inclusion of questions on student feedback questionnaires whose relation to teaching quality is oblique even in the abstract. For example, questions are included on many student surveys about the use of digital technology, 'flipping', or 'blending' courses, that are wholly unrelated to learning or teaching quality. Some types of material may be better delivered using digital technology, or in flipped or blended format, and others not; some teachers may teach better with the assistance of digital tools, and others are more effective when using more tried-and-tested tools like whiteboards or document cameras. There is nothing inherently of higher quality in the teaching that goes on in a class using digital technology relative to one that does not use digital technology specifically because of the use of that digital technology *per se*.

Questions about the degree of student participation in a given course are also arguably unrelated to the quality of teaching and learning, if we accept that in some classes – likely more theoretically or mathematically rigorous ones, that arguably carry higher potential educational value for students than less rigorous courses – more material must be communicated from teacher to student over the course of the semester, leaving less time for students to 'participate' (discuss case study applications, give presentations in class, etc.) because they have to spend more time listening to the material and absorbing it.

There is also no capture of value-added and no comparison to a counterfactual in the student evaluation surveys in use today. To generate a student-perceived proxy for value-added, one might ask, in a similar vein as the value-added questions used in many American universities, 'How much more do you know about <subject X> today than you did at the start of this course?,' or, 'Are you more interested in this subject now than at the start of the course?' Similarly, instead of enrolling at university, a valid alternative learning avenue for modern students is to go online and look up resources for themselves. Hence, a question asking students to compare the teaching they have experienced to a relevant counterfactual might be worded as, 'Compared to the alternative of learning this material on your own, did you experience enhanced learning because of this teacher?'

One alternative measure of teaching quality to which Australian educators and administrators ascribe value is the teaching award system. Awards for university teaching are given out in Australia by bureaucracies at many levels, from the school or department level to the faculty level to the university and national levels. Australia's national teaching awards are administered via the Australian Awards for University Teaching (AAUT) program, whereas lower-level awards are administered through individual universities and groups within them. It may appear on the surface that these awards capture independent (and, hence, somewhat objective) judgments upon what is good teaching and what is not, akin to the way that other award systems such as the Nobel prizes or critical book prizes are seen to capture other dimensions of quality as perceived by outside observers. Unfortunately, the reality is that awards for university teaching in Australia are made only after a laborious process of self-nomination and self-justification to the bureaucracy administering the award, rather than via nomination and write-up by a star teacher's supervisors or peers. While being awarded for teaching in an Australian university (particularly at higher levels) is probably somewhat related to in fact being a good teacher, receiving such an award is also a signal that the awardee had the ability and willingness to spend the time and effort at self-trumpeting required to lodge an application in the first instance – time and effort likely to have been re-directed from other academic activities.[10] This spells selection problem, which in turn spells lack of confidence that those receiving teaching awards are the teachers whose teaching performance is of the highest quality amongst all teachers at Australian universities.

Notably, students' evaluations of teaching are not directly included in the international university ranking schemes that university administrators target. They make no appearance in the criteria used to judge university quality by the Times Higher Education rankings, the QS rankings, or the ARWU rankings.[11] So why do university

---

10 I feel able to write candidly on this matter as a former winner myself of teaching awards at the school, faculty, university, and national levels.

11 For a review of the criteria used by these schemes to rank universities, see httpspp.//www.timeshighereducation.com/world-university-rankings/methodology-world-university-rankings-2018, httpspp.//www.topuniversities.com/qs-world-university-rankings/methodology, and httppp.//www.shanghairanking.com/ARWU-Methodology-2018.html, respectively. Student-faculty ratio does appear as a criterion in the first two schemes as an explicit proxy for teaching quality, and global prize-winning by alumni is used in the ARWU ranking scheme to indicate teaching quality.

administrators pay attention to student evaluations of teaching quality, as evidenced by their use in career and promotion discussions?[12] One probable reason is that the 'student experience' is a well-publicised input into domestic rankings, and students' satisfaction with teaching is seen as a core driver of students' reports about their learning experiences.[13] There may also be a suspicion that some other inputs to global university ranking schemes, such as institutional reputation, are driven indirectly by aspects of students' experiences in classes.

Another, less benign reason to rely upon student evaluations to measure teaching quality is that holding teachers to account using measures with significant interpretational problems leads to an environment of uncertainty for academic staff, which assists with controlling them. People coping with uncertainty are less likely to have the energy needed to speak up against bad policies or practices, so the use of reductionist and dubious teaching quality measures is a conveniently energy-sapping distraction device for administrators who would prefer to avoid the headache of being held accountable to academic staff as regards their own (administrative) performance.

Alternative measures of teaching quality

What might we do to measure the quality of teaching more accurately in Australian universities?

To address the problem of low response rates that in turn leads to interpretational uncertainty due to small and unrepresentative samples, we might turn to the fundamental advice of basic economics, to adjust the incentives. Basic services that enable students to continue to interact with the university at which they are being educated, such as having their marks released or being able to enrol in further courses, could be made conditional on the completion of teaching

---

12 Darwin (2017) argues that teaching quality measures are used more for promotion and monitoring than for pedagogical improvement.
13 Students can compare the overall 'student learning experience' on offer at different Australian universities at the following website: https//www.qilt.edu.au/about-this-site/student-experience

evaluations. The Australian nation recognises the power of incentives in getting out the vote, as evidenced by the fine payable for people registered to vote who do not cast a ballot. Why should we not use our knowledge of incentives to deliver more accurate assessments of, at the very least, what students think or feel about the teaching at our universities?

Naturally, the thoughts and feelings of those on the receiving end of education may evolve over time. Students' immediate reactions to a course may be influenced by ephemeral concerns or dimensions of the course that are either unrelated to, or even diametrically oppose, the amount or quality of learning received. They may respond positively to an end-of-term question about their degree of satisfaction with 'teaching quality' when a teacher was entertaining or gave high marks, for example, or negatively when a teacher set high expectations or gave low marks, even though we might guess that the latter combination would be more likely to yield more and/or higher quality student learning.

To address this problem, we could ask imminent degree graduates to reflect on the courses they have taken during their entire career, and to provide feedback about which were in hindsight the most useful and least useful in progressing their learning. This is notably not asked in the current SES or GOS, described above although, if added and made linkable to those prior courses, these questions would make those instruments significantly more potent in highlighting good and bad teaching or course quality within university programs. Although a lengthy gap between course and evaluation introduces other measurement concerns, other measures of teaching quality could be supplemented by following students even further in life using post-graduation surveys, allowing an even longer and wider scope of hindsight to inform students' reflection on the quality of the education they received in different courses.

Instead of relying only on students' evaluations of teaching quality, we could also avail ourselves of the wealth of information that is collected by universities as students move through their degrees. This information can be massaged into analysable micro-data at the student-course-semester level, as has been done in prior research (e.g., Foster 2012), and then used to examine the predictors of all manner of educational outcomes. Do students who took Professor Smith's Chemistry 1 course do better or worse in their chemistry courses in the following year than students who took Professor Kelly's Chemistry 1 course? Is there a difference in these two student cohorts in time to graduation, total GPA, or anything else we might care about? The data to answer such questions are sitting in the universities' data banks and being updated every semester.

Each of the above suggestions has the drawback of introducing a lag between the moment of teaching and the moment at which teaching quality is measured. To circumvent this problem in a way that also puts judgments about teaching quality into the hands of people arguably most skilled at making those judgments, universities could engage their own academic staff in formal, institutionalised peer-to-peer teaching evaluations. Such programs need to be designed carefully so as to ensure peer evaluators' expertise is being channelled effectively, to avoid administrative capture, and to minimise the interpersonal frictions or negative impacts on morale that could arise from less than stellar rankings given by colleagues. Done well, however, institutionalised peer-to-peer teaching evaluation programs hold perhaps the most promise across all possible approaches to delivering reliable, pedagogically relevant, real-time feedback about the quality of teaching and learning.

An even more radical idea is to supplement direct measures of teaching quality with inference based on the quality of teachers' research. Recent research has found that research quality correlates with teaching quality across people (Cadez et al. 2017). While it would be foolish to treat it as a comprehensive measure of teaching quality, and while it is clearly vulnerable to the phenomenon of the career-oriented researcher who does not care about teaching, a broad measure of research quality may be useful in identifying teachers at higher-than-average risk of poor teaching performance.

Barriers to implementation

The barriers to increasing the size of student evaluation samples are political and administrative. The push to digitise student evaluations and the notion that students should not be 'compelled' in any way to respond to teaching evaluations, both of which directly suppress student response rates, are both sourced in the doctrines of university administration. While high-effort coal-face workarounds do exist – from using pencil-and-paper evaluation forms in one's classes without full administrative support, to linking in-class assessment item return to the completion of those forms – the fact that they are high-effort and carry the flavour of going against the norm mean that very few teachers will opt for them. What is required here is for high-level teaching and learning administrators to champion higher response rates, and unapologetically lobby their universities to move back to paper-based evaluations or require students to submit teaching evaluations as a condition of progressing normally through their programs, or both.

The barriers to tracking students over time within universities could also be lifted with political will. Universities' administrative systems and protocols are typically not set up to track students over time at the micro-level and thereby make it easy to relate their later academic progress to their performance in courses taken early in their programs. At a typical modern Australian university, a high-level champion of this idea would be needed to obtain the resources necessary to re-tool these systems and protocols to support wide-scale student tracking. Of course, once micro-level student tracking becomes possible, other dimensions of a university's performance become more visible – from the progress of its indigenous and socio-economically disadvantaged students, to the differences in enrolment and performance between men and women, younger and older students, international and domestic students, or students from different entry pathways, in its various degrees and courses – and this opens the door to broader accountability of the university for the education it is providing to the tax-paying community.

Is it realistic to measure teaching quality in part using research quality measures? Research and teaching quality metrics are increasingly seen as independent, as evidenced by the fact that teaching-only positions are becoming more palatable to university management. This increased palatability is arguably a response to the increased casualisation of teaching after a certain point, it becomes politically infeasible to continue offering repeated short-term contracts to casual teaching staff, so universities are forced to offer such staff permanent positions. The separation of teaching and research that is implied by the creation of teaching-only positions means that teaching quality for such staff cannot be indicated by research-based measures, since research is not a primary dimension of teaching-focussed roles.

Casualisation itself, mentioned frequently in the higher education literature as a potential quality depressor (Lama and Joullié 2015), brings another particularly vexing and subtle barrier to the production of secular improvements in teaching quality, regardless of what teaching quality measurement system is implemented. When courses are taught by casual staff on short-term contracts, they are more likely to be handed about to more lecturers in any given window of time, due to the insecurity of involvement and the stop-gap nature of the work performed that is signalled by the causal contract. This inhibits the growth in teaching quality both within a course and within a person over time.

Suppose, for example, that feedback about teaching quality in a course taught by Teacher A in Period-1 is collected but that Teacher B is assigned to teach that course in Period-2. Even if she receives the feedback from Period-1 – unlikely, due to the confidence in which teaching evaluations are often held – Teacher B is likely to place less weight on the Period-1 feedback than would Teacher A, since the feedback was generated about a teaching setting that did not involve her. Being taken off the course in Period-2 also means Teacher A is deprived of the chance to attempt an improvement to his teaching quality within the same course. Even if he is assigned to some other course in Period-2 and attempts some changes in that setting intended to improve teaching quality based on the Period-1 feedback, he will be less confident that any changes he makes are responsible for differences in Period-2 feedback relative to Period-1 feedback differences in the mix of students, the level of the course, the size of the course, the degree of familiarity he has with the course content, his level of interest in the content, and so on may all influence the feedback he receives. For these reasons, a steady state with heavy casualisation and frequent rotation of staff across courses is likely to feature teachers and courses 'treading water' rather than actively pursuing a trajectory of positive change towards higher teaching quality.

'Teaching quality' has been shown to be reasonably fixed within person over time (Marsh and Hocevar 1991), which carries the policy implication for any given institution that recruitment of good teachers is likely to be more effective in delivering high quality teaching in the long run than attempts to improve the teaching quality of bad teachers. This in turn implies that for the best long-run outcome, assessment of teaching quality should be made at point of hiring and given significant weight in the hiring decision. This is to some extent done already through the usual process of candidates giving seminars, at which their communication and organisational skills as well as their level of enthusiasm for their subject can be assessed. Nevertheless, outstanding perceived research quality can lead to discounting of poor soft skills by hiring committees whose incentives are formed with reference both to international scholarly norms and to Australia-specific measures of quality that directly inform university resourcing, such as those delivered by the Australian Research Council's Excellence in Research in Australia (ERA) assessment.[14] The weak link between teaching ability and qualities that are sought in academics by those in a position to offer them high-status jobs or money for their research is another institutional barrier to the improvement of teaching quality over time at Australian universities.

Some hopeful signs

Although digitising student evaluations is often associated with severe reductions in response rates, as noted already, increasing digitisation

---

14 https//www.arc.gov.au/excellence-research-australia

more generally brings a greater ability on the university's side to implement a requirement for students to submit feedback as a precondition for the release of marks or for enrolment into courses for the ensuing term. Online responses can be tracked at the student level through creative means that do not compromise their confidentiality, and then used to trigger processes that release marks or turn on enrolment eligibility for students who have submitted their responses. With more reliance on digitised records, universities also have more opportunities to target higher student response via emails, social media messaging, texts, and other means when certain indicators are observed digitally (e.g., 'student about to graduate' or 'student has failed this course'), in order to promote better measurement of teaching quality.[15]

The tracking of students across time and further into their lives – particularly when they transfer universities mid-degree or enrol in successive degree programs at different universities – would be greatly facilitated by the assignment of a single number that sticks to students throughout their educational careers and beyond. The Commonwealth Higher Education Student Support Number (CHESSN) initiative is a start in this direction, although it is limited by the fact that CHESSNs are only given to Commonwealth-supported (i.e., domestic) students.[16] This idea could be taken further by a whole-of-sector commitment to student tracking that commences with a student's first interaction with a higher education provider, at which point he is assigned a unique student identifier for life that is made available to both universities and educational researchers. For political reasons, such a commitment is unlikely to be forthcoming, but it could instead be mandated by the Commonwealth, with compliance by each university required as a condition of receiving Commonwealth funding.

The possibilities offered by utilising peer review of teaching as a measure of teaching quality and a vehicle for improving teaching and learning are described in Sachs and Parsell (2014). This recent volume

---

15 See https://www.chronicle.com/article/Colleges-Are-Getting-Smarter/245457
16 https//www.monash.edu/enrolments/government-loans/chessn

offers both theoretical musings and practical advice for universities considering the implementation of a peer review system. While a decade ago, Harris et al. (2008) could claim (3) that 'peer review is an infrequent and generally piecemeal activity' at Australian universities, this has been slowly changing. The Australian Learning and Teaching Council supported an investigation into using peer review of teaching for promotion purposes in 2009, and at time of writing, all four of the universities involved in producing that project's final report have now formalised peer reviews of teaching – two (the University of Adelaide and the University of New South Wales) to the point of encouraging or requiring them as part of promotion applications.[17] While peer observation can suffer from its own biases (Campbell and Ronfeldt 2018), done well it offers a constructively critical assessment of what occurs in a class that can complement other measures of teaching quality and, given its source, is likely to be respected by teachers.

Finally, the Australian Research Council's recent expansion of the measures used to evaluate research quality, embodied in its Engagement and Impact assessment exercise,[18] holds the potential to effect improvement in teaching quality as well. Engagement and impact are inherently social activities that involve the wider public, and the skills required to achieve high levels of these broader measures of research quality are arguably more similar to teaching skills than are traditional measures of research quality, such as the counts of A* journal articles that researchers have published.[19] Hence, teaching quality may be indirectly rewarded if and when the Commonwealth

---

17 https//teaching.unsw.edu.au/summative-peer-review, https//www.griffith.edu.au/learning-futures/our-practice/professional-learning/peer-enhancement-of-teaching-and-learning, https//www.uow.edu.au/dvca/ltc/teachdev/PeerReview/index.html, and https//www.adelaide.edu.au/learning/teaching/peer-review/teaching-review/

18 https//www.arc.gov.au/engagement-and-impact-assessment

19 Although it has fallen out of favour in some circles, the Australian Business Deans Council's quality ranking of academic journals (http//www.abdc.edu.au/master-journal-list.php), in which A* is the highest rank and C the lowest, is the source of the 'A* journal' terminology and is still used at many departments throughout Australia to judge research quality.

begins to reward universities for their achievement of research quality as measured more broadly as the degree of research-related engagement and impact.

Conclusion

Measuring the quality of teaching is no simple task, as documented in many of the articles cited in this chapter and published in a recent issue of *Studies in Educational Evaluation* entitled 'Evaluation of Teaching Challenges and Promises,' edited by Fadia Nasser-Abu Alhija. The weaknesses of relying solely on student evaluations of teaching to judge teaching quality, and particularly of focusing on a single question answered by a small number of students – which many Australian universities still do – are becoming clearer as time passes. Complementary approaches that rely on digitised records, student tracking over time, peer review of teaching, and the use of broad measures of research quality are all within reach for Australia from a technical standpoint. The barriers to implementing better teaching quality measures and using them to improve the quality of teaching and learning in our universities mainly relate to political will and the incentives of administrators and, to a lesser extent, the incentives of teachers and students. With leadership from the ranks of university administration, change is possible.

References

Alderman, Lyn, Stephen Towers and Sylvia Bannah (2012), 'Student Feedback Systems in Higher Education, a Focused Literature Review and Environmental Scan', *Quality in Higher Education*, 18(3), 261-280.

Baik, Chi, Ryan Naylor and Sophie Arkoudis (2015), 'The First Year Experience in Australian Universities. Findings from Two Decades, 1994-2014', Melbourne Centre for the Study of Higher Education, The University of Melbourne.

Cadez, Simon, Vlado Dimovski & Maja Zaman Groff, 'Research, Teaching and Performance Evaluation in Academia, the Salience of Quality,' *Studies in Higher Education*, 2017, 42(8), 1455-1473.

Campbell, Shanyce L. and Matthew Ronfeldt, 'Observational Evaluation of Teachers: Measuring More Than We Bargained for?' *American Educational Research Journal*, 2018, 55(6), 1233-1267.

Capa-Aydin, Yesim, 'Student Evaluation of Instruction Comparison Between in-class and Online Methods,' *Assessment and Evaluation in Higher Education*, 2016, 41(1), 112-126.

Carrell, Scott E. and James E. West, 'Does Professor Quality Matter? Evidence from Random Assignment of Students to Professors.' *Journal of Political Economy*, 2010, 118(3).

Challice, Graham, Shane Compton and Natasha Vickers, '2017 Student Experience Survey Methodological Report,' Social Research Centre at the Australian National University, 2018.

Darwin, Stephen, 'What contemporary work are student ratings actually doing in higher education?' *Studies in Educational Evaluation*, 2017, 54, 13-21.

Darwin, Stephen, *Student Evaluation in Higher Education: Reconceptualising the Student Voice*, Springer International Publishing, 2016.

Demediuk, Therese and van Gramberg, Bernadine, 'Quality Teaching in a Managerialist Setting: Higher Education Challenges in Australia,' *Transylvanian Review of Administrative Sciences*, 2011, 32, 98-113.

Foster, Gigi (2011), 'Academics as Educators in Australian Universities Power, Perceptions and Institutions.' *Economic Papers*, 30(4), 568-575.

Foster, Gigi, 'The Impact of International Students on Measured Learning and Standards in Australian Higher Education,' *Economics of Education Review*, 2012, 31(5), 587-600.

Guder, Faruk and Mary Malliaris, 'Online Course Evaluations Response Rates,' *American Journal Of Business Education,* 2013, 6(3), 333-338.

Harris, Kerri-Lee, Kelly Farrell, Maureen Bell, Marcia Devlin, and Richard James, *Peer Review of Teaching in Australian Higher Education: A Handbook to Support Institutions in Developing and Embedding Effective Policies and Practices*, Centre for the Study of Higher Education at the University of Melbourne and the Centre for Educational Development and Interactive Resources at the University of Wollongong, 2008.

Harvey, L., 'The Nexus of Feedback and Improvement.' in *Student Feedback. The Cornerstone to an Effective Quality Assurance System in Higher Education*, Nair, C.S. and Mertova, P. (eds), University Press, Oxford, 2011.

Haugh, Michael, 'International Students and the "English problem" in Australian Universities. A Discursive Perspective', in *International Education and Cultural-Linguistic Experiences of International Students in Australia*, Australian Academic Press, 2015.

Hoffman, Kevin M., 'Online Course Evaluation and Reporting in Higher Education', *New Directions for Teaching and Learning*, 96, 25-29, 2003.

Hornstein, Henry A., 'Student Evaluations of Teaching are an Inadequate Assessment Tool for Evaluating Faculty Performance', *Cogent Education*, 2017, 4(1).

Lama, Tek and Jean-Etienne Joullié, 'Casualization of Academics in the Australian Higher Education. Is Teaching Quality at Risk?', 2015, *Research in Higher Education Journal*, 28.

Linse, Angela R., 'Interpreting and Using Student Ratings Sata: Guidance for Faculty Serving as Administrators and on Evaluation Committees', *Studies in Educational Evaluation*, 2017, 54, 94-106.

Marsh, Herbert, 'Students' Evaluations of University Teaching: Dimensionality, Reliability, Validity, Potential Biases, and Utility', *Journal of Educational Psychology*, 1984, 76(5), 707-754.

Marsh, Herbert W. and Dennis Hocevar, 'Students' Evaluations of Teaching Effectiveness. The Stability of Mean Ratings of the Same Teachers over a 13-year Period', *Teaching and Teacher Education*, 1991, 7(4), 303-314.

Nasser-Abu Alhija, Fadia. 'Teaching in Higher Education. Good Teaching through Students' Lens,' *Studies in Educational Evaluation*, 2017, 54, 4-12.

Nulty, Duncand, 'The Adequacy of Response Rates to Online and Paper Surveys: What Can be Done?', *Assessment and Evaluation in Higher Education*, 2008, 33(3), 301-314.

Productivity Commission, 'University Education' *Shifting the Dial: 5-year Productivity Review*, Supporting Paper No. 7, Canberra, 2017.

Quality Indicators for Learning and Teaching (QILT), '2016 Student Experience Survey. National Report', 2017.

Quality Indicators for Learning and Teaching (QILT), '2016 Graduate Outcomes Survey. National Report,' Technical report, 2016.

Ramsden, Paul, 'A Performance Indicator of Teaching Quality in Higher Education: The Course Experience Questionnaire.' *Studies in Higher Education*, 1991, 16(2), 129-150.

Sachs, Judyth and Mitch Parsell, (eds), *Peer Review of Learning and Teaching in Higher Education: International Perspectives*, Springer, 2014.

Sulis, I., Porcu, M. and Capursi, V., 'On the Use of Student Evaluation of Teaching. A Longitudinal Analysis Combining Measurement Issues and Implications of the Exercise', *Social Indicators Research*, 2018.

Svinicki, M., & McKeachie, W. J. (eds), *McKeachie's Teaching Tips. Strategies, research, and Theory for College and University Teachers* (13th ed.), Belmont, CA. Wadsworth Cengage Learning, 2011.

Uttl, Bob, Carmela A. White and Daniela Wong Gonzalez, 'Meta-analysis of Faculty's Teaching effectiveness: Student Evaluation of Teaching Ratings and Student Learning are not Related',*Studies in Educational Evaluation*, 2017, 54, 22-42.

8

Same Policies, a Different Country
How English Universities have Developed in an Era of Loans, Growth and Globalism

Alison Wolf

Until very recently English universities seemed to be enjoying a glorious 21st century: growing, well-funded, respected and highly ranked. Now, quite suddenly, the sector looks politically isolated and unstable. This has little to do with Brexit, and a lot to do with government policies which have tracked Australia's in key respects. They have unleashed changes which were predictable but unpredicted, and which have threatened standards, and made university funding a highly disputed and high profile political issue. On this latter point I must declare an interest. At the time of writing, I am a member of an independent panel established as part of a government review of Post-18 Education and Funding in England, which will report early in 2019.[1] This chapter does not and cannot provide a preview of the panel's conclusions. It can, and does, however, explain how policies that will be familiar to Australian readers – on fees, foreign students, and 'demand-led' growth – have affected English universities.

Higher education in the UK

Higher education forms a major part of the economy in all parts of the United Kingdom. Our universities' combined annual turnover is now in excess of £37 billion – on a par with legal services, and half as much

---

1 The Review's Terms of Reference can be found at https://www.gov.uk/government/publications/review-of-post-18-education-and-funding-terms-of-reference

again as pharmaceuticals. Notwithstanding, within the sector there is considerable variation, not only in size but also in levels of income per student, research intensity, and prestige. Indeed, the country has one of the clearest, and most publicly discussed, prestige hierarchies in the world. It also boasts far more 'top' institutions than size would suggest. For example, in the most recent *Times Higher Education* list of the world's top 25 universities, England is the only country aside from the US with multiple entries and it outperforms the US in number of top-ranked institutions per head of population. To a very large degree, this is a function of research reputation, and of a distinctive approach to public research funding.

The UK government funds research councils which award grants, competitively, for specific projects. Moreover, it also provides large research block payments to individual institutions Around £2bn 'quality related' funding is handed out annually, on the basis of research performance, in order to support 'research infrastructure'. The allocations, which are highly unequal, depend on periodic peer assessments of every research-active academic in the system. These assessments are aggregated across an institution to determine the total grant: and, unlike specific research grants, this money is the university's to do with as it wishes. (The last 'Research Excellence Framework' exercise was in 2014: the next is due in 2021.)

Evaluations of research quality date back to the mid-1980s but the high-intensity, high visibility policy of today dates back to the early 1990s, when student numbers were being expanded at speed, and government funding per student was plummeting. Ministers and regulators concluded that, to maintain research quality, they must channel most research support to a few select institutions. And so 'quality-related' funding was born.

These periodic national research evaluations provided an official, inclusive, university-by-university ranking that anyone could access. In the last two decades, we have all become used to global league tables, and to governments around the world obsessing over having universities in the 'top 200'. Well before that, however, Britain's research league table was important in turning what was a rather moderately hierarchical system into one which is marked by an ever-steeper and more visible ranking of institutions by prestige. Allocations are highly unequal: for example, of the 120 plus universities which are eligible for such funding, just six, all in the 'golden triangle' of Oxford, Cambridge and London, attract a good fifth of the pot. Moreover, since 1994 – just after the big expansion referred to above – the UK's large research universities have had their own organisation and lobby group, the 'Russell Group', comparable to Australia's 'Group of 8'. [2]

Within the UK, the term is increasingly well-known, so that families will monitor carefully how many students proceed from a school to a Russell Group university, and not just how many proceed to higher education,

Research funding and policy are decided at UK level. By contrast, other aspects of university policy and spending are the responsibility of the 'devolved administrations'. Schools have traditionally been a devolved function, with Scotland in particular having a completely distinct and distinctive system, but Welsh and Northern Irish school systems are also significantly different from England. At university level, divergence is more recent, but has become increasingly marked, especially since the very late 1990s when major changes were made in English fee and payment policy. England, demographically by far the largest constituent part of the United Kingdom, accounting for 85% of the population, has followed a path of increased 'marketisation' and encouragement of competition, up-front student fees, and demand-led growth which echoes much of Australia's recent policy. The other three countries have done so to lesser and varying degrees, and Scotland least of all. The following sections concentrate largely on England.

The next section examines developments in post-war higher education in order to explain how successive decisions created a system driven in large part by three features. These are the income-contingent student loan system through which an overwhelming

---

[2] The relevant Vice-Chancellors first met in London's Russell Hotel, hence the name.

proportion of funding for UK student teaching now flows; the growth in international student numbers; and the recent 'lifting of the cap', which to Australians will be more familiar as a policy of allowing 'demand-led' student numbers.

Getting to the present

England entered and left the Second World War with just 16 universities. Today there are 120. Then almost a third of its university students were in Oxford and Cambridge, another third in London, the rest scattered across a number of redbrick 'civic' universities in the larger cities: only 2% of the population attended. But post-war, in a fast-growing economy, middle-class parents (and voters) were ambitious for their children. Successive governments responded to the electorate's demands by both expanding numbers and opening a considerable number of new institutions, as they did throughout most of the developed world. In fits and starts, a mix of individual ambition, voter pressure and Whitehall paternalism drove a long expansion continued over the next 25 years (see especially Carswell 1985). By the mid-1960s 10% of the 19 year old age cohort was entering higher education. By 1990, it was 25%.

Until 1990, however, this expansion was only partly through universities. In the 1950s, 'Colleges of Advanced Technology' (CATs) were created. Teacher training colleges were expanded and upgraded, offering a wider range of subjects, and turning teaching into a fully graduate profession. In the 1960s, a complete new set of universities opened (including Warwick, Sussex, York), but the government also created a whole new set of higher education institutions. The 'polytechnics' were designed to specialise in technical education and offer large numbers of two year 'Higher National' qualifications as well as three year bachelor's degrees.

Today, the CATs, the polytechnics and the Colleges of Higher Education (the old teacher training institutes) have all either merged with universities or, more often, become autonomous universities in their own right. Any commitment to an institutionally more complex sector, and to a specifically vocational pathway within higher education, was abandoned. England is now a country in which almost all higher education takes place in fully-fledged universities, but where there is also a very steep hierarchy of prestige within the university sector.

This contrasts with Scotland[3] (let alone most of Europe, or North America) though again, Australia is similar. One result has been that, for 18 year olds at the end of full-time secondary schooling, there is a more or less total divide between those going into higher education to start a full (and almost always full-time) degree, and those for whom there is effectively no educational progression route.[4] Higher technical qualifications, which used to be offered, have more or less disappeared in England (although the government is in principle committed to resuscitating them). More generally, a consistent pattern of cutting budgets and underfunding activity in 'Further Education' has facilitated generous funding for universities.[5] As mentioned at the start of this chapter, universities in England in recent years have been funded generously by international standards, reaching higher real levels per student than for many years before. This is true on almost any measure used, and is directly linked to the country's move to levying student fees, backed by income-contingent loans. This move is, as noted above, one of three developments which determine to a large degree how the current system operates.

The move to student fees

Twenty years ago, the current success and wealth of the English higher

---

3 In Scotland, a large number of school leavers enter higher education courses in Colleges which lead, after two years, to a 'Higher National Diploma'. Many HND holders then transfer to universities, with credit, to complete the final two years of a full honours degree.

4 Apprenticeships are overwhelmingly at lower levels although traditional craft apprenticeships are increasingly entered at age 18 rather than the traditional 16, and continue to offer good job prospects.

5 Wolf et al, 2016. In Scotland, where home undergraduates do not pay any up-front fees, there have been major direct cuts in the further education budget to help fund universities. Scottish universities are also currently funded at considerably lower levels than those in England.

education sector would have seemed unlikely. During the 1950s and 1960s, government funding was extremely generous. Students paid no fees; maintenance grants were high; and the total level of teaching expenditure per student has, in real terms, not been matched since (Wolf et al. 2016). Places were also limited, with the funding council allocating numbers of places to each individual institution.

This level of expenditure could not survive expansion, let alone the economic crises of the 1970s and 1980s. Year after year, governments imposed 'efficiency savings' in the 'unit of resource', meaning, in ordinary English, that less was spent on each student. Governments also cast around for ways to fund yet more students while restraining total costs: means-tested maintenance grants for living costs were scaled back, and subsidised maintenance loans introduced instead. But charging fees remained unthinkable: when Thatcher's mentor, Sir Keith Joseph, did think about it, he was quickly slapped down.

With more students, but less money per student, class sizes rose and teaching hours per student fell. Politicians hoped, as they do today, for technology-driven savings, but teaching and research remained stubbornly labour-intensive. With rising productivity pushing up pay for highly-skilled hires elsewhere in the economy, UK higher education faced a bad case of the 'cost disease': the fate of any low-productivity sector competing for highly qualified and mobile staff (Baumol 2012). Save British Science, which started in 1986 with a 1500-signature letter to *The Times*, was probably the single most effective force in convincing politicians that quality was falling calamitously. Money was needed.

A decade later, Labour and the Conservatives reached an agreement that would transform the university sector. Whichever won in 1997 would introduce student fees to inject additional, private funding, which—on winning—Labour duly did. They also set themselves a goal of getting 50% of young people into higher education – a goal the country has just now reached.

Opponents of fees warned this was the 'thin end of the wedge', and so it has proved. Since the early, modest fees of £1,000 a year, England has moved to 'home' fees[6] of first £3,000, and now over £9,000 a year. Each change has been fraught. In 2004, Tony Blair had a majority of over 160 in the House of Commons. For the legislation authorising fees of up to £3,000 for students (while also establishing the income-contingent principle), the majority fell to just five.

Both in 2005, when £3,000 fees were introduced, with income-contingent repayments; and in 2010-11, when they were sharply raised, there were widespread predictions that applications would fall sharply, especially from the less well-off. This did not happen: and at the moment, we are experiencing a continuing steady increase in the proportion of the cohort applying to, and attending, university. (There is a demographic dip which means that absolute numbers of home students have dropped somewhat from their high point.)

The 2004-05 changes felt, at the time, like a workable long-term settlement, splitting the cost of undergraduate degree provision between student fees and a still substantial government 'teaching grant'. The decision to impose a large and sudden jump in fees just six years later was unexpected. An incoming Conservative-Liberal Democrat coalition government introduced a 'maximum fee level' of £9,000, expecting, naively, that most institutions would charge less. In fact, £9,000 became the norm, with only a very few courses charging less. This was, as explained below, entirely predictable and, indeed, predicted (by this author among others) but recurring gaps between official predictions and reality have been a repeated feature of higher education policy since at least the 1980s.

The fee increase came very soon after the 2010 election, and was deeply unpopular with students and young people: the response included mass demonstrations and a genuine riot in London. Although the possibility of an increase in fees from either a Conservative or a Labour government was trailed during the campaign, this level of

---

6 Any EU member state must make university places available to all EU citizens on the same basis as it does to its own. So, at present, any EU citizen accepted by an English university can access fee loans in precisely the same way and on the same terms as a UK national

increase certainly was not. Indeed, the Liberal Democrats had made heavy play with a pledge to abolish fees, in pursuit of student votes. Instead, as partners to the Conservatives in the 2010-15 coalition government, they signed up to, and were in consequence heavily attacked for, the very large increase. This 'betrayal' is generally seen as one significant factor in the collapse in the LibDem vote in subsequent elections.

Opinion polls show a high level of public acceptance for the idea that students should contribute to the cost of their education. The British Social Attitudes Survey tracks public attitudes to important policy areas on a rolling basis, and the 2014 survey – coming after the introduction of £9,000 fees – found that a large majority agreed that some (not all) students and their families should 'pay towards tuition costs' (sic) and around half that it was reasonable for students to take loans to help with maintenance while studying.[7] Nonetheless, having fees at all remains politically controversial.

The Labour Party under Blair had introduced income-contingent loans. The Labour Party, under the left-wing anti-Blairite Jeremy Corbyn, has taken a completely different position. During the 2017 general election campaign, the Labour Party pledged to abolish student fees altogether. This remains official party policy.

In this 2017 election, the Conservative Party lost the overall majority it had gained in 2015. This has made the Conservatives very nervous about current tuition policy and fee levels, but it is not clear how much difference, if any, the Labour pledge made. Britain currently has a huge age-related gulf in voting patterns and support – far greater than usual (Piketty 2018) – and this is probably related in large part to age-related differences in support for Brexit. What is true, however, is that the student vote was critically important in some seats. The Labour pledge also responded to a growing groundswell of concern over *levels* of student debt. At (now) £9,250 a year, fee plus maintenance loans pile up large levels of indebtedness: students can easily leave university with over £50,000 in debts.

---

[7] www.bsa.natcen.ac.uk/media/38917/bsa32_highereducation.pdf

In addition, elements of the funding model now resemble nothing so much as a Ponzi scheme. First, as explained next, the current balance of funding between government grants and fee income is as much a product of government financial rules and political smoke-and-mirrors as it is of any coherent thoughts on higher education policy. Second, a set of wildly over-optimistic beliefs about the 'returns' to a degree and, therefore, more recently, on the likelihood of loan repayment, has now been driving English education policy for decades now, and continues to do so. These beliefs are, however, rapidly losing credibility within the wider population.

The current funding system

As already noted, England currently operates with a system of 'income-contingent loans' for higher education students paying university fees. These are administered by the Student Loans Company, a not-for-profit organisation owned and funded by central government. Any eligible student who is offered a place in an approved English higher education institution – normally a university – is automatically eligible for a loan to cover the full cost of fees (which is itself regulated and subject to a maximum).[8] These are paid directly to the university by the SLC. Students may also take out maintenance loans which are very generous by international standards. Repayment starts only if and when a graduate's earnings exceed a threshold (currently £25,000), with repayment rates rising gradually thereafter.

The system of income-contingent loans which is used in England has the same logic and structure as in Australia, although the details differ quite substantially – and those details have a very large impact on repayment rates and schedules. What is true of any such system, however, is that it discourages price competition. In both

---

[8] There are a number of exceptions and complications: small private providers in particular may not have a full-fledged 'access' agreement, which involves efforts to increase participation by disadvantaged groups, in which case the maximum fee they can charge is lower. English students may also receive loans to study elsewhere in the UK.

2004 and 2010, when the major changes in fee policy occurred, the relevant government ministers predicted with confidence that price competition between universities would ensue.[9] This happy assumption was presumably built into the government's fiscal projections. No such competition followed. For very good reasons, the maximum fee of £9,000 became near-universal.

First of all, the whole point of an income-contingent system is to reduce price-sensitivity, especially for poorer and more risk-averse students. In a system of income-contingent loans, it makes no sense to choose a university because it is cheap. If you turn out to have made a bad choice, you won't earn a lot and won't have to repay anyway. And even if a student chose a course that was, say, 25% cheaper than the maximum, and eventually earned enough to repay everything, the amount saved is likely to be a small percentage of total costs once maintenance, and foregone earnings, are factored in.

Second, there are very few ways to make university education more 'efficient' – i.e. to deliver the *same quality* of education for less money. As noted earlier, education is a classic case of a sector which cannot deliver big productivity increases, but needs employees whose cost rises because other sectors can – the 'cost disease' identified by Baumol and referred to earlier. No-one has yet developed a model of effective teaching which is not highly dependent on individual teachers' time. Charging less than the maximum therefore means having less money for good staff, or small classes, as well as less for facilities, than institutions which charge more.

Moreover, prospective students have very little clear information on the quality of institutions. An institution which charges little is therefore signalling that it is not getting many applicants, and so is not worth much, and worth a lot less than 'top' universities which

---

9 David Willetts, for example, the Higher Education Minister who oversaw the move to a £9,000 a year maximum, expected most degrees to incur fees of about £7,000-£7,500.

cost more. In this environment, as research confirms,[10] price signals quality. Recent English governments have tried, and are trying, to provide more data, but current indicators of 'quality', such as the annual National Student Survey, are rightly criticised for both a lack of validity and for creating perverse incentives such as persistent grade inflation, discussed below (Royal Statistical Society 2018).

So, not surprisingly, there is virtually no price competition in the current English undergraduate 'market' any more than in other comparable systems. What there is, however, is a ballooning cost which will land on future taxpayers and about which the government has been in total denial.

I noted earlier that the huge fee rise announced in 2010 was unexpected. So why did it occur? Not because of any coherent policy or thought about what sort of provision the country might want or need, and who should pay for what. It was, instead, the result of 'austerity' politics, plus Treasury (comparable, in this instance, to Department of Finance) rules that, to a normal human being, appear to be straight out of *Alice in Wonderland*.

These rules, and their impact on higher education policy, have been discussed in a number of publications (Wolf et al. 2016). But for a perfect summing up, I would turn to the BBC's education correspondent.

> Question: How can you lend someone almost £120bn and not have a hole in your budget?
>
> Or how can you give out £17bn, only receive back £3bn and not be any worse off?
>
> Answer: When you're the government and it's the student loans system.[11]

It is clear that, on anything approaching current terms, a very large part of that loan book will never be repaid, piling up a liability

---

10 A number of institutions are well known in the sector for using price increases as a way of driving up their reputation successfully (see Askin and Bothner 2016).
11 https://www.bbc.co.uk/news/education-45421621

for the taxpayer instead. It represents real expenditure, for which the country taxed and borrowed. So what has been going on?

When the Conservative-Liberal Democrat Coalition came to power in 2010, it was in the wake of the 2008 financial crisis. The growth projections on which future government spending, and projected national borrowing and debt levels had been based, were clearly not materialising. The then-Chancellor of the Exchequer, George Osborne, proclaimed the need for 'austerity' and demanded big cuts from government departments.[12] Among the departments being pushed hard for very large cuts was the Department of Business, Innovation and Skills (BIS), which at that time also held the university brief.

At that point, in 2010, the total amount being paid directly to universities, as 'teaching grant', was larger than the amount they collected, via the Student Loan Company, from home students' fees – as is the case in many countries which combine fees with central grants. But a government accounting convention meant that student fees and direct teaching payments were treated differently in the accounts. Grants were expenditure. But fees paid through student loans were not. Because it could be assumed that the loans would be repaid, they did not 'count', whereas teaching grants did.

For the officials and politicians concerned, this seemed like a win-win situation. They could slash the teaching grant for undergraduate degrees, earning gold stars for their 'austerity cuts'. But they could also not merely maintain but, indeed, increase, university funding by tripling undergraduate fee levels – and the amount government paid over to the Student Loan Company. University quality would be protected and, indeed, universities have, since then, enjoyed the highest real level of teaching-income per home student in over 30 years (Wolf 2015). And the income contingent nature of the loans

---

12 Support for this approach was far from total, with many commentators arguing for a very different and more Keynesian response to the crisis.

meant that students would be protected too. So that is what they did.[13]

The trouble was, and is, that whether or not it appears on the books when first lent, this is real money, raised from taxes or borrowed by the government, and a great deal of it is simply not going to be repaid.[14] The precise amounts which will not be repaid vary considerably depending on assumptions about the economy, the distribution of earnings, and on whether or not governments decide to vary loan terms retrospectively – as they are able to do. But on any currently credible assumptions, *only 30% of students are expected to repay their loans in full.* The Office for Budget Responsibility monitors government spending and revenue and, in his notes to their 2018 fiscal sustainability report, the head of the OBR observed that,

- 'The loan book is large and growing rapidly, with net outlays forecast to reach £20 billion by 2022-23. The value of the outstanding loan book is set to rise to around 20 per cent of GDP by the 2040s;' and
- 'if we take into account the cost to the government of financing the loans, it makes a loss of almost £10 billion on ... (the 2017-18) single cohort.' (Chote 2018).

With every year since 2012, there has been growing awareness of these huge looming write-offs. The Office for National Statistics (ONS) announced in summer 2018 that it was reviewing the way the loans are treated in the national accounts, and in December 2018 gave its expected decision. The full amount of student loans can no longer be treated as an 'asset' – i.e., something that will be repaid in full,

---

13 For arts and humanities subjects, any direct teaching grant ended: this complete switch from a mixed to a fees-only payment system is, to the best of my knowledge, unique for publicly-funded universities. Some teaching grant remains for science and other 'high cost' subjects but is much reduced.

14 This is especially true for loans to women, because the current loan conditions provide for unpaid balances to be written off after 30 years. Many graduate women interrupt employment, or work part-time for salaries below the repayment threshold during child-rearing years.

with interest, and therefore costs the taxpayer nothing. Henceforth the Treasury must distinguish between the amount which it is confident will be repaid and the amount that will be written off and is therefore public expenditure (Office for National Statistics 2018).

Suddenly, loans are no longer a magic answer to the challenge of funding higher education, allowing endless expansion at no cost. They are at one and the same time a looming financial problem, a terrible weight on students facing an uncertain labour market and soaring house prices, and a somewhat underhand way to fund universities more favourably than any other parts of education. Universities' relatively privileged financial position, compared to other parts of education, and other public services, was already receiving increasingly hostile scrutiny, especially with respect to Vice-Chancellors' salaries and a spate of new and expensive building programs. The ONS decision can only increase this scrutiny.

International students

At the start of this chapter, we identified three key characteristics of current English education, which together account for a great deal of its recent development. The first was the fees regime. The second – which is shared with the rest of the UK – is the importance of international students.

While international student fees are perhaps slightly less important than in Australia, many universities are enormously and increasingly dependent on overseas intakes and, in total, they currently contribute over a quarter of teaching and tuition income.[15] Sector organisations monitor obsessively the relative performance of the UK in recruitment, compared to the other 'Anglo-Saxon' countries which currently dominate high-fee international student markets, namely the US, Canada, Australia and (to a smaller degree) New Zealand.

International fees and international student numbers are entirely uncapped – and, in the case of fees, effectively unregulated – and have

---

15 Higher Education Statistics Agency (HESA) https://www.hesa.ac.uk/data-and-analysis/providers/finances

been ever since Margaret Thatcher ended the practice of treating international and home students alike for fee purposes. (At the time, there were no up-front fees, and international students were included in the overall numbers cap). While virtually every university recruits some international students and, indeed, is extremely keen to do so, there are enormous differences in how large a proportion of the student body comes from outside the EU – and can therefore be charged what the market will bear.[16] For example, at the London School of Economics, 44% of students are international: it is 35 per cent at UCL, and 27% in Edinburgh, one of Scotland's two members of the Russell Group.[17] That plummets to 10% in the 'new' universities of Northumbria or Lincoln, and just 3% in Staffordshire or Gloucestershire.

Today, in a huge and expanding global higher education market, the higher a university's reputation, the more international applicants it can attract, the more selective it can be, and the more it can charge international students. This 'virtuous circle' is evident in every country which –like the UK and Australia – recruits large numbers of international, and especially Chinese and other Asian, students.

The resulting differences within the sector are manifest on any number of fiscal measures. In a recent analysis, a colleague and I estimated that English 'Russell Group' universities currently pull in an average of £3,000 more teaching income per student per year than the rest of the sector (Wolf and Jenkins 2018). Since fees for home students are controlled, this is a result of both the proportion of international students and the (highly variable) level of fees they pay.

Differences between individual universities are accounted for in very large part by whether they appear in global league tables, and in what position. And since global leagues are accounted for in overwhelming part by research reputation, it is their research

---

[16] This is a senior university finance officer's description of how he and his peers set international fees.
[17] There are currently 24 Russell Group universities: two in Scotland, one in Wales, one in Northern Ireland and 20 in England.

reputation which makes the Russell Group average so high (Hazelkorn 2015).

For many years, the UK enjoyed a unique position in Europe with respect to international fee income. Other countries limited recruitment, and/or offered international students access on the same very cheap terms as they did home recruits. By 2007, 16% of overall teaching and tuition revenue in England already came from international student fees; by 2014, 24%. Although other European countries are now competing for this market, often offering English-language programs, the UK still recruits more, and charges more. For example, Russell Group international undergraduate fees of, typically, £17,000 to £20,000 a year (AUD$31,000-36,500), are more than twice the Dutch or Swedish level.

As in Australia, this money is paying for academic staff, libraries, sports facilities, for ambitious building programs and, also, critically, for research. Teaching cross-subsidises research to a large extent in both countries (Norton 2015), and this is possible because of the high level of international fees. As we have just seen, research outcomes also drive prestige and market position, domestically and internationally. This 'virtuous circle' means that, in spite of governments' publicly-stated desire to create competitive environments in which hierarchies shift and innovative institutions thrive, the hierarchy of UK universities is highly stable. This seems again to mirror the Australian position.

Lifting the cap

Australia, New Zealand and the UK have had a strong tendency, in recent decades, to borrow policies from each other, especially in the field of tertiary education (university and vocational). The third major influence on current higher education in England – though, again, not Scotland – is a policy which Australia implemented a few years before England. It lifted any general restraints on student numbers in universities,[18] and provided government funding for as many students

---

18 There continue to be restrictions on certain courses, notably in medicine and other health-related occupations.

as universities chose to admit. In Australia, there is a 'demand-led' system. In England, the government 'lifted the cap'.

We may discover, when the relevant papers enter the public domain, whether or not anyone inside government took overt notice of Australian experience, and whether our politicians were consciously copying Australia. Certainly, some members of the higher education policy community were aware of Australian developments, and of the problems that demand-led funding had brought and were correspondingly aghast at the lack of attention being given to the problems that had arisen there.[19]

The relevant English policy is known as 'lifting the cap' because that is the term generally used to describe the number of home students that a given university (and, therefore, the overall system) could admit at undergraduate level. (Overseas numbers and postgraduate numbers had been 'uncapped' for many years.) It was lifted completely unexpectedly in 2013, when the government announced that, from 2015, any and all universities could recruit as many 'home' undergraduate students as they liked, all of whom would be eligible for standard student finance. Members of Cabinet were, apparently, told shortly before the announcement with the explanation being that 'anyone who can benefit' from higher education should be able to attend,[20] but there was no external indication that this massive change was imminent and the sector was taken by surprise.

Until the surprise announcement, the number of funded 'home student' places in English universities had been centrally controlled (as is still the case in Scotland) and allocated to individual universities.

---

19 The annual lecture sponsored by the Higher Education Policy Institute (HEPI), the English think tank which specifically focuses on higher education, was given in 2014 by Paul Wellings, Vice-Chancellor of Wollongong. In a well-attended lecture at Australia House he highlighted some of the challenges and problems that had attended recent deregulation in Australia. As someone who was at that lecture I do not remember there being any indication, from discussants, of how, if at all, English government policy had been designed to address these.

20 Personal communication.

This meant that overall costs were predictable centrally, and that the financial viability of all institutions could be secured.

Between 2011 and 2014 the government introduced a number of changes which meant that universities could, in effect, compete for some places, with the most successful and attractive growing in relative size: but total numbers remained capped. Then, as noted above, the cap on numbers was lifted completely. Since there are no formal restrictions on recruitment standards, and universities may admit whomever they wish, this meant that, in principle, anyone could attend if they could find a university to accept them.

Just three years on, the results of lifting the cap have been not just predictable but also extraordinarily rapid. Universities are far from being slow, ponderous institutions, wedded to tradition: on the contrary, they respond with alacrity to each and every fiscal incentive.

Funding per home student is, as noted, currently quite generous, and increasing home numbers is therefore more attractive, relative to increasing international numbers, than was the case a few years ago (although international students still pay more). Higher status universities have moved rapidly to increase their home intakes, and their overall student numbers. Durham, Exeter, University College London and my own institution, King's College London, are among the Russell Group universities expanding at speed. Meanwhile, a number of 'new' universities are facing plummeting levels of application and enrolment, in spite of pouring money into marketing: overall, more than a quarter of the sector has fewer students than a decade ago. To recap – England's is a strongly hierarchical system, where students very often leave home to study, and where, as shown, there is virtually no incentive for students to pay, or universities to charge, less than the maximum permitted fee. What is rational, therefore, is to attend the highest-prestige institution you can – and they mostly do.

Competition can be a huge force for efficiency and innovation *under the right conditions*. It can also drive down quality, reward rent-seeking and incentivise fraud. The type of competition currently prevalent in English universities has probably been good for research activity, but it has certainly not been good for the maintenance of academic standards.

We have no objective data on the performance of students across universities and across time, although surveys of English academics find that the large majority of academic staff believe the standards required for a given grade or degree class have declined.[21] We do, however, know that there has been an enormous increase in the proportion of First Class and 2.1 degrees awarded throughout the sector, and that it is well nigh impossible to explain this as anything other than grade inflation. English degrees are given a 'classification': a First class degree is the top, follow by a 2.1, a 2.2, or a Third.

The vast bulk of the increase in student numbers, over the last 10 years, has been the result of lower-achieving young people entering university, not of rising standards in schools (Bekhradnia and Beech 2018 and UCAS 2018). The higher education regulator published a report into degree standards in December 2018, looking at how far changes in degree patterns could be explained by standards on entry: since England sets external examinations at the end of upper secondary education, and the standard of these is monitored and secured from year to year using extensive statistical checks, this is relatively straightforward.

The regulator concluded that a very large proportion of the increase in First and 2.1 classifications was 'unexplained' – meaning that it could not follow from rising standards at entry – and that 'The analysis corroborates concerns about grade inflation across the higher education sector' (Office for Students 2018). This was true across the sector and for the large majority of individual institutions. One large research university in Southeastern England, the University of Surrey,

---

[21] A good number of professional bodies, including the medical professions, set national examinations. It is not clear whether standards here have gone up, down or stayed the same, although strong efforts are made to maintain consistent levels. What we do know is that, for the main medical examinations, there is no correlation between the performance of students from a given university and 'National Student Survey' scores of student satisfaction – but a strong correlation with pre-university attainment.

gave first-class degrees to half of its total graduating class in 2017. Across the sector, the percentage had risen to 27%: as recently as 2000 it was below 10%.

Grade inflation is not specific to England, but the speed with which it has proceeded almost certainly reflects not only the pressures from students who have 'paid' for a degree, but also the imperative to score well on National Student Survey. This measures student 'satisfaction' and is increasingly used by government for regulatory purposes. Other changes relate much more directly to recruitment, and the need to get enough students enrolled to stay solvent.

There has consequently been an enormous growth in unconditional offers, outside the 'top' part of the prestige hierarchy. Applicants are offered places regardless of their academic results in an effort to secure firm acceptances.[22] More recent still is a surge in marketing and offers for a 'Foundation' Year: a pre-degree year, tied to a particular degree in a particular university, which is, in effect, a repeat final year of school, enabling students, if successful, to proceed onto the degree. The difference between a Foundation Year and repeating the final year of school is that it is funded at a full £9,250, under a student loan. This is significantly more than schools receive: it means that the student incurs and the institution receives four years of fees instead of the normal three. Given the target 'market', much of this is highly unlikely, on present earnings evidence, to be repaid.

Overall, the result of lifting the cap is that the higher education sector is in a state of serious disequilibrium. Since this was highly predictable, why did government ministers think it was a good idea? The fundamental reason is a faith in the power of higher education to generate economic growth, which translates into a belief that the more university students, the better. Higher education is supposedly a magic bullet – a cure-all for the economy which will more than pay for itself,

---

22 The integrated application system for undergraduate education means applicants can only 'hold' two offers and will be highly tempted to make at least one of those an unconditional one. UCAS, the application agency, reports that, in 2017-18, a quarter of applicants received at least one unconditional offer.

however large it becomes. This is joined to a belief, held especially but not only on the right, that it will be good for quality and price if universities 'compete' in a market, and that the more institutions and the more new entrants there are, the better.[23] But it is the supposed link between higher education and growth which is key, and has driven higher education policy in this country since the early 1990s.

The growth illusion

Given the developments outlined above, why has the government been so keen to increase university enrolments and open more universities?

Universities are not just training institutions, existing to serve labour market demand. In England today, however, they are discussed, overwhelmingly, in economic terms. And looked at in this way there are, crudely, two major ways in which education has a direct impact on the economy. First, there is the investment in skills — that is learning to do new useful things or, in the jargon, 'developing human capital'. This is usually a good idea and, if it is not prohibitively expensive, makes us more productive. Second, there is 'signalling' and 'sorting' of a very general kind. People sink time and money into proving, via education, that they are more desirable to employers than others: that having more qualifications, more bits of paper, means they should move right up the shortlist. And the more prestigious the institution from which they were obtained, the harder it was to get into that institution, the further up you go.

This works for individuals, if it helps them into a higher-paying job. Signalling of this sort can also make hiring cheaper and more efficient for employers if it genuinely indicates which applicants will be quicker to learn, or more likely to work hard. But signals are not always very accurate; and, when education is used in this way, there is also, always, a risk of an expensive and wasteful spiral. If everybody spends years re-certificating skills they already have, just to land a job they could already have done, or taking qualifications simply to

---

23 For a sophisticated presentation of these arguments, by the minister who lifted the cap, see Willetts 2017.

stay ahead of the next person, then society is wasting a lot of time and money that could be better used elsewhere.

For many years now, English politicians have ascribed all the results of university attendance to skill acquisition. Graduates appeared consistently to earn more than non-graduates. Therefore, they were more skilled. Therefore, if we had more graduates, they would all go on earning the same as their predecessors, and the whole country would get richer, and richer, and richer. Therefore, university expansion was an unequivocally good idea and a superb investment.[24]

There was a deep confusion here between relative and absolute earnings: a lifetime gap between the average earnings of graduates and the unqualified does not actually tell you what either group is in fact earning: they (and the country) could all be getting richer or all getting poorer. But the belief that 'returns to a degree' were all the result of graduates being more skilled and generating economic growth, and that this would go on being true for future graduates in a much larger system, became deeply embedded in government, among both politicians and officials.

One of the UK Parliament's last actions before the June 2017 election, which heralded a period of exclusive concern with Brexit, was to pass a new *Higher Education and Research Act* (UK). Its principal purposes, as expressed by its ministerial sponsor, were to ease the setting-up of new universities, and give new players, including private ones, faster access to the government's fee-and-loan-based regime: this was designed to increase competition among institutions for students, and further boost degree enrolments. Drawing on a single cross-country regression analysis, the preceding White Paper proclaimed:

> Doubling the number of universities per capita is associated with over 4 per cent higher future GDP per capita.
>
> (Department for Education 2016).

That statement, if taken literally, would mean that dividing each of our large universities into three or four smaller ones would more

---
[24] See Wolf 2002 for a fuller discussion of these arguments

than compensate for the worse post-Brexit scenarios. That is palpably absurd. But it encapsulates what was, for a quarter century, the dominant policy mind-set.

Ever greater numbers of university students and institutions make it harder and harder for anyone to have good quality information on what each degree or university actually does, and, therefore, on what a given individual graduate has learned and can do. In that environment you would expect signalling of quite a general kind to be more and more evident: and so it is. Where you study, and what subject you take, are increasingly important in the labour market.

In England, as described above, students typically graduate with hefty debts, a system justified by the argument that having a degree 'pays' in later life. Yet there are universities in England where average graduate earnings are no higher than those for non-graduates. And in every subject, graduates' future incomes – the 'returns' to their degree – vary enormously and are strongly related to where they studied. The highest earnings go, predictably, to graduates from institutions at the top of the well-known and well-established prestige hierarchy.

The most thorough published analyses, to date, have been carried out by the Institute for Fiscal Studies (Britton et al. 2016; Belfield et al. 2018). They show that the returns to a degree vary enormously by university and by subject studied. For example, economics is one of the top 'earners' (no doubt because so many graduates go into banking and financial services). But for economics graduates of the University of Central Lancashire, median earnings five years out are just £18,900 (or almost £10,000 below full-time median adult earnings). At Kingston they can expect £27,400; at Essex £34,000. But LSE economics graduates, five years into work, have a median salary of £55,200 – and for the upper quartile, it is £120,000.

This sort of detailed information obviously reinforces the pressure to attend 'top' universities, and, over time, the value of their 'signal'. Moreover, the information will be more and more accessible in future years, as the government makes it available to prospective students and employers through its 'LEO' website.²⁵ The reasoning is that, once students know about differences in future earnings, they will make more 'informed' choices, and by enrolling increasingly in the courses which offer the best returns, will make the whole economy more 'productive'. But this is only true if the differences are actually a reflection of differences in the skills that students acquired during their degrees, rather than, in large part, a function of prior attainment and signalling. Governments have believed this: the general public is less and less inclined to do so – and also more inclined to see much university education as a waste of time and money.

In the last year or two, in part because high fees have made universities so politically 'live', there has been growing scrutiny, by media and parliamentary committees, of the current settlement. They have not liked what they found. Vice-Chancellors' salaries have become a toxic subject for the sector. So has the building boom on university campuses – linked, in good part, to both absolute growth and the desire to enrol high-fee (and affluent) overseas students, but taking place against a background of financial stringency and falling real spending for schools and vocational programs. Parliamentary committees have criticised the fees regime, including not only the treatment of government debt but also the interest rates that students have been charged; and also argued that spending is too heavily tilted towards full degrees and away from technical and vocational education. ²⁶

Nor is this criticism confined to the traditional right wing press, which has for years railed against 'Mickey Mouse' degrees. The following two quotes are from columnists for the left-of-centre *Guardian*, whose readership includes a large proportion of the country's public sector professionals, and from the sober *Financial Times*.

> In any other area it would be called mis-selling. Given the

---

25 https://www.officeforstudents.org.uk/data-and-analysis/graduate-earnings-data-on-unistats/

26 House of Commons Education Committee 2018; House of Commons Committee of Public Accounts 2018; House of Lords Economic Affairs Committee 2018.

sheer numbers of those duped, a scandal would erupt and the guilty parties would be forced to make amends. In this case, they'd include some of the most eminent politicians in Britain. But we don't call it mis-selling. We refer to it instead as 'going to uni'.... For two decades, Westminster has used universities as its magic answer for social mobility. Ministers did so with the connivance of highly paid vice-chancellors, and in the process they have trashed much of what was good about British higher education (Chakrabortty 2018).

For universities, the simple incentive (is) ... to maximise revenues with bums on seats. Hapless students enrolled in low-quality, cheap-to-provide degrees. ... The consequence of policy... has been universities offering lousy courses, a dysfunctional market in degrees, grade inflation (Giles 2018).

In summary, the English university system is facing a combination of criticism from the political and media elite, disequilibrium created by policy change, and an understandably 'consumerist' student body, invited both to pay up and to see education largely in terms of financial pay-offs. In this climate, further disruption, and increased government interference, both seem a near certainty.

References

Askin, N. and Bothner, M. 'Status-Aspirational Pricing: The "Chivas Regal" Strategy in US Higher Education, 2006–2012', *Administrative Science Quarterly,* 2016, 61(2).

Baumol, W. J., *The Cost Disease: Why Computers Get Cheaper and Health Care Doesn't,* Yale University Press, New Haven, 2012.

Bekhradnia, B. and Beech, D., *Demand for Higher Education to 2030* HEPI, Oxford, 2018.

Belfield, C, Britton, J., Buscha F., Dearden, L, Dickson, M., ven der Erve, L., Sibieta, L., Vignoles, Walker, I. and Zhu, Y., *The Relative Labour Market*

Returns to Different Degrees, Institute for Fiscal Studies and Department for Education, London, 2018.

Britton, J., Dearden, L., Shephard, N., and Vignoles, A., *How English Domiciled Graduate Earnings Vary with Gender, Institution Attended, Subject and Socio-economic Background* (No. W16/06), Institute for Fiscal Studies, London, 2016.

Carswell, J., *Government and the Universities in Britain*, Cambridge University Press, Cambridge, 1985.

Chakrabortty, Aditya, 'Mis-sold, Expensive and Overhyped: Why Our Universities Are a Con', *Guardian*, 20 September 2018.

Chote, Robert, 'Fiscal Sustainability Report 2018 and Accounting for Student Loans', *Office for Budget Responsibility*, 2018.

Department for Education, *Higher Education: Success as a Knowledge Economy* (White Paper), London: DfE, 2016.

Giles, Chris, 'Student Finance Distortions Show Official Statistics Are Awry', *Financial Times*, 20 December 2018.

Hazelkorn, E., *Rankings and the Reshaping of Higher Education: The Battle for World-class Excellence*, 2nd ed., Palgrave Macmillan, Basingstoke, 2015.

House of Commons Education Committee, *Value for Money in Higher Education*, House of Commons, London, 2018.

House of Commons Public Accounts Committee, *The Higher Education Market*, London: House of Commons, 2018.

House of Lords Economic Affairs Committee, *Treating Students Fairly: The Economics of Post-School Education*, House of Lords, London, 2018.

Norton, A., *The Cash Nexus: How Teaching Funds Research in Australian Universities,* Grattan Institute, Melbourne, 2015.

Office for National Statistics, *New Treatment of Student Loans in the Public Sector Finances and National Accounts*, 2018.

Office for Students, *Analysis of Degree Classifications Over Time: Changes in Graduate Attainment*, Office for Students, 2018.

Piketty, T., *Rising Inequality and the Changing Structure of Political Conflict. (Evidence from France, Britain and the US, 1948-2017)*, 2018.

Royal Statistical Society, *Response to the Teaching Excellence and Student Outcomes Framework Subject-Level Consultation,* Royal Statistical Society, London, 2018.

UCAS (Universities and Colleges Admissions Service), *End of Cycle Report,* UCAS, Cheltenham, 2018.

Willetts, D., *A University Education,* Oxford University Press, Oxford, 2017.

Wolf, A., *Does Education Matter? Myths about Education and Economic Growth,* Penguin Press, London, 2002.

Wolf, A., *Heading for the Precipice: Can Further and Higher Education Funding Policies be Sustained?,* King's College London, The Policy Institute, 2015.

Wolf, A., Dominguez-Reig, G. and Sellen, P., *Remaking Tertiary Education: Can we Create a System that is Fair and Fit for Purpose?,* Education Policy Institute, London, 2016.

Wolf, A. and Jenkins, A., 'What's in a Name? The Impact of Reputation and Rankings on the Teaching Income of English Universities', *Higher Education Quarterly,* 2018, 72.4 286-303.

9

A Canadian Perspective on Higher Education in Australia

Charles M. Beach and Frank Milne

While Canada and Australia share much in common, this chapter highlights their often quite different higher education systems. This chapter compares higher education sectors in the two countries out of a wish to offer lessons for the direction of higher education policy they are facing. The discussion is largely based on comparative statistics since 2000 and current policy stances, and the incentives they reveal.

Distinctive features of the Canadian higher education system

First off, it should be noted that in Canada constitutional responsibility for education – including for tertiary, post-secondary, or higher education (terms used interchangeably in this study) – lies with the provinces. So rules, regulations, funding and demographic pressures for institutions of higher education vary somewhat across the ten provinces, and especially so between the province of Quebec with its francophone majority and language-based education systems and the rest of the provinces.

The federal government does not directly support teaching activity in the post-secondary sector. The areas of direct federal government involvement in higher education since 1996 have been in research grants and research chairs, student aid, and occasional fits of infrastructure investment. So, in 2016, for example, federal government grants and contracts accounted for 9.4% of total university revenue compared to 40.0% from (essentially) provincial sources (CAUBO 2018, Report 1.1). This compares to 8.6 and 44.7%, respectively, in 2000, and 11.7

and 42.8% in 2005 (ibid.). The federal share has generally bounced around in response to intermittent federal initiatives, while the provincial share has broadly declined as funding sources have generally shifted to the private sector.[1]

A second major point of context is that the higher education sector in Canada has a binary structure which includes universities as well as an extensive array of community colleges (henceforth 'colleges'). Universities are 'Institutions offering Bachelor's, Master's and/or PhDs', while colleges are 'Institutions offering Applied Master's, Applied Bachelor's or Master's, Bachelor's college diplomas, attestations d'études collégiales (AEC) in Quebec, Associate Degrees and other college programs. Does not include vocational schools' (CAUT 2018, Table 4.2).[2] College programs typically run two to three years and have much in similarity to the US state college systems, while university bachelor programs are typically four years. The general role or purpose of colleges has been seen as (i) offering more ready access with lower learning barriers to continuing education that could lead into universities, and (ii) providing programs of a more applied nature designed to address specific workplace needs better (Skolnik 2005, 61).

There are currently 121 accredited universities (including a few university colleges) – 92 public and 29 private (almost all non-profit) – in Canada and 159 colleges – 132 public and 27 private (all non-profit) (ibid.). The higher education sector is thus relatively decentralised. Canadian universities also range very much in size from about a thousand students or less (e.g., King's College University in Halifax) to about 75 thousand (University of Toronto spread over three campuses). Forty universities have 10 thousand or more students (comparable to 38 in Australia – Universities Australia 2018), 15 between five and 10 thousand, and seven less than one thousand (Wikipedia 2018). Thus the university system is quite heterogeneous in size as well. A popular

---

[1] Federal share of community college revenues is less than 2% compared to provincial funding share of 62% (CAUT 2018, Table 1.1).

[2] The system examined in this study thus does not include trade schools offering trades certificates or registered apprenticeships.

ranking of Canadian universities has traditionally categorised them into primarily undergraduate schools, comprehensive schools that offer a wider range of programs, and medical/doctoral schools with major doctoral and professional programs (Mueller and Rockerbie 2005).

The higher education sector is of substantial size in the Canadian economy. In 2015-16, there were 2.008 million students enrolled in tertiary education out of a Canadian population of 36.3 million (vs. 1.457 million students – Universities Australia 2018 – out of a 22.9 million population for Australia). A number of summary higher education statistics for Canada are provided in international comparison in Table 1. The Universitas 21 ranking of national higher education systems as a whole places Canada at eighth in 2018, down from sixth in 2015 (vs. Australia close by at tenth). Public expenditures on tertiary education as a percentage of GDP in Canada is 1.7%, compared to 1.3-1.4% in Australia, the United States, the United Kingdom and the OECD average. Thus total expenditure in the higher education sector can be estimated (in comparable US dollars) as $62.5 billion in Canada vs. $55.3 billion for Australia.[3] As a fraction of total government expenditure, the share is also relatively high in Canada. But, interestingly, this higher share comes from Canada spending much more on college training (what the OECD refers to as short-cycle tertiary education) than most other countries. As a result, the proportion of 25-34 year olds with tertiary education is again markedly higher than for the other comparators. But a more refined breakdown shows that this is due to a much higher fraction with college education. The fraction with a bachelor's education, while higher than the OECD average, is lower than in Australia, the US, and the UK. The fraction with advanced degrees in Canada is also below that in the US and UK. However, a relatively high proportion of 30-44 year olds with non-tertiary education parents attain tertiary education in Canada compared to the OECD average (OECD 2017; Canada Study, 3), so the opportunity for advancement into a tertiary education is considered relatively high.

---

[3] Calculations are based on lines 1 and 4 of Table 1 multiplied by US dollar GDP figures for 2015 in *The Economist*.

Public funding for higher education is somewhat higher in Canada than in Australia. The government share of tertiary education funding in Canada at 48% is higher than in the other three comparator countries, though well below the OECD average of 71%. The flip side is that the private sector share (largely tuition and fees), at 52%, is relatively lower than for the comparators though well above the OECD average. The pattern is generally similar for annual expenditure per student in the tertiary sectors: while the figure for Canada exceeds that for Australia, and is well above the OECD average, it is also below that for the UK and well below that in the United States.

Over the last decade or so, higher education in Canada has come to be seen – in addition to all its standard roles – as a pathway to attract high-skilled young immigrants to Canada. Like many developed countries, Canada is facing a natural rate of population growth below the replacement level, so that, with immigration, both the economy and the population grow. Seeking to retain some of the international post-secondary students helps address many high-tech job vacancies that Canadian employers say they have difficulty finding the skilled talent they need to grow – especially in the key STEM disciplines. Skilled immigration also complements and advances current production processes and increases the supply of entrepreneurial talent. With these considerations in mind, a new Canadian Experience Class immigration program was set up in 2008 to target highly skilled temporary foreign workers and recent foreign post-secondary graduates of Canadian schools with qualifying Canadian work experience.

Foreign students, though, play an even larger role in the Australian higher education system than in Canada. The proportion of international students in higher education in Canada at 11% in 2016 is lower than in Australia (at 26% – Grattan 2018, 27) and in the United Kingdom, though well above the OECD average. The proportion rises with the level of tertiary education in all countries.

Bachelor-level tuition fees for domestic students in Canada are about the same as for Australia, much lower than for the US International student fees, however, in Canada are more than triple domestic fees and thus exceed those paid by foreign students in both Australia and the United States.

The overall level of R&D expenditures as a fraction of GDP has long been chronically low in Canada as compared, say, to Australia, the United States and even the OECD average. In Canada, this comes to about 1.6%, compared to Australia's 2.1% (STIC 2015, 23; APRFS 2017, 50). This has long been a public concern and attributed to the relative importance of natural resources in the Canadian economy and to the private sector in Canada operating as a branch plant to the United States where multinational companies traditionally have invested much more in R&D activities. A portion of the best Canadian technical talent typically moves to the US each year where there are more opportunities and funding available. The level of *higher-education sector* R&D expenditures as a fraction of GDP, however, is well above the OECD average and considerably higher than that in the United States or United Kingdom. So higher-education sector research activity in Canada stands up well, but cannot make up for the traditionally very poor business sector research activity level. Over the 2009-14 period, Canada ranked ninth in the world in terms of research publications, down from its previous seventh place position over 2003-08 (CCA 2018, xviii). In terms of average citation of research publications relative to population size, Canada ranked sixth internationally over 2009-14, compared to Australia's ranking of fifth (CCA 2018, xx; APRFS 2017, 50).

Table 2 provides some background information on the *growth* of the higher education sector in Canada since 2000. Numbers of students enrolled in higher education has risen pretty steadily since 2000, though the number of domestic students has started to fall off in the last five years essentially for demographic reasons. The relatively rapid growth of foreign students in universities has kept the total student numbers rising. These increases are driven by a rising demand for higher education due to higher average incomes and recognition of the job market benefits of higher education, by rising labour market needs for skilled labour as technology and trade evolve, by expanding the number of university and college positions available in the tertiary sector and, in Canada's case, by relatively high levels of immigration (similar to Australia) where immigrants have traditionally worked hard to see that their children get a university education.

Total university and college revenues in Canada have also risen steadily. The key feature, though, is the declining share of provincial funding over 2000-2016 from 43.1 to 39.1% for universities (and from 64.6 to 60.7% for colleges), and the increasing share of revenues from student tuition and fees from 18.8 to 27.9% for universities (and from 18.3 to 25.8% for colleges). There has thus been a substantial shift in funding for higher education in Canada over this period from public sources towards direct student or household payments for their education.

Public funding and government direction in post-secondary education[4]

In light of these basic background results, several major challenges or stresses are evident that create a mix of incentives that need to be better understood.

Public expenditures on higher education under pressure

Provincial government budgets in Canada – the major source of public revenue for the tertiary sector – are being squeezed by rising costs of health care with an ageing population and from other infrastructure and social needs for a growing urban population, while trying to maintain competitive tax rates relative both to other provinces as well as to the United States to the south. As a result, revenues from governments per student in universities in Canada have declined in real terms by about 15% between 2010-11 and 2015-16 (row 3 of Table 2). A large portion of this decline was also a fall off in direct federal contributions

---
4 A more detailed discussion is provided in Beach and Milne (2018).

as the federal government sought to reduce its deficit. Total university expenditures per student (in real terms) also declined since 2010-11, but by a more muted 3.4% (Table 2, row 4). With public sector funding has come public sector equity and other program requirements (without additional funding), and more extensive reporting/monitoring review and administrative costs. Tertiary sector costs also generally go up faster than the CPI used in calculating the above per student figures (Ehrenberg 2005).

As student numbers have risen, so also has the number of university faculty, but less than proportionally. The result has been a substantial increase in the overall ratio of students to full-time teaching faculty (row 7) from 22.5 in 2000-01 to 34.8 most recently. Corresponding figures for Australia show an increase from 18.1 in 2001 to 20.7 in 2013 (Universities Australia 2015, Fig. 49). This is consistent with larger class sizes, less access to faculty, reduced use of term papers and essays, increased reliance on multiple-choice assignments and exams, and generally reduced quality of post- secondary education (Mahboubi 2017).

At the same time, universities are reducing the proportion of faculty who are permanent full-time and increasing their use of lower-cost temporary, adjunct and part-time employees (row 8). This has been a major issue in several faculty union strikes that have occurred. University spending on scholarships and bursaries (in part government mandated) has also steadily risen from 3.6% of university expenditures in 2000-01 to 5.7% in 2015-16 (CANSIM, Table 477-0059). These funds were thus not available to spend on teaching and research.

The biggest revenue change, however, has been the rising component of tuition and fees (row 5) – essentially set by provincial governments – as governments have shifted costs of higher education increasingly to students and households. Between 2000-01 and 2015-16, real tuition and fee costs per student rose by 56.7% for universities, and between 2001-02 and 2015-16 went up by 45.4% for colleges. Such major shifting of the costs of higher education has serious efficiency and equity concerns (Boadway 2005; Barr 2005).

One of the leading concerns of reduced government funding and rising user costs is accessibility to post-secondary education. There are at least two aspects of accessibility here. One operates from the supply side of the tertiary sector and affects the availability of student positions or capacity of post-secondary institutions. The other operates from the demand side of the education market and reflects how higher tuition and fees can reduce student access for those who cannot afford to attend (i.e., unequal access), especially for lower- and middle-income households, and more so for those potentially attending universities than colleges. Fortin (2005), using Canadian and US data, estimates both these effects separately and finds that (i) a 1% increase in university tuition levels reduces enrolment rates by about 0.15%, while (ii) a 1% decrease in provincial funding levels to universities (in terms of per student-age person) yields a decrease in enrolment rates of 0.25%. The decreased funding effect to universities is thus considerably larger than the negative tuition effect on students.

A worrisome consequence of rising student contribution levels has been increasing student debt levels. Large amounts of student debt can reduce a graduate's financial independence and lead to postponed fertility and home ownership, and it can bias a graduate's choice of field of specialisation and jobs towards those that are more remunerative than rewarding. There is a complex mix of student loan options with both federal (Canada Student Loans) and provincial (e.g., Ontario Student Assistance) programs. In 2013-14, the proportion of full-time university students receiving a Canada Student Loan was 37.0% (CAUT Almanac 2018, Table 3.3) and average government debt owed at graduation by bachelor's students was $22.3 thousand in 2010-11 (Statistics Canada CANSIM Table 477-0068).

Historically low interest rates may be a contributing factor as well. Rising student debt levels are more a problem of university graduates than of college graduates, though this also reflects the higher expected earnings levels of the former. There is every reason to expect these figures to be considerably higher now because of big jumps in tuition and fee levels. In contrast to Australia's HELP program, Canada also does not have an income-contingent student loan system despite repeated researcher suggestions to consider one.

A further concern is the incentive to bring in foreign students. Funding arrangements concerning foreign students differ across provinces. In Ontario, for example, the provincial government does not provide funding for foreign undergraduate students, but allows the universities to charge much higher tuition fees to foreign students and to keep almost all this tuition revenue for the university's operations. At the margin, then, there is an incentive to raise revenue by increasing foreign student numbers. This generally benefits the better known universities. But foreign student numbers are still considerably below those in Australia or the United Kingdom, perhaps because many Canadian schools are not well known internationally or are considered as close substitutes for US schools. Some recent research suggests, however, that, while foreign students trained at Canadian schools do well in the Canadian labour market, their relative earnings performance has been deteriorating – consistent with a lowering of average foreign student quality as 'post-secondary institutions and governments have reached deeper into pools of prospective international students ... to meet their demands for students and new immigrants' (Chen and Skuterud 2018, 222).

Role of government direction in post-secondary education

The funding system for post-secondary education in Canada arose not through any grand plan based on best principles of public finance, but through an evolution or history of piecemeal developments. And the incentive schemes built in reflect that.

Major sources of federal funding towards post-secondary education in Canada are the Canada Social Transfer and federal-provincial equalisation payment programs, both of which are unconditional block transfers to help equalise government expenditure opportunities across provinces, including for tertiary education. But there is no requirement that such funds actually are spent on tertiary education. To the extent that university participation rates are much higher for higher-income families than for lower-income families (Corak et al. 2005), these transfers provide a regressive subsidisation of university students and their families. Interestingly, the college participation rates are pretty flat across family income groups (op. cit.). Since education rules vary from province to province, there is no equivalent of Australia's ATAR results for Canada. Registered Educational Savings Plans (RESP) instituted by the federal government since 1998 also provide tax-sheltered vehicles (to which the government contributes) for parents saving for their children's future tertiary education. But, again, the take-up rates rise strongly with family income since low-income households have difficulty finding funds to set aside for future education and high-income families treat this as a tax-reduction opportunity. Thus, at the undergraduate and college levels of post-secondary funding, the role of the federal government is largely indirect.

The largest portion of direct federal funding of Canadian universities comes through research-related grants from three major granting councils – the Natural Sciences and Engineering Research Council, the Canadian Institute of Health Research, and the Social Sciences and Humanities Research Council. These correspond in Australia to the National Health and Medical Research Council and the Australian Research Council. Two other sources of federal post-secondary research support are the Canada Foundation for Innovation (which helps support equipment and overhead costs) and Canada Research Chairs (which helps retain and attract top research talent to Canadian universities) programs. All these programs are essentially based on evaluating competitive applications, not on block grants. Canadian universities face direct competition from US schools for top talent; and when the Canadian dollar slips significantly below the US dollar, such competitive pressure intensifies and the environment for top talent becomes more precarious (APRFS 2017, 34).

The great majority of public funding for Canadian tertiary institutions is direct provincial transfers (or 'provincial operating grants') paid directly to universities and colleges. These essentially correspond to the Australian system's Commonwealth student grants (which are also paid directly to universities). These operating grants are based on the number of students enrolled ('basic income units' or BIUs) weighted by program enrolled in, part-time vs full-time status, and perhaps year in the program. These are universal programs that apply uniformly to all universities and separately to all colleges within a province, irrespective of quality. The size of the per student (or capitation) transfer varies across provinces. Since post-secondary institutions have substantial overheads (particularly with respect to plant and research equipment), and it can be argued that there are economies of scale in operating a university, marginal costs of admitting an extra student are well below average costs. So a university may wish to raise revenues by increasing the number of students. But the provinces typically limit such increases through multi-year corridor funding arrangements (involving funded student caps) with each university.

With the declining demographics of young people in some regions (such as the Atlantic provinces), this may be less a concern on the upside and more a problem of attracting students from higher-growth regions (such as Ontario) to fill available spaces. Alternatively, universities may wish to increase revenues by raising student tuition levels (or other related costs such as residence fees). But the provinces, in effect, have caps on what tuition the schools can charge, so they have in effect set tuition levels that can vary somewhat across academic programs – higher fees in fields where graduates' incomes are higher and program delivery costs are more expensive – but much less so across schools. On the other hand, some professional university programs (such as an MBA) are not capped in some provinces, so their fees can be much higher (by a factor of 6-10) and vary substantially between schools.

Universities can thus compete for quality of students, but not much on student fees (except in some professional programs), and the provincial transfers they receive are capitation-based and do not reflect any interactions between research and teaching. Consequently, the Canadian university system is relatively homogeneous across schools in terms of the quality of their undergraduate programs as compared to the United States or United Kingdom systems, and has relatively little differentiation or hierarchical ranking between schools at the undergraduate level. Performance funding at the undergraduate level is essentially not part of the system. Large schools certainly have more program and course options and there is a whole collection of smaller schools only offering undergraduate programs. They do compete for outside private-sector and government infrastructure and occasional specific-program subsidies with varying degrees of success depending on research excellence (e.g., University of Toronto), historical establishment (e.g., McGill University), entrepreneurial success (e.g., University of Waterloo), and geographic location (e.g., University of Alberta and University of Windsor).

But there are no Canadian schools at the very top of the world university rankings. The top, the University of Toronto, was ranked 22nd in *The Times Higher Education* ranking, and 28th in the QS world university rankings in 2018. The other frequently top ranked schools in the top 50 international rankings are the University of British Columbia and McGill University. Australia has five schools in these top 50 rankings. In the Shanghai Jiao Tong university rankings, Australia has one school in the top 50 and Canada two. And *The Times Higher Education* rankings lists two Australian schools in the top 50 and Canada with three. There are also virtually no 'research only' academic staff positions in the Canadian system. This compares with over 15 thousand faculty in Australia in research-only roles (Universities Australia 2018, 41). Top faculty in Canada can use some research funds to buy off some teaching release time, but typically carry on some teaching and often extensive graduate research supervision.

While revenues from foreign student fees have helped subsidise research activity and hence improved the international rankings of Australian universities (Grattan 2018, 3), Canadian school rankings have generally held their own or slipped in recent years.

On the other hand, the early career average earnings of bachelor's graduates from the bottom third set of universities in Canada are not much different from those of graduates from the top third set of universities, certainly nowhere nearly as great as average earnings differences between different fields of study (Finnie et al. 2016). So the Canadian market does not distinguish much between undergraduate school program quality.

Recently, the Ontario government has begun a major initiative to better differentiate the universities (and the colleges) and have them concentrate more on their self-chosen specialised focus. Through a series of multi-year Strategic Mandate Agreements (Ontario, 2018) between each university (and each college) and the province, the former need to decide on how they are going to be assessed on their particular strengths and focus and whether they are going to be assessed as research-intensive or more teaching-intensive, and then, in follow-up SMAs, agree on a set of performance metrics (e.g., total tri-council funding per faculty member, number of papers published per faculty member, and number of citations per paper over, say, five years). Future operating grant funding, then, will be dependent on numbers of students, but also on how well the university (or college) performs on the agreed-upon metrics.

The Canadian higher education sector is already relatively decentralised compared to Australia and the United Kingdom (though less so than in the United States with 50 states and its extensive set of private colleges and universities). This partly reflects that post-secondary education is largely a provincial responsibility in Canada and the uniform capitation funding system used. But the closed-shop union system (i.e., all faculty at a school must become union members) present at most Canadian schools and a tenure-stream tradition at many universities provide some local faculty resources and possible resistance to prospective central planning-like government regulation of the system (Polster and Amsler 2017).

Academic salary rules in Canada also are school-specific and can differ very much across universities, far more than is the case in Australia (Grattan Institute 2018, 40). Academic salaries can vary substantially between top urban-located schools – that continually face US competition for faculty – and smaller-town universities, as well as between disciplines and within departments (depending on individual performances). Academic salaries are not centrally set and follow more a US market-driven model.

Background influences on Canadian and Australian tertiary education systems

Demographic, social and competitive influences in Canada

Following the post-World War II baby boom – which was particularly strong in Canada – the Canadian university system expanded rapidly. Similar expansions occurred in Australia, UK, Europe and the US. Because of its proximity to the US, Canada was strongly influenced by its university system. Although there has been some influence from the UK, faculty hiring and course structures increasingly followed US practice. Canadian undergraduates could seek admission to any Canadian university or apply to US universities. Similar competition occurred at the graduate level, where it was common for outstanding Canadian graduate students to study in the best US graduate schools. The top Canadian universities hired junior faculty from the top US and Canadian graduate programs. In effect, the Canadian university system was semi-integrated into the US system.

Canadian provinces played the same role as US states in funding and competing for students and faculty in the North American university market. Clearly these factors have played a major role in determining Canadian undergraduate fees, faculty hiring practices and salaries. A major difference was that the US had elite private universities, whereas Canada had the equivalent of the US state university system.

The competitive pressures have not been uniform, in that they were more obvious for the best and most ambitious Canadian universities. In particular, the competition was most intense in STEM disciplines (engineering, physical and biological sciences, and mathematics), where technical skills were easily transportable across international boundaries. This is reinforced by the fact that large STEM projects require heavy infrastructure and major funding, which is easier to obtain in the US because of their much larger research funding base. This can make it harder to keep top faculty in the Canadian STEM disciplines than in some other disciplines. As academic priorities shift towards STEM fields, the pressure of such competition will only increase. Generally there is less international mobility in some of the humanities, social sciences and law where cultural differences are more locally specific and less internationally transportable.

Canada has long developed a tradition of accommodating differences, at least in part because of the role of Quebec in the Canadian political system and being a close neighbour during the US Civil War upheaval, but also because of large regional differences in traditions, economies and perspectives.

Accommodating differences has a perceptible impact on the tertiary education sector and its operations. Constitutionally, education is provided by the provinces, while the power of the federal finances and unrestricted taxation (especially following World War II) meant a mixed and diffused system of tertiary education funding and operations, where differences have to be accommodated – whether in language, religion, regional history, or perspectives and priorities. Committees that make funding allocation decisions always have regional representation which tends to accommodating differences.

The Canadian federal system is quite different from a single-authority top-down decision-making style. It more closely follows the US style of decision-making where there are fifty states and a great variety of different types and qualities of universities. This mode of operation has also been influenced by the so-called more risk-averse nature of Canadians. The Canadian system traditionally has been more reliant on long-run planning and a broad human capital improvement perspective. It has been wary of adopting various pop trends – which would be harder to implement in such a diffuse system. It has also been argued that there is a greater sense of responsibility for others and stronger preference for a more even or fairer distribution of resources – often as an explicit regional requirement – than, say, in the United

States. And, again, this works against a centralised uniform system of operation.

A possible problem occurs in the incentive system set up by the presence of large numbers of foreign students, who pay much higher fees than domestic students. By 2016, Canada had over 181 thousand foreign tertiary students and Australia had 391 thousand (Statistics Canada, 2017, Table C.1.2; Universities Australia 2018, 27). Of these totals, for Canada about 11% came from Africa, 10% from the Americas, 61% from Asia (32% from China), and 13% from Europe. For Australia, the respective shares are 7%, 5%, 82% (37% from China) and 3%, respectively (op. cit.).

Universities can become dependent on maintaining this flow of revenue, especially when governments reduce their funding, requiring foreign fees to cross-subsidise domestic students. Within the traditional academic disciplines, foreign students – especially Asian students – tend to be more concentrated in business schools and STEM disciplines, perhaps because their knowledge is more 'transportable' back home. In Canada, 27% of foreign students are enrolled in management and public administration programs and 19% in architecture, engineering and related technologies (Statistics Canada 2016, 9). In Australia, just under half of all international students are registered in commerce-related studies (Grattan 2018, 27). In some areas, such as business schools where tuitions are typically very high and disciplines covered are quite mixed in terms of their technical and language proficiency requirements, some foreign students may face difficulties adjusting and completing their studies. This potentially puts the schools in an incentive bind where they are averse to losing the high tuition revenue from foreign drop-outs. They may find it easier to accommodate these students by revising requirements and standards. This can have a deleterious effect on the general quality of education provided to the student body as a whole and can eventually lead to reputational effects. There is also the risk of exposure to sudden revenue loss. Saudi Arabia, for example, just days before the current academic year began, withdrew all 6,000 or so of its students at universities in Canada because of offence at a Canadian Foreign Affairs tweet about human rights. If universities are to rely on such foreign student revenues, they should thus seek to diversify their intake mix across many countries rather than rely heavily on a few.

There have been numerous complaints by faculty members in the US, UK, and Canada that the number of university administrators has grown faster than faculty numbers. Numerous reasons have been given for the rapid growth in administration: some are related to increasing government involvement in monitoring research, and requiring social objectives such as inclusiveness and transparency. There is also evidence that administrative salaries are among the highest of academic salaries. (Ontario, for example, annually publishes all individual public sector (including in higher education) salaries above $100,000, along with names.)

Demographic, social and political influences in Australia

The Australian tertiary education system has long followed features of the UK system. Historically, one can think of the Australian system as a provincial copy of the UK system. This has been true of the UK departmental structures with professors, readers, and senior lecturers and lecturers with their salary grade increments. This system has begun to evolve as the US system has become more common internationally and scholars became more international mobile.[5]

Australia, like most Western countries, expanded its tertiary education system rapidly in the 1960s and 1970s. Growth stagnated in the late 1970s and most of the 1980s. But beginning in the later 1980s, it has grown rapidly in a sequence of bursts to accommodate a larger cohort of domestic and foreign fee-paying students. These expansions have largely been instigated by federal government policies. These policy innovations have very much followed UK policy fashions. For example, the large increase in fee-paying foreign students was presented as a way to expand export revenues. A second example

---

5 See Milne (2001) for a history of the Australian university system and associated policy issues up until 2000.

was introduction of income-contingent loans for students. A third example was increasing use of various metrics attempting to influence undergraduate/graduate teaching and research in a top-down system of federal government funding and control (see below). A fourth example was active conversion of tertiary colleges into universities in the late 1980s, ostensibly to increase university competition.

More recently, universities have begun to copy some US structures without acknowledging that the US system is highly variable in quality and function. For example, it may not be widely recognised that some of the most prestigious (private) universities in the US have small undergraduate numbers. Furthermore, these universities have accumulated very large endowments over long periods of time that are used to fund outstanding faculty, provide generous means-tested scholarships for top undergraduate and graduate students, and construct state of the art scientific and engineering facilities. In addition, the US has a number of prestigious private liberal arts colleges that provide excellent undergraduate degrees in the humanities and social sciences. Class sizes in these colleges are generally far smaller than in the large US, Canadian, and Australian universities, which use the revenue from large classes in other fields to cross-subsidise the very expensive sciences, engineering and medical schools (Ehrenberg 2005).

Unlike Canada, Australia has no equivalent of the province of Quebec that has placed restrictions on acceptable national policies. As a general rule, Canadians try to gain consensus in policy decisions, while making due allowance for cultural and regional differences.[6] Given that the provinces have control of the tertiary education sector (with federal research funding), there is more inherent diversity of funding sources in Canada. Australia (modeled on the UK) adopted a centralised tertiary education system in the late 1950s, controlled by a federal minister overseeing a large department in Canberra. A major cause of the problems in the Australian tertiary education system is

---

6 Canadian culture and social interaction is typically more restrained and diplomatic than Australian culture. This observation is based on numerous conversations with Canadian professionals who are familiar with Australia.

the centralised, top-down system of funding and policy interventions. It can stifle diversity, using crude metrics in attempts to oversee the system. But implementing these metrics can often have unintended consequences as well (see below).

Australian universities are very reliant for their financial viability on foreign fee-paying students for undergraduate and graduate programs. This has been an implicit government policy since the late 1980s. This heavy reliance on fee income creates serious incentive problems.

First, fees and government subsidies are predicated on graduation numbers. This can create an incentive for universities to lower standards so that failing students are allowed to graduate. The implication is that there could be a major decline in standards. Second, fee-paying foreign students cluster in fields that are seen to provide a direct commercial return and where skills are readily transferable internationally. Many of these students are clustered in commerce and business-related disciplines. There is thus a strong incentive for universities to use these faculties as cash cows, diluting quality for both foreign and domestic students.

Third, given the highly competitive international market for foreign students, there is a strong incentive to indulge in marketing practices to entice students into the Australian universities. These practices may include implicit expectations of becoming an Australian citizen on completion of a degree, universities indulging in manipulation of data to enhance rankings in international university league ladders, and incentives to increase 'research output' as measured by indices of research productivity.

Although these metrics appear to enhance quality, attracting fee-paying students to apparently prestigious universities, they can potentially induce precisely the reverse result over a longer time horizon as students may realise that the claims are not consistent with their experience, thus resulting in a loss of reputation. The gross revenue from foreign student fees are also significantly reduced by extensive supporting administration marketing and catering for foreign students.

A perverse consequence of the substantial reduction in training in trades and vocational skills[7] has been serious labour market distortions: numerous newspaper articles complain of serious shortages in skilled trades, and significant oversupply in some professional areas. Attempts to anticipate labour markets via centralised training plans have a very poor record in many countries. The best one can do is to allow the universities and colleges to be sufficiently flexible so that they can respond rapidly to changes in labour market demands. In addition, it is obvious that tertiary education should encourage intellectual flexibility and skills so that graduates can adapt to changes in labour market demands, driven by technological changes and other factors.

Australian research funding is dominated by the Australian Research Council and, to a lesser extent, more specialised (e.g., the National Health and Medical Research Council) research funding programs. These funding sources, controlled federally, determine research funding for all disciplines. The Canadian system has separate funding bodies for the various research fields. This is an attempt to cater to the different types of research and their associated postgraduate training. The Australian system appears to be much less flexible, dominated by the major sciences and technology, and their research and funding requirements.

Complaints about the increasing corporatisation of universities have been commonplace in the US, UK, and Canada. Australia has been no exception. But subjective judgments, based on numerous observations by Australian faculty and visiting Canadian scholars suggest that the degree of bureaucratic control is relatively great in Australia.

---

7 Australia has evolved a Technical and Further Education (TAFE) or Vocational Education and Training (VET) system of colleges and institutes to cater for vocational training. The TAFE/VET system awards an array of certificates and diplomas for training in various trades and vocations. The TAFE system is primarily funded by the states. There have been numerous recent complaints that the TAFE system is under-funded, is demoralised and lacks a coherent governance framework. For an analysis of the policy problems see The Productivity Commission Report of 2011 – https://www.pc.gov.au/inquiries/completed/education-workforce-vocational/report/vocational-workforce.pdf. It is revealing to compare that report with a critique of the UK vocational training system analysed by Wolf (2011).

This occurs at two levels. First, the federal bureaucracy continually interferes in general university and research funding and the size and composition of student admissions. Canberra is constantly tinkering, thus making long-term university planning difficult.

Second, university administrations are continually aware of government surveillance through extensive reporting requirements and other interventions. Political fads and fashions may be imposed on hiring, admissions and research topics, requiring government mandated support groups, monitoring the imposed objectives. The power emanating from the ministry distracts university administrations forcing them to lobby Canberra and address political demands.

There have also been media complaints that Australian Vice-Chancellors earn much larger salaries compared to many other overseas university principals or presidents. Senior administrative salaries in Australia appear on a much higher scale than is the case in Canada (see Table 3, reproduced from Kneist (2017)). As Australian faculty salaries are more comparable to Canada, there should be an independent analysis of the relative cost of senior Australian university administration.

Problems in the use of metrics in tertiary education[8]

During the last three or four decades there has been increasing use of metrics (statistical measures) of organisational performance. In order for these to be really useful as indicators of institutional performance, the user will require a detailed knowledge of the sources and construction of these summary metrics. They can, with due care, be used with other softer sources of information to shed light on poor performance or problems that had been hidden in standard reporting. Economists and other social scientists familiar with private and pub-

---

8 This section draws extensively on Muller (2018), especially chapters 1-7 and his bibliography. For a highly insightful and early analysis of the abuses of metrics and their unintended consequences for tertiary education policy, see Wolf (2002). See also Edwards and Roy (2017) for a penetrating critique of the perverse incentives of the use of metrics in rewarding scientific research in the US.

lic sector decision-making understand the strengths and weaknesses of metrics, their appropriate application, and dangers in the hands of unfamiliar users.

Metrics became popular early in management science, measuring workforce productivity in simple, repetitive tasks on production lines. They were used in time and motion studies and related fields. The methodology gravitated into management taught in business schools where financial indicators of profitability and performance, and corporate bonus systems, were promoted as providing high-powered incentives. The obsession with quarterly earnings and forecasts, feeding into executive bonuses, became ubiquitous in the 1980s up until the recent financial crisis. It was well-known from research that these indicators were seriously flawed and often led to perverse short-term incentives.

The use of metrics has been bolstered by the growth and complexity of private and public organisations. Senior management wanted simple, reliable measures of productivity and performance in large scale organisations. But these organisations and their activities are often difficult to understand, even by senior management. Complex, technical tasks undertaken by workers several layers below are not observed by senior management, who rely on reports by intermediate management. Often the complexity of technical tasks undertaken by subordinates may not be understood or appreciated by senior management. This is compounded by senior management concern that subordinates may manipulate data and performance indicators.

As senior management increase surveillance and reporting metrics, relying on them to reward lower levels in the organisation, there is a strong incentive for employees to respond by manipulating behaviour to conform to management requirements. Even worse, the metrics can erode trust, weakening professional integrity and codes of behaviour. As many researchers have observed, the incentive is to increase performance in measured activities and reduce performance in unobserved or unreported activity. The latter activities can be important or vital to the long run output of organisations that produce complex, physical products or subtle multi-faceted services.

Management and political ideology combined by arguing that the effectiveness of 'high-powered' private sector incentives, driven by selective metrics, could be introduced to transform 'inefficient' public sector organisations. Keen observers and researchers of public enterprises had long understood that services of most of these organisations are complex, multi-faceted and hard to capture in a few simple metrics. Attempts to use simplistic metrics for incentives and rewards can thus easily produce unintended perverse outcomes (Miller 1992; Miller and Whitford 2016).

The rest of this section examines the use and abuse of metrics in tertiary education.

Increasing the percentage of high school students going to university: a free lunch?

In the late 1990s and early 2000s, a new political fad appeared and became popular in the US, UK, Australia and Canada. The basic idea is an apparently self-evident economic argument: because the average graduate earns more than the average non-graduate, then providing financial and other incentives to increase the percentage of any secondary school graduating class going to university, will increase general productivity in the economy. This hypothesis appears to be supported by aggregate statistics. But it is very much a partial truth (see Wolf (2002) for a lucid discussion).

First, aggregate statistics disguise wide variations in graduate salaries across fields and across graduates of different departments and universities. In a well-functioning university system, professional reputations are crucial in attracting good undergraduate and graduate students. It is well known that, in technical fields, private and public-sector employers have their own rankings of university departments. Some employers even contact individual faculty (who are highly respected in teaching and research) when hiring graduates.

If the increased undergraduate numbers are dominated by weaker students, admitted in the expanded scheme, they will gravitate to less demanding programs, and graduate to less skilled jobs and relatively low salaries. But, in addition, they will crowd out non-degree workers for jobs that do not utilise graduate skills. In this case, a university degree is a very expensive signaling device, replacing the cheaper and perfectly adequate high school or vocational college educated student. Second, if the incentives are to increase student numbers across disciplines, then universities may be faced with a dilution of the average ability of any class – especially in more intellectually demanding disciplines. The consequence is that there are disciplines where there can be very serious pressures to lower standards, especially when funding is tied to class-size numbers and numbers graduating.

Third, even if the extra students graduate from high demand/high quality programs, and the increase in graduate supply exceeds the increase in demand in the field, salaries will be reduced. The original high salary, observed by the incoming university student, is a retreating chimera that induces extra graduates into a field. But when the cohort graduates, they may find a crowded job market, and reduced financial prospects.

Rewarding universities by counting graduates produced

In the late 1980s and early 1990s, Australia adopted an incentive scheme for the 'production' of undergraduates: universities were rewarded by the number of students they graduated. This incentive scheme, with a one-dimensional metric, had very perverse incentives. There were no incentives to promote quality. The incentives were to lower standards and graduate as many students as possible. University administrators can point to the lower drop-out rate and much higher graduating numbers as metrics that demonstrate a remarkable increase in the quality of students and instruction. Sadly, much anecdotal evidence reported in the media suggests otherwise.

One might argue that the scheme produced more graduates, but it did not reduce the numbers of high-quality graduates. However, there are too many indications that mass classes and multiple-choice exams are reducing the quality of education for all students in the core disciplines.

Another unintended consequence is that there may be incentives to reduce the commercial value of upper-level undergraduate courses, transferring the same material into masters and other graduate programs. This incentive is amplified when graduate programs in commercially related fields are rewarded with far higher fees than the undergraduate courses they have displaced.

Incentives to produce more research

The UK introduced periodic research rankings for universities and departments. The rankings counted faculty research output, weighting articles by the prestige of the journal. These types of rankings again can introduce perverse incentives. Just before the ranking period, departments could try to induce faculty with long CVs to join their department. Hiring may be calculated to boost the department's score, placing it in a higher category with increased funding. The new hire's salary would be more than compensated by the increased research funding reaped by the department. The result would be a disruptive churn in faculty for a discipline just before a ranking process. Even worse is the incentive to attract high-profile researchers for short periods at lucrative salaries and then claim them (and their research record) as faculty members.

Similar systems in Australia and elsewhere have induced increased quantities of research of possibly dubious quality. For example, researchers can create circles where members capture a journal, citing and publishing each other's research. Niche field journals can spring up to cater for this demand. Some are legitimate and are of reasonable quality, but many are low quality journals aimed at research quantity (Muller 2018, chap. 7).

If research rankings rely on journal articles, this biases the ranking towards fields that rely mainly on journals for disseminating research.

Conversely, the rankings devalue disciplines (e.g., the humanities and some social sciences) that rely extensively on detailed monographs and books, requiring long periods of research and gestation, exploring topics in depth.

When research rankings are used as an input to rank universities for international league ladders, administrators will have strong incentives to bias their research record upwards, favouring disciplines that produce large numbers of articles in 'high ranked' journals. The incentive is to have multi-authored short articles that slice the research into as many articles as possible. The rewards can be great if the university has the freedom to set fees, as international fee-paying students often rely on rankings when applying to programs. A university may have many famous researchers, while relying on adjuncts and/or graduate students to teach most of the undergraduate courses in large classes.

Conclusions

This paper has examined aspects of the Canadian system of higher education, exploring possible lessons for the Australian situation. It has also raised concerns about some policy directions in the post-secondary sector in both countries, especially with respect to public-sector funding incentives and growing use of performance metrics.

Several lessons can be offered from comparative experiences in post-secondary education systems.

- A more centralised tertiary education system is more likely to be vulnerable to government funding providers' imposed cross-system regulation and use of performance metrics.

- Competition between tertiary education institutions for good students, research funding and the best faculty is a good thing in that it drives excellence, efficiency, responsiveness, and delivery of best product for the students. Allowing schools to differentiate their products

so they can better compete based on their relative advantage is definitely worthwhile.
- Funding colleges to help develop a vibrant system of skilled trades to go with traditional tertiary white-collar training will benefit resource allocation in the labour market and flexible output potential for the economy.
- The incentives embodied in the funding arrangements for foreign students should be carefully examined in order to bring about a reasonable balance of benefits for all students and to diversify risks.
- Heavy reliance on top-down imposed simple performance metrics as a basis of funding within a complex tertiary education environment can have major negative unintended consequences. Weight should be put on measures that cannot be so easily manipulated and should reflect peer-group judgment, such as entry student admission cut-off grade averages, peer-reviewed research funding, success measures of graduating students, and within-discipline department and faculty evaluations.

Table 1
Canadian Higher Education Statistics in International Comparison

	Canada	Australia	United States	United Kingdom	OECD Average
1) Public expend. on tertiary education as pctg of GDP- all tertiary	1.7	1.4	1.4	1.3	1.3
2) Public expend. on tertiary education as % of total gov. expend.					
short-cycle	1.6	0.7	n.a.	n.a.	0.3
bachelor's and above	3.1	3.1	n.a.	n.a.	2.7
all tertiary	4.6	3.8	3.5	3.0	3.1
3) Educational attainment of 25-64 year olds in 2016: pctg with					
short-cycle	26	12	11	10	8
bachelor's	21	25	22	23	16
master's	10	6	11	12	12
doctoral	<1	1	2	1	1
4) Share of funding in 2014: pctg					
public sources	48.4	38.8	34.7	27.9	70.9
private sources	51.6	61.2	65.3	72.1	28.8
5) Annual expend. per tertiary student in US$(PPP) in 2014	$21,326	$18,038	$29,328	$24,542	$16,143
6) Share of international students in 2014-15: pctg					
bachelor's	10	13	4	14	4
master's	14	43	9	37	12
doctoral	30	34	38	43	26
all tertiary	10	15	5	18	6
7) Avg. annual tuition fees for FT domestic public school bachelor's students in 2015-16 in US$(PPP)	$4,939	$4,763	$8,202	n.a.	n.a.
8) Avg. annual tuition fees for FT international public school bachelor's students in 2015-16 in US$(PPP)	$17,498	$15,678	$16,066	n.a.	n.a.
9) R&D expend. as share of GDP: pctg	1.6	2.1	2.7	1.6	2.4
10) Higher edn. R&D expend. as share of GDP: pctg	0.65	0.63	0.39	0.43	0.43

Sources: OECD Education at a Glance 2017; CAUT Almanac (2018).

Table 2
Canadian Higher Education Statistics 2000-2015 (Selected Years)

	2000-01	2005-06	2010-11	2015-16
1) Tertiary enrolments ('000)[1] University - Can. students	805.4	969.2	1,128.0	1,137.1
- Inter. students	45.7	80.9	107.6	168.6
College - Canadian students	490.4	560.4	692.4	647.5
- Inter. students	13.9	22.1	34.3	53.2
2) University revenue sources (millions of dollars)[2] Federal	1,554	2,833	3,855	3,245
Provincial	6,989	10,084	13,504	13,577
Tuition & fees	3,053	4,944	7,001	9,695
Total revenues	16,225	24,705	32,554	34,762
3) Revenue from governments per student (2000$)[3] - Universities	$10,038	$11,082	$11,516	$9,753
4) Total expend. per student (2000$)[4] - Universities	$18,016	$20,489	$20,784	$20,076
Tuition & fees per student (2000$)[5] Universities	$3,587	$4,241	$4,644	$5,621
Colleges	$2,127	$2,311	$2,303	$3,093
6) Full-time university teachers[6]	30,399	36,831	41,934	37,551
7) University student-full-time faculty ratio[7]	22.5	28.5	29.5	34.8
8) % of university faculty in permanent full-time employment[8]	73.6	66.9	64.7	69.1
% of university faculty in temporary part-time employment[8]	12.2	13.4	15.0	15.4

Sources:

1. Statistics Canada, CANSIM, Table 477-0031.
2. Statistics Canada, CANSIM, Table 477-0058. Figures in millions of current Canadian dollars.
3. All figures are expressed in real 2000 dollars (based on the CPI deflator).
4. Total expenditures from CANSIM Tables 477-0059 and 477-0061. All figures are expressed in real 2000 dollars (based on the CPI deflator).
5. All dollar figures have been deflated by the CPI.
6. Figures in columns 1-3 from CAUT Almanac 2014-15, Fig. 2.1; figure in column is for 2016-17 from the current CAUT Almanac, Table 2.4.
7. Column 1 from CAUT Almanac 2003-04, Table 3.3; columns 2-4 from rows 1 and 6.
8. CAUT Almanac, Table 2.12; figures in column 4 refer to the 2014-15 academic year.

Table 3
Vice-Chancellors' and Presidents' Salaries

	$A	Local Currency	Year
Australia: G15	1,060,000	1,060,000	2015
Australia: All	860,000	860,000	2014-2015
US: Private	685,000	515,000	2014
UK: Russell Group	670,00	366,500	2015-16
US:Private	600,000	450,00	2014
UK: all	495,000	330,000	2014-15
Canada: U15	440,000	275,00	2013
New Zealand	340,000	375,000	2014-15
Canada:all	300,000	295,000	2013

A$1.00 = C$0.98 = $NZ1.10 = £0.55 =US$0.75

Source: Paul Kniest, 'Australian Universities ... Top Ranking for VC Pay', National Tertiary Education Union, 2017.

References

Advisory Panel for the Review of Federal Support for Fundamental Research (APRFS), *Investing in Canada's Future: Strengthening of Foundations of Canadian Research*, 2017.

Barr, Nicholas, 'Higher Education Funding', in Frank Iacobucci and Carolyn Tuohy (eds), *Taking Public Universities Seriously*, University of Toronto Press, Toronto, 2005.

Beach, Charles M. and Frank Milne, 'Challenges to Higher Education in Canada and Australia', QED Working Paper No. 1407, 2018.

Boadway, Robin, 'The Rae Report and the Public Finance of Postsecondary Education', In Charles M. Beach (ed.), *A Challenge for Higher Education in Ontario*, John Deutsch Institute for the Study of Economic Policy, McGill-Queen's University Press, Montreal & Kingston, 2005.

Canadian Association of University Business Officers, *CAUBO Financial Information of Universities and Colleges*, 2018.

Canadian Association of University Teachers, *CAUT Almanac of Post-Secondary Education in Canada 2014-2015*.

Chen, Zong Jia and Mikal Skuterud, 'Relative Labour Market Performance of Former International Students: Evidence from the National Graduates Survey', *Canadian Public Policy*, 44 September 2018, 207-225.

Corak, Miles, Garth Lipps and John Zhao, 'Family Income and Participation in Postsecondary Education', In Charles M. Beach, Robin W. Boadway and R. Marvin McInnis, eds, *Higher Education in Canada*, John Deutsch Institute for the Study of Economic Policy, McGill-Queen's University Press, Montreal & Kingston, 2005.

Council of Canadian Academics (CCA), *Competing in a Global Innovation Economy: The Current State of R&D in Canada*, 2018.

Edwards, Marc A. and Roy, Siddhartha, 'Academic Research in the 21st Century: Maintaining Scientific Integrity in a Climate of Perverse Incentives and Hypercompetition,' *Environmental Engineering Science*, 2017, 4(1), 51–61.

Ehrenberg, Ronald G., 'Key Issues Currently Facing American Higher Education', in Charles M. Beach, Robin W. Boadway and R. Marvin McInnis, eds, *Higher Education in Canada*, John Deutsch Institute for the

Study of Economic Policy, McGill-Queen's University Press, Montreal & Kingston, 2005.

Finnie, Ross, Kaveh Afshar, Eda Bozkurt, Masashi Miyairi and Dejan Pavlic, 'Barista or Better? New Evidence on the Earnings of Post-Secondary Education Graduates: A Tax Linkage Approach', Education Policy Research Initiative (EPRI), University of Ottawa, 2016.

Fortin, Nicole M., 'Rising Tuition and Supply Constraints: Explaining Canada-US Differences in University Enrolment Rates', in Charles M. Beach, Robin W. Boadway and R. Marvin McInnis (eds), *Higher Education in Canada*, John Deutsch Institute for the Study of Economic Policy, McGill-Queen's University Press, Montreal & Kingston, 2005.

Grattan Institute, *Mapping Australian Higher Education, 2018*, by Andrew Norton and Ittima Cherastidtham, 2018.

Kneist, P. 2017 'Australian universities top world rankings ... for VC pay', http://www.nteu.org.au/article/Australian-universities-top-world-rankings...-for-VC-pay-(Advocate-24-01)-19415.

Mahboubi, Parisa, 2017. 'Talkin' 'Bout My Generation: More Educated but Less Skilled Canadians', C.D. Howe Institute E-Brief (November 14). Toronto.

Miller, Gary J., *Managerial Dilemmas: The Political Economy of Hierarchy*, Cambridge University Press, Cambridge, UK, 1992.

Miller, Gary J. and Andrew B. Whitford, *Above Politics: Bureaucratic Discussion and Credible Commitment*. Cambridge University Press, Cambridge, UK, 2016.

Milne, Frank, 'The Australian Universities: A Study in Public Policy Failure', QED Working Paper No.1080, 2001.

Mueller, Richard E. and Diane W. Rockerbie, 'Do the Maclean's Rankings Affect University Choice?: Evidence for Ontario', In Charles M. Beach, Robin W. Boadway and R. Marvin McInnis, (eds), *Higher Education in Canada*, John Deutsch Institute for the Study of Economic Policy, McGill-Queen's University Press, Montreal & Kingston, 2005.

Muller, Jerry Z., *The Tyranny of Metrics*, Princeton University Press, Princeton, 2018.

Ontario, www.ontario.ca/page/2017-20-strategic-mandate-agreements, 2018.

Organization for Economic Cooperation and Development, 2017, *Education at a Glance 2017: OECD Indicators*.

Polster, Claire and Sarah Amsler, 'Waking Up to the Reality of Canadian Higher Education', 2017, *Academic Matters* (Winter issue).

Science, Technology and Innovation Council, *State of the Nation 2014: Canada's Science, Technology and Innovation System*, 2015.

Skolnik, Michael L, 'The Case for Giving Greater Attention to Structure in Higher Education Policy-Making'. In Charles M. Beach, Robin W. Boadway and R. Marvin McInnis, (eds), *Higher Education in Canada*. John Deutsch Institute for the Study of Economic Policy, McGill-Queen's University Press, Montreal & Kingston, 2005.

Statistics Canada, *International Students in Canadian Universities, 2004/2005 to 2013/2014*, Cat. No. 81-599-X, 2016.

Statistics Canada, 2017, *Education Indicators in Canada: An International Perspective*, Cat. No. 81-604-X. Statistics Canada. 2018. CANSIM Database, Tables 176-0003, 358-0001, 358-0159, 384-0037, 477-0021, 477-0031, 477-0032, 477-0058, 477-0059, 477-0060, 477-0061, and 477-0068.

Universitas 21, 'Ranking of National Higher Education Systems'. Accessed 2018-08-26, Universities Australia, 2018, 'Data Snapshot 2018'.

Universities Australia, 2015, 'Higher Education and Research: Facts and Figures'. Wikipedia, 2018, 'List of Universities in Canada'. Accessed 2018-02-15.

Wolf, Alison M., *Does Education Matter?: Myths About Education and Economic Growth*, Penguin, London, 2002.

Wolf, Alison M., *Review of Vocational Education: The Wolf Report*, UK government report, 2011.

10
Then and Now

Peter Drake

Two aphorisms to begin:

- The purpose of a university education is to learn the difference between a fact and an opinion.
- More means worse.

The first was given to me as a student around 1960 by Alan Boxer, art collector and economics lecturer, then lately returned from postgraduate study in Oxford. The second comes from the novel, *Lucky Jim*, that marvellous parody of academic life by Kingsley Amis.

It may be unfashionable to say so, but there is merit in these two aphorisms.

Sixty years ago I entered academic life as a first-year student in the University of Melbourne. The university then was the only one in the city, and the state of Victoria, and it had about 4,000 students. One of my student colleagues, Graeme Little, later wrote, accurately, that in most streets of Melbourne suburbia there was no university student. How times have changed!

I had an excellent education in the University of Melbourne of the late1950s and early 1960s, and later the Australian National University, and I remain committed to their ways of education. At Melbourne we were taught in the standard way of the time: face-to-face lectures and tutorials; *plus* out of classroom discussion with our teachers and fellow students, and considerable reading, both in the splendid main library of the university and the smaller specialist one in the Faculty building. Honours students at Melbourne were particularly well-treated, thanks to good leadership of the department and the watchful eyes of Associate Professor Jean Polglaze over the progress of each student in the honours group (10 in my day but 20 in the subsequent year). A feature was the annual honours retreat when students and staff gathered for a week-end in the beautiful Dandenong Hills and met distinguished guests from commerce and industry with whom to discuss career opportunities. In my year we had 'Nugget' Coombs, Governor of the Reserve Bank of Australia.

In those pre-internet days the only way to learn was by personal effort. Assessment was entirely by written essays and end-of-year examinations. This regime required students to knuckle down to the hard work which resulted in individual mastery of the subject matter. Indeed, the whole flavour of the education was deeply personal, with strong contact among students and with teachers.

Our teachers were generally well-read and up-to-date in their subjects. Naturally, the quality of classroom instruction was rather varied. There was no spoon-feeding, but most teachers were lucid, knew their subjects and had taken pains to prepare for classes. At the nether extreme, my group experienced one lecturer who was knowledgeable but incomprehensible. This forced me and my student colleague, Bob Gregory (now perhaps the most eminent living Australian economist), to work extremely hard on the books and journal articles relevant to the subject, with the result that we both did very well in it.

Few lecturers of that time bothered with original research, and yet they were dedicated scholars. Many had no PhD, nor wished for one. But most had graduate experience, often in the UK or USA, at the MA or BLitt level. There was no imperative to publish and there were very few learned journals. In economics there were but half-a-dozen general international journals (and some specialist ones) and Australia's *Economic Record*. It was a respected achievement to get an article into any of the highly regarded and widely read overseas journals. Sole author books were prized and were manifold at ANU and not uncommon in Melbourne.

At the ANU my doctoral research was entirely individual though guided by my supervisors in reading, research methods and discussion. Again, I was fortunate in the quality of my research scholar colleagues but we each had to work very hard to pursue our individual projects. It took me about a year to define and refine the subject of my thesis.

One of the sadnesses of modern higher education seems to me to be the great decline of inter-personal connections between students and teachers and even among students.

Each Australian university had been established by legislation and thereby endowed with total, independent authority. There was no government regulator but internal university governance was strong. There are some good things about TEQSA but it indulges in over-regulation, micro-management and intrusion into individual institutions. Moreover, its work is conducted by bureaucrats who seldom have any personal experience of university teaching or research.

But of the many weaknesses in modern higher education, the demise of true academic leadership is above all else. And the rot starts at the top. Vice-Chancellors are now more likely to be chosen for their corporate management abilities than for their academic understanding, achievements and personal leadership. They should and need to be of sufficient academic standing to be recognised, respected and influential leaders in their institutions. From outside, nowadays, it appears that many or most VCs are 'external' rather than 'internal' in focus and delegate much of their true responsibilities to others. In many universities there is a bloated and expensive senior bureaucracy with a plurality of DVCs, PVCs, Assistant and Associate VCs, each with a platoon of administrative assistants. There are several studies that reveal that, in many universities, more money is spent on administration than on teaching and research.

Next comes academic appointments, which are largely conducted by internal administrators or external recruitment firms. Many applicants for jobs give my name as a referee; but I am seldom contacted by the prospective employer, and almost never asked for a written reference. The consequence of this is that the appointment process is steered by people who may lack a detailed academic opinion of the applicants.

There are also too many journals. Many are of doubtful quality and are self-interested in the sense that the founders create outlets for their own writings and those of their associates. The vast number of journals (possibly inferior) obscures the landscape for the notable and readily recognisable publications that really inform the development of any subject.

There is also less recognition of sole-authored books, which represent true scholarship.

Does more mean worse for the universities?

Around 1960 there were, in Australia, one million of population to one university. Now there are about half a million people in proportion to one university. It is debateable whether the nation has too many universities but surely it has too many university students. There appears to be substantially excessive enrolments as business (not a discipline) and law, to the neglect of the humanities. One wonders if all the graduates from such vocational courses will find satisfying employment. Admission standards are not strict. As one senior university administrator said to me very recently, 'all that is required to get in is a pulse'. I am convinced that the average quality of students admitted has been debased. Also, standards of achievement have been lowered because it is very hard – in this litigious age – to fail anyone, especially international students whose fees provide the universities with very large revenues. Grades are also debased. First class honours were very hard won in the past; nowadays most honours degree students hope for a first and feel disappointment or even failure with a lower second or a third, and yet those grades are indicative of superiority over pass degrees. A common practice now is 'blended learning'. This mixture of classroom teaching and the provision of concepts and information by electronic means gives rise, however, to problems of plagiarism and rote learning, as evidenced by the submission of virtually identical assignments from different students. I do not know of the completion rates of today's university students, but I do now that many of the graduates cannot write plain English with clarity and persuasion.

What of that of which I have had much experience in the last 10 years: private higher education? In these institutions there is an inevitable and eternal tension between the financial 'bottom line' and the quality of education. I see a triangle of tension among the three corners of profit, quality, and student welfare. While some university people have a condescending or disparaging attitude to private higher education, there is much to be learned from it.

First, these institutions have strong departments for student support and learning, which diligently monitor the progress, or lack of it, of individual students. Early identification of student weakness enables prompt corrective advice or action. Progression rates, retention rates and completion rates are statistically recorded and reported to the academic board and the governing body. Class sizes are generally smaller than in universities, and this assists the monitoring of students; but classes of uneconomic size are not maintained.

The greatest weakness of private higher education is the scarcity of full-time academic staff available every day to students. Part-time and casual teachers are the norm because their hours are flexible and they are considerably cheaper to employ than full-time appointees. But this prevents the development of academic collegiality which, in my view, saps the educational experience of students and the intellectual development of staff.

Finally, and perhaps controversially, I do not think that universities have any institutional remit to pursue social or economic goals, though individual academics must be free to pronounce from their disciplinary expertise. As long as admission procedures are fair and transparent, society must accept that inevitable differences in individual intellect and application must lead to unequal graduate results.

References

Carrigan, Frank, 'Forget Rules – Start Teaching', *The Australian*, 11 April 2017.

Spicer, Andre, 'The Knowledge Economy is a Myth. We Don't Need More Universities to Feed it', *The Guardian*, 18 May 2016.

11

Culture, Utility, and Critique

The Idea of a University in Australia

Stephen A. Chavura

> The first point will be to secure every Child the means of acquiring a good practical English Education; and on that basis it will be easy to establish, progressively, such improvements and refinements as the progressive State of Society may render necessary.... and ultimately of an Establishment of the nature of an University
>
> – Bathurst [1823] 1917, 140.

The above-quoted letter of 1823 of the 3rd Earl Bathurst to Thomas Brisbane, Governor of New South Wales, is perhaps the earliest documented reference to a university in Australia.[1] Nearly thirty years later Australia's first university was realised. The University of Sydney – incorporated in 1850 – was deemed 'expedient for the better advancement of religion, morality, and useful knowledge... .' (New South Wales Legislature 1850). It was to be a 'regular and liberal course of education' that would culturally elevate the colony of New South Wales. Other universities followed: Melbourne (1853), Adelaide (1874), Tasmania (1890), Queensland (1909), and Western Australia (1910).

Australia's first Professor, John Woolley, described a 'liberal education' as 'one which cultivates and develops in their due and harmonious proportion what the Romans called 'humanitas,' all those faculties and powers which distinguish man from the inferior creatures.'

---

[1] Three years later, Archdeacon Thomas Hobbes Scott (1826, 316) could also speak of building up the existing education institutions in New South Wales, and ultimately of establishing 'one of a greater magnitude'.

(Woolley 1862, 15-16). Others offered lofty visions of the purpose of a university. William Charles Wentworth assured the NSW Legislative Council that the purpose of the intended Sydney university was 'to enlighten the mind, to refine the understanding, to elevate the souls of our fellow-men' (cited in Barcan 1975, 378). Wentworth saw the university as a path for every child, rich or poor, to 'greatness and usefulness.'

At the laying of the foundation stone for the University of Adelaide in 1879, the South Australian Minister of Education said, 'I cannot sum up my feelings in relation to this University better than by expressing the hope that the intellectual education which it will be the means of imparting may enable the mind, in the very beautiful words of Dr. (now Cardinal) Newman, "to look out into the world right forward, steadily, and truly" ' (King 1879, 24). The above ideas of a university describe its aims in terms of several ideals: knowledge, morality, character, religion, and usefulness. In short, both culture and utility. Culture, utility and, later, critique have been the three ideals that have competed for the soul of universities in Australia.

The tension between culture and utility has always bedevilled Australian education in general, and university education in particular. Glyn Davis has said that 'The unworldly university has always been rare. Professional training dominated Australian universities from their earliest expression' (Davis 2013).[2] Even if this is true, we must remember that much of the professional training still included large doses of the more other-worldly subjects, with doctors and lawyers being trained not only in their professions but also in philosophy, Greek, and Latin. Part of the decline in the Humanities must be attributed to the ever-increasing specialisation of law and the sciences. Specialisation leaves little or no time to indulge in other-worldly intellectual pursuits. Philosophical High Court justices like John Latham (1877-1964) or prime ministers like Gough Whitlam (1916-2014), who could scribble in Greek, are extinct birds.

The early practical bent of Australian universities was not merely

---

2 Davis provides a good overview of the history of universities in Australia. The most comprehensive history is Forsyth (2014).

because they were being founded during the period in which criticism of the medieval nature of English universities was strong, but was also owing to the kind of culture that had emerged in the colonies by the mid-nineteenth century. Colonial culture was shaped by the kind of people who would come to a place like Australia – practical people bent on making money. Some of these people could even become statesmen and seriously ask, 'what philosophy had done for this country. Had it ever discovered a single payable gold-field in the colony?'(Victorian Legislature 1859, 224).[3] Still, always fighting against the conception of the university as a useful training ground for lawyers and doctors, and serving the needs to the ever-changing economy, was the idea of the university as preserver of culture.

The university as preserver of culture: Sir Robert Menzies

Few people today accuse the universities of being too lofty in their concerns, too carried away with the pursuit of ideas and dead languages for their own sake. Utilitarian thinkers in the nineteenth century like Robert Lowe[4] mocked British universities for having little or nothing to do with the latest science, remaining mired in a medieval curriculum of dead languages, metaphysics, and mathematics. This could not be said of the Australian universities. By the 1930s universities in Australia were being criticised for being overly vocational and barely interested in knowledge for the sake of knowledge. By the mid-1930s Australian historian, G. V. Portus, saw how modern complex society and its need for experts was turning the university into something very different from its lofty ideal:

> A citizen in a modern democracy is faced with an increasing complexity of facts, all of which may be, and many of which certainly are, very important in their bearing on

---

[3] The comment was made during a parliamentary debate on granting £2,000 to establish a Philosophic Institute. The grant was approved by 21 votes to 10.

[4] Lowe (1811-92) was a classics tutor at Oxford in the 1830s before coming to Australia as a barrister in 1842, returning to England for good in 1850. Lowe was fiercely critical of the Oxbridge universities as essentially medieval, and became an educational reformer in the Gladstone government. See Knight (1967).

his life. They find the university departmentalised, and seldom discover the relation between subjects taught in different departments. The result is that our graduates are professionalised rather than educated (Bailey 1936, 90).

The Second World War accelerated the vocational transformation of universities, training future experts with an emphasis on technology as essential for keeping up with a world economy flying forward in the optimistic spirit of post-war reconstruction (Macintyre 2015). The technological demands of post-Second World War industrial growth as well as competetive trade opening up among decolonised states meant that universities were fast focusing on the sciences rather than the humanities.

The tension between the utilitarian and the cultural view of the university is evident in the life and career of Sir Robert Menzies (1894-1978), the Prime Minister who most admired the universities. In fact, Menzies' own conception of a university was fully developed half-way through his studies while he was editor of the *Melbourne University Magazine* in 1916. Menzies' idea of a university harked back to the twin emphases of Woolley and Newman: truth and character. In an article he wrote when he was 21, called 'Education and Truth', Menzies rejected what he called 'the more utilitarian conceptions of education which are current today' in favour of education as 'the eternal quest for Truth....' He went on: 'Education is thus essentially ethical in purpose; it is the cultivation of the highest in man, and the negation of all those lower elements which would drag him down'(Menzies, 1916, 4). 'As a University we dare not look lower than this for our ideals.... Indeed, to adopt any other position would, so surely as the seasons pass, bring us to the doleful conclusion that our studies are conducted but in a blind alley, and end in falsehood and lying' (Menzies 1916, 4-5).

Twenty-three years later, on 26 April 1939, the same day he became Prime Minister for the first time, Menzies gave the key address for the annual commencement of the Canberra University College. In 'The

Place of a University in a Modern Community,' Menzies envisioned the university as working to preserve high culture – truth, beauty, and goodness – while also operating as a place of respite or asylum for those who live in the 'real world'; that they – doctors, lawyers, engineers, businessmen, politicians – may return regularly for re-inspiration (Menzies 1939). Again, for Menzies, the great threat to the university was the utilitarian or commercial spirit. These utilitarians 'have weighed the classics, literature, and philosophy in their commercial balances and found them wanting because unprofitable' (Menzies 1939, 12).

Menzies also emphasised the university as a unique place of free enquiry and freedom of speech: 'I have never been able to understand the notion of a heresy hunt at a University. It may be necessary under some circumstances in an organised society to set some limits to what a member of that society may say or do. But I am clear that he must never be prevented from coming at the truth' (Menzies 1939, 31). Ultimately, Menzies' conception of a university had not changed since he was an undergraduate; a university was to be 'a home of pure culture and learning,' and this required freedom of speech and freedom from the demands of utility (Menzies 1939, 11).

For the most part Menzies believed the great threat against universities was the utilitarian acid that washes away anything unable to withstand an economic justification, not to mention the dominating spirit of science which increasingly looked down on anything unquantifiable. Interestingly, Menzies did notice something else emerging. Speaking of the temptation among teachers to use their platform as a means of political indoctrination, Menzies said: 'No man can be a great, or even a good, teacher, who yields to this temptation. Yet there are those, in schools and universities, who do. To teach history, for example, so as to justify some current and personally held political theory, is to deface history and obscure the lessons it can teach to the uninhibited and unbiassed mind' (Menzies 1961, 11). No doubt Menzies was aware of ideologues in the universities much earlier, but by 1961 he could see that the universities were being increasingly influenced by leftists.⁵ Even nine years earlier, in 1952, Liberal MP William Wentworth, great-grandson of the founder of Sydney University, could say in Federal Parliament that 'the Australian National University has become deliberately, according to a planned scheme, a nest of Communists who are busy building up their own organisations to subvert the institutions of this country, to frustrate the desires of governments and to destroy proper administration' (cited in Crowley 1973, 264). By the late 1960s, there was a struggle between three competing ideas of a university: the cultural, the utilitarian, and the critical.

Two kinds of critique: Andersonians and leftists

Against utilitarianism Menzies offered the sweetness and light vision of the purpose of a university, but there was another, which in the end would oppose both utility and culture: critique. The university as an institution of social critique was not necessarily incompatible with the conservative notion of cultural preservation and construction. Yet, when detached from classical humanism – Woolley's *studia humanitatis* – and attached to Marxist and Post-modern conceptions of human relations as power-relations, all analysis becomes an exercise in political activism, and the quest for truth, beauty, and goodness – culture – becomes at best misguided, at worst oppressive.

John Anderson (1893-1962) was not a product of Australian education or of a critical conception of the university, but was formed in the wide-ranging system of his native Scotland, with its austere Calvinist demand for system, depth, breadth, and rigour.⁶ Whereas the conservative ideal of the university followed Newman and Matthew Arnold, emphasising truth and culture as the end of the university, Anderson emphasised critique:

The work of the academic, qua academic, is criticism;

---

5 By 1962 Peter Coleman could write of 'the standard radical-leftist interpretation of Australian history which is given in nearly all textbooks....' (Coleman 1962, 6).

6 This section on Anderson is informed by Ian Tregenza's discussion in Chavura et al (2019, 213-17).

and whatever his special field may be, his development of independent views will bring him into conflict with prevailing opinions and customary attitudes in the public arena and not merely among his fellow professionals (Anderson 1980, 214).

Anderson had his exemplar:

Socrates did not deny, but rather gloried in the fact, that he had striven by example and precept to inculcate the spirit of criticism, to encourage the questioning of received opinions, and traditions.... The Socratic education begins, then, with the awakening of the mind to the need for criticism, to the uncertainty of the principles by which is supposed itself to be guided (Anderson [1931] 1962, 206).

In describing Socrates, Anderson was describing himself. Anderson found himself fighting a difficult battle against both political conservatism – the young Anderson was a communist – and moral conservatism – Anderson was also a sexual libertine. Anderson himself went through a profound change and, like Menzies, came to see the spirit of science as the greatest threat to the preservation of culture and excellence. This, and the oppressive tendencies of Marxism, which Anderson eventually abandoned, would lead Anderson to emphasise culture or 'classicism' as much as critique.

Certainly, in the mid-1950s, the political and moral conservatism of the universities was strong enough to end the career of University of Tasmania philosopher Sydney Orr and play a part in Russel Ward's failure to obtain a position at the University of New South Wales (Pybus 1993; Forsyth 2014). Ten years later, when the appointment of Frank Knopfelmacher – a prominent anti-communist – was overturned by the Sydney University Senate, accusations of leftist domination of the university started to fly (Franklin 2003, 283-86). Even if the Knopfelmacher case was ambiguous in terms of whether the withdrawal of the appointment was ideological or due to Knopfelmacher's alleged uncollegial personality, it was around this time that conservative academics were noticing a far more assertive and dominant leftism in Humanities departments. Marxists were taking over, and their Baby-Boomer students would finish the job of transforming universities from preservers of culture to critics of culture. Like his ideal of a British Australia, Menzies' ideal of the university as a place of cultural enhancement and the pursuit of truth, beauty, and goodness had become untenable not long after he retired in 1966.

Donald Horne's observations, published in 1964, of 'the academic' are telling in terms of a transition that was taking place in the universities:

> Before the Second World War the general line of belief of the most influential Australian academics was, on the whole, conservative.... There is still some of this conservatism left, although it is necessarily changed in style, but on the whole Australian academics now hold orthodox Australian liberal opinions: they are critical of censorship, licensing laws, hanging and the police; *in politics they would tend to distrust the Liberal party, hate the Democratic Labor Party and despair of the Labor Party*.... (Horne [1964]1968, 225).[7]

For Horne, the average academic, if not yet a radical, was certainly left-leaning. Their students would become radicalised by the end of the 1960s, mainly owing to introduction of conscription (selective national service) and the Vietnam War and the incredible opportunity it provided for Marxist critique to grab the imagination of the youth (not to mention celebrities like Jane Fonda and John Lennon). In fact, Horne's full discussion of the academic and the university in *The Lucky Country* still largely rings true today, and repays re-reading. In all the present conservative talk of leftist ideology destroying the universities, we must bear in mind that one of the great agents of cultural destruction was the rapid vocationalisation and bureaucratisation of the universities after World War II and then, again, from the late-

---

7 Italics added.

1980s, with the neoliberal Dawkins reforms under the Labor Party (Melleuish 2018).

Anderson himself underwent a conversion, albeit a gradual one, from communism to an anti-communism that valued classicism in the university. In any event, Anderson's emphasis on critique was never slavishly Marxist, which enabled him eventually to turn against communism itself and become something of an elite cultural conservative, seeing the university as a crucial preservative against the tendency of the sciences – themselves strongly linked to utility – to declare all disciplines deemed unscientific as arbitrary, obscurantist, and indulgent.

In some ways Anderson's view of the university turned out to be not so different from Menzies'. In the end, according to Anderson, it was the hegemonic status of the sciences that fatally wounded the university. By 1960 he could lament that 'neither the notion of culture nor the classical outlook is now accorded any great respect even in reputedly educated circles' (Anderson 1962, 189). The emphasis on critique survived Anderson but became divided between the Andersonians and the neo-Marxists; the latter would come to dominate humanities faculties from the 1960s, eventually morphing into the Post-modernists from the late-1980s.

Critique or critical dogma?

The shift in emphasis from truth to critique in university education, though seemingly subtle, is difficult to underestimate in terms of its subsequent impact on university culture. If an emphasis on truth may lead students to accept propositions uncritically as dogmas,[8] an emphasis on critique could also lead the average student to care more about exposing error than discovering truth. From a character perspective, encouraging the youth to critique has also encouraged a kind of irreverance to all things accepted – precisely Anderson's earlier goal, not to mention the goal of contemporary Post-modernists

---
8 Even though the quest for truth does demand scrutiny and critique, so that truth rather than error is affirmed.

who see education as an emancipatory project from the patriarchal, homophobic, racist, and, now, 'cisgendered' discourses that apparently animate the world. Perhaps describing the purpose of education in terms of either truth or critique is misguided from the beginning.

One cannot pursue truth without being able to critique, for how does one distinguish good ideas and arguments from bad ones, truth from falsehood? At the same time one cannot critique without presupposing some things taken to be true – the laws of classical logic at the very least, which warn against accepting a contradictory proposition as true. But critical thinking *must* presuppose certain propositions judged to constitute knowledge, for upon what basis do we launch a critique if not on facts we already suppose that we know? Most critique in the universities is social critique, but to launch any kind of social critique presupposes a lot of knowledge that comes from a lot of hard *constructive* work.

Take the example of economic inequality.[9] To say that the present degree of economic inequality in Australia is unjust presupposes that one knows roughly how much economic inequality in a country like Australia is just. Or, perhaps, the contention is that *any* economic inequality is unjust. But this presupposes that one knows that economic inequality is ultimately grounded in power and selfish interest rather than in, say, the brute facts of human psychological and physical difference, or the free choices of individuals. To grant that human beings are individually different in capabilities but that social institutions are unjustly skewed to reward those with certain capabilities and traits over others is to argue that institutions and vocations could function just as well if they were not so skewed. But this presupposes a very detailed and robust social theory that will be informed at least by psychology, history, and economics.

Also to keep in mind is that any readjustment of social institutions or human psychology needs to be done in a way that does not destroy human freedom. For example, if removing economic inequality meant instituting a state that could control every aspect of our lives from the

---

[9] The rest of this paragraph could speak just as well to the notion of gender inequality.

way we raised our children to the economic transactions we engaged in, that is, removing choice from nearly every aspect of individual and social life, would we not start to think that economic inequality is a legitimate – necessary – state of affairs owing to the dehumanising results its absence must involve? Inequality would take on a kind of tragic legitimacy which would render many critiques of it at best superficial, at worst redundant.

The above paragraph does not even begin to touch on an even more fundamental question, the answer to which is necessary for the above discussion even to begin: What is justice? This question, going at least as far back as Plato's Socrates, is still debated by philosophers. The point here is that the proposition that Australian economic inequality is unjust presupposes a mountain of economic, sociological, and psychological knowledge, not to mention the ability to think about the human condition from more philosophical and theological perspectives.

Perhaps the main problem with the critical view of the university has to do with intellectual disposition and virtue. If students are taught over and over again that the point of the educated mind is to critique – that is, to uncover falsehood – will the mind be groomed to be so sceptical that truth, beauty and goodness will not be recognised or admitted when encountered? And how can one even launch a critique of anything when one's intellectual disposition has become so critical that the very knowledge – factual, psychological, sociological, moral, philosophical, and theological – required for the kind of social critique mentioned above is occluded? Ironically, an emphasis on truth rather than critique could be the best foundation for effective critique. Is it telling that neither Marx nor Anderson were themselves products of education systems animated by their own philosophies of critique? It may be the case that the faculty of critique is best developed indirectly through pursuit of truth, beauty, and goodness.

To say that an education is about either truth or critique is problematic. It is about both, and they presuppose each other. However, it may make a world of difference if one is *emphasised* over the other. Is it likely that an emphasis on critique as the goal of university education will actually produce individuals who will be able to critique competently? Anyone who has worked in a humanities department will know that their barely-educated students are critiquing all the time. In reality, the critical disposition often found in university classrooms is little different from the critical disposition once upon a time directed towards Roman Catholicism – by Protestants.

Critique: By its fruits you shall know it

Admittedly, the emphasis on truth probably contributed to the intolerance against so-called heretical ideas in the universities for hundreds of years. Having said that, the emphasis on critique has proven to be rather intolerant itself, with no shortage of academics finding themselves on the outer because they critiqued the wrong things, that is, they critiqued the critical dogmas. The Geoffrey Blainey case in the 1980s at Melbourne University and the Stephen Buckle case at Sydney University in the late-1990s demonstrate the point (Franklin 1999). Conservatively-inclined scholars will testify to many more undocumented instances of bullying, bastardry, and victimisation by fanatically leftist colleagues over the past thirty years (Shaw 2017). More recently, the controversy surrounding Germaine Greer and the Ramsay Centre for Western Civilisation indicates that the critique of critical academics (and students) is now far removed from anything John Anderson had in mind.

Germaine Greer, once a firebrand of the women's liberation movement, is now judged by many to be reactionary, not because she has abandoned her feminism, but because she criticises the transgender rights movement as largely unreflective and ideological. That is, Greer rejects the idea that gender is a subjective matter, and that the average so-called transgender really knows what it is like to be a member of the gender opposite to their birth-assigned gender. Despite the fact that she still stands by her quasi-Marxist critique of gender-relations as outlined in *The Female Eunuch* (1970), she is now deemed by many students to be a reactionary whose views must be quarantined by 'no-platforming'(Lehmann 2015).[10] Greer's case is paradigmatic. What we often find in the universities is that critique is encouraged until the critics are critiqued from a point of view deemed 'uncritical', that is, when current leftist critical dogmas are taken apart from standpoints deemed 'conservative'. Critique of leftist ideas from an outside perspective is frequently not judged to be critique but reaction, as in the Greer case above. 'Reactionary' is the new term for that doxastic vice that was in the Dark Ages termed 'heresy'; much better to be 'critical' or 'radical'.

The intolerance historically exercised by many critical academics is now aped by their students who do not think certain views should be given oxygen on campus. Recent examples of censorship and disruption on Australian university campuses serve to show how the 'critical' ethic of the university is really not critique at all but a whole panoply of dogmas. At Sydney University, in September 2017, a small group of Christian students hosting a stall opposed to same-sex marriage were verbally and physically attacked over over a period of hours by dozens of protesting students (Fox Koob 2017). The University of Sydney did nothing to reprimand those protesting students. In July 2018 La Trobe administrators refused to approve a request from the university's Liberal Club to host a talk by critic of modern feminism, Bettina Arndt. The ban was based on the content of Arndt's message, which claimed that claims of a rape culture on Australian campuses were wildly exaggerated. The university administrators said that Arndt's message went against the university's own message on that topic (Hutchinson 2018). A clear case of speech-content censorship by university bureaucrats. The university changed its position after conservative media exposure, but Arndt's lecture tour was continuously interrupted by vocal protestors trying to make it as difficult as possible for the lectures to take place.

These are just two cases of leftist censorship or interruption of heterodox views on university campuses. Perhaps nothing reveals the

---

10 For a canonical example of leftist pro-censorship, that almost reads as parody, see Duc-Chong 2018.

dogmatic nature of contemporary critique more than the fact that as 'critical' ideas have increasingly taken hold of university departments, bureaucracies, and students over the past thirty years, they have become more, not less, moralistic. Critical academics and students are more certain than ever as to how people ought to think and live.

The saga over the Ramsay Centre for Western Civilisation is depressing and telling in terms of the effects that dogmatic critique can have on a university culture. The Vice-Chancellor of the University of Sydney, Michael Spence, has assured the media that the university will not countenance any course that attempts to rank or 'score' civilisations.[11] Apparently university classes can engage in critique of religion (well, Christianity), traditional morality, traditional gender relations, America, Western civilisation, patriotism, Israel, and the family but not critique the dogma of cultural and civilisational equality, incommensurability, or relativism.

Spence says that any attempt to do so would be 'intellectually bogus' (*Sydney Morning Herald* 2018). Maybe, but this is not obvious, and there are plausible reasons to question it. For example, the critique of the idea that Western civilisation is the best focusses on certain misdemeanours committed by Western civilisation – colonialism, oppression of women, racism, economic inequality, environmental destruction, etc. In other words, Western civilisation is attacked for exemplifying certain injustices and moral vices.

But would not this mean that we could rank different civilisations and cultures based on the extent to which such injustices and vices are exemplified in them? So a civilisation that never practised colonisation would rank more highly, all other things being equal, than one that did? A civilisation or culture that did not exploit and destroy the environment would rank, all other things being equal, higher than one that did? Does not the whole program of bringing human rights – especially LGBTQ and women's rights – education,

---

11 The pivotal claim of the Ramsay Centre is not that the West is the best, simply that the West has ideals, achievements, and practices that are so noble and enriching that they are worth studying and preserving.

and hygiene to the Global South pressupose that these countries are lacking something good that we and not they possess? Would not this mean that *at least in this respect* the way we do things here in the West is better? Hypothetically, one could study the practices of a set of civilisations and cultures, monitor the extent to which the goods and evils are exemplified in them, and come up with a ranking of civilisations from best to worst.

Now this may be an obscure exercise, generating more trouble than it is worth, but the point is that the notion of superior and inferior large-scale living practices is not as obviously intellectually bogus as many might assume. Indeed, the critics of the Ramsay Centre themselves furnish the premises for such an excersise. And yet the quick – reactionary? – dismissal of it shows how deleterious to open enquiry the 'critical' approach to university education can be.[12]

But, as I have argued, the kind of critique that has taken hold of universities over the past forty years is really just an exercise of criticising ideas and institutions which are themselves critical of certain dogmas – feminism, multiculturalism, environmentalism, anti-heteronormativity. It is not critical in the Andersonian sense of exposing ideas, institutions, and practices that arbitrarily stifle the quest for truth and the striving towards excellence. It is little wonder that Germaine Greer, one of the last vestiges of Andersonianism, is a pariah on many university campuses.

Conclusion

From the beginning, university education in Australia exhibited a tension between culture and utility. This tension was inevitable in a

---

12 Some may say that the critique of Western civilisation is not so much based on an objective list of goods (and evils) that *all* civilisations are accountable to, but on the West's own ideals. In other words, we condemn Western civilisation based on its own criteria of what is good. But this means that we critique colonialism and environmental destruction not because it is evil in some objective sense, or in any sense, but simply because it is inconsistent – a practical contradiction – with Western ideals of universalism and human dignity. But critics of Western civilisation speak in such a morally condemnatory tone that it is clear that they are not accusing the West of mere inconsistency, but of something much worse.

society largely populated by convicts and their heirs and immigrants whose main motive for settling in the Antipodes was to get ahead. In some ways little has changed in Australian universities, which are now significantly funded by foreign students taking vocational degrees in business and commerce, with myriad vocational degrees such as tourism and management fast multiplying. Over the past few decades, as classics and philosophy departments have either shut down completely or merged with other departments, the humanities in universities have been eviscerated.

The tension between culture and utility was joined by a third competitor – critique. But there are historically, in Australia at least, two kinds of (secular) critique, Andersonian and dogmatic, the latter being historically anchored to the neo-Marxism of the New Left which morphed into Post-modernism in the 1980s. The latter has licensed self-indulgent academics to transform many humanities units into niche gender, sexuality, and race studies units.

All of this represents something of a crisis for universities in Australia, one that is also characteristic of universities in the UK, Canada, New Zealand, and the US. Many see this crisis as an opportunity to start afresh with new privately-funded institutions which return to the ethic of the university as preserver of culture, of the greatest intellectual achievements of humankind, particularly in the Western traditions. Unfortunately, Australian universities stand at a massive advantage in certain respects, making it nearly impossible for new private institutions to compete.

First of all, private tertiary institutions receive no public funding, relying solely on fees which are frequently more expensive than public university fees. Second, Australian pragmatic culture may be too inhospitable for private liberal arts colleges; we lack the college tradition that so characterises American tertiary culture. Third, Australia's population is small, meaning that even the few private institutions that seek to resuscitate the traditional ideal of the university struggle for students. Fourth, the secular nature of Australian society means that the religious universities and colleges that are common in

America and do so much to preserve the liberal arts struggle to find a market here. Perhaps the best that can happen is for the universities to continue to degenerate, for humanities faculties to continue down the path of critical theory, for campuses to be inhospitable to the free exchange of ideas, and for academics to continue in their intolerance towards venures like the Ramsay Centre for Western Civilisation. Maybe only then will the prospect of sending our children to the major public universities become so objectionable for enough students and their parents that alternative institutions will flourish.

Most likely is that Australian universities will neither mend nor die but will limp on, becoming increasingly vocationalised, all to the general indifference of a pragmatic public in a lucky country.

References

Anderson, John, 'The Place of the Academic in Modern Society', in *Education and Society: John Anderson*, D.Z. Phillips (ed.), Basil Blackwell, Oxford, 1980.

Anderson, John, *Studies in Empirical Philosophy*, Angus and Robertson, Sydney, 1962.

Bailey, K. H., 'Discussion', in W. G. K. Duncan (ed.), *Educating a Democracy*, Angus and Robertson, Sydney, 1936.

Barcan, A., (ed.), 'Speech on Moving the Second Reading of the University Bill, 4 October 1849', *Sydney Morning Herald*, in *Sources in the History of Australian Education 1788-1970*, Angus and Robertson, Sydney, 1975.

Bathurst, 'Bathurst to Brisbane', *Historical Records of Australia*, series I, 10, 30 October 1823, The Library Committee of the Commonwealth Parliament, Sydney, 1917.

Chavura, Stephen A., John Gascoigne and Ian Tregenza, *Reason, Religion and the Australian Polity: A Secular State?*, Routledge, New York, 2019.

Coleman, Peter, 'Introduction: The New Australia', in Peter Coleman (ed.), *Australian Civilization*, F. W. Cheshire, Sydney, 1962.

Crowley, F. K. (ed.), *Modern Australia in Documents, vol.2, 1939-1970*, Wren Publishing, Melbourne, 1973.

Davis, Glynn, 'The Australian Idea of a University', *The Conversation*, 23 August 2013.

Duc-Chong, Liz, 'Why Germaine Greer is Not Entitled to a Place at the Brisbane Writers' Festival', *SBS Sexuality*, 30 August 2018.

Forsyth, H., *A History of the Modern Australian University*, UNSW Press, Sydney, 2014.

Forsyth, H., 'The Russel Ward Case: Academic Freedom in Australia during the Cold War, *History Australia*, 2014, 11/3, 31-52.

Fox Koob, Simone, 'Yes, No Camps Clash at Sydney University', *The Australian*, 14 September 2017.

Franklin, J., *Corrupting the Youth: A History of Philosophy in Australia*, Macleay Press, Sydney, 2003.

Franklin, J., 'The Sydney Philosophy Disturbances', *Quadrant*, 43/4, April 1999.

Greer, Germaine, *The Female Eunuch*, Paladin, 1970.

Horne, D., *The Lucky Country: Australia in the Sixties*, Penguin, Ringwood, 1968.

Hutchinson, Samantha, 'La Trobe University Lifts Ban on Bettina Ardnt Talk....', *The Australian*, 2 August 2018.

King, Thomas, in *Addresses Delivered at the Laying of the Foundation Stone ... July 30 1879*, Adelaide, 1879.

Knight, R. L., 'Lowe, Robert (1811-1892)', *Australian Dictionary of Biography*, National Centre of Biography, 1967.

Lehmann, Claire, 'Germaine Greer and the Scourge of 'No-Platforming', *The Drum*, 28 October 2015.

Macintyre, S., *Australia's Boldest Experiment: War and Reconstruction in the 1940s*, Newsouth Publishing, Sydney, 2015.

Melleuish, Greg, 'The Machiavellians in our Universities', *Quadrant*, February 2018.

Menzies, R. G., 'Education and Truth', *Melbourne University Magazine*, 10(1), May 1916.

Menzies, R. G., *The Place of a University in the Modern Community*, Melbourne University Press, Melbourne, 1939.

Menzies, R. G., 'The Challenge to Education', in *The Challenge to Australian Education*, The Australian College for Education, F. W. Cheshire, Melbourne, 1961.

New South Wales, 'An Act to Incorporate and Endow the University of Sydney', in John Thompson (ed.), *Documents that Shaped Australia's History: Records of a Nation's Heritage*, Millers Point, NSW: Pier 9, [1850], 2010.

Pybus, Cassandra, *Gross Moral Turpitude: The Orr Case Reconsidered*, William Heinemann Australia, Melbourne, 1993.

Scott, Thomas Hobbes, 'Report on the Church and School Establishments by Archdeacon Scott', *Historical Records of Australia*, series I,12, 1 May 1826. The Library Committee of the Commonwealth Parliament, Sydney, 1919.

Shaw, George, 'How They Wrote History out of Australian Universities', *Quadrant*, May 2017, 61/5, 64-7.

Sydney Morning Herald, 'Puerile Culture War Battering Ramsay Centre Negotiations, says Sydney Uni Boss', *Sydney Morning Herald*, 29 September 2018.

Victoria, *The Victorian Hansard, containing the Debates and Proceedings of the Legislative Council and Assembly of the Colony of Victoria, Session III, 1858-1859*, William Fairfax and Co, Melbourne, 1859.

Woolley, 'Oration at the Inauguration of the University of Sydney, Oct. 11 1852', in *Lectures Delivered in Australia*, Macmillan and Co., Cambridge and London, 1862.

12
The Academic Social Welfare Dysfunction

Ruth F. G. Williams

'Academic social welfare dysfunction' is a play on words. The social welfare function is a technical tool that conceives of social welfare as a function of the variables that govern the nation's welfare. The tool is useful when a ranking is deemed necessary over alternative *social* arrangements, some more desirable, others less desirable. Pondering the academy's propensity for harm is incongruous with the strong belief that the academy contributes to social welfare positively. The purpose of this chapter is to contend that an academic dysfunction can develop that lowers the welfare of nations.

How one can conceive of academia lowering social welfare

The initial step involves answering a question of how the claim made here, that academic dysfunction can lower social welfare, is approached. The contention will now be re-stated by employing some welfare economics. Doing so also makes the value judgments herein explicit.[1]

The welfare of nations involves economic and non-economic factors. There is an oft-quoted definition from Pigou (1932) which states that economic welfare is '[…] that part of social welfare that can be brought directly or indirectly into relation with the measuring-rod of money' (11). Pigou notes also that there is no clear demarcation line

---
1 There is a clear and concise account of the value judgments associated with these conceptions about a nation's economic welfare in Nath (1969).

between the economic and non-economic factors that affect social welfare, and that 'the outline of our [economists'] territory is, therefore, necessarily vague' (11).

A distinction is also relevant between 'the welfare of the community' or general welfare, W, and 'economic welfare', E. Economic welfare is determined by market-priced inputs, such as labour, non-labour inputs and goods consumed. All variables have prices, and thus are captured by Pigou's 'measuring-rod of money'. Following Bergson (1938), the economic welfare function, E, is conceived of by way of the individual utility functions of the people who comprise the community, that is:

$$E = f(U_1, U_2, ..., U_j) \quad (1)$$

for $i = 1, 2, ..., j$ where i is the ith member of the community, and the arguments of each utility function $(U_1, U_2, ..., U_j)$ are commodities and/or services consumed. The meaning of Equation (1) is that economic welfare for a community is determined not by a dictator or dictating class of people but by the individual utility levels of the people who comprise the community.

In addition to these economic variables, Bergson notes in a footnote that general welfare is also determined by non-economic factors. Bergson's examples are the weather and specific political factors. What Bergson means here is that changes in the weather, for example, affect economic welfare, such as when there is windy and rainy weather (some non-economic factors), coats and umbrellas are brought into W via E; or where a locality is, say, drought-prone, governments can construct, say, a suitable dam (E) to store the water needed for W. In regards to Bergson's 'overturn of the government', there are many illustrations where the living standards of nations currently and historically are affected. Bergson's additional aggregate conception of W is relevant to this discourse:

$$W = f(E, r, s, t...) \quad (2)$$

where E is economic welfare, and r, s, t, ... are the non-economic factors determining general welfare. The conception in Equation (2) is that E is a part of W. In other words, it is not assumed '[...] that economic welfare is an independent element which may be added to other welfare to get total welfare' (Bergson 1938, 313).

Let us now re-state the purview of this chapter in terms of Bergson's social welfare function. The discourse here observes the academy becoming the means of securing hegemony, which has an impact on W through E, due to overlooked variables in r, s and t. In the context here, 'overthrows of government' is not relegated to a footnote like Bergson's $n.$ 7.

Are the social effects of universities ever negative?

A type of social myopia can thrive in universities if protection affords it a refuge. There can, for instance, be an ethos of lofty learnedness pumping the heartbeat of social progress. Such imagery is apparent in some university marketing. Utopia has had a place in Western thought since the Middle Ages (Lasky 1976); but political implications exist over Utopian thinking.[2]

The risk of the social effects of universities is seldom palpable: it can be underestimated or simply ignored. The following sections elaborate on this type of risk in contemporary times. Let us first identify various intellectual traditions that criticise the maldirected academy.[3]

Adam Smith, Cardinal Newman and J. S. Mill

Perhaps the oldest of these traditions is associated with Adam Smith, John Henry Newman and John Stuart Mill (each of whom also wrote on economics) due to some scholarship about the nineteenth century academy (e.g., Cook 2009). Incentive mechanisms within wealthy academies rewarded 'idle monks' and induced the over-allocation of resources to certain divisions of scholarship or ways of thinking at the expense of others. Cook discloses John Stuart Mill's view on Cambridge: 'a corrupt institution failing to make proper use of its not inconsiderable resources' (63).

---

2 See Lasky (1976). Voltaire's *Candide* is also a satirical rejection of Utopianism.
3 Cornford (1953) describes a particularly sardonic side of these risks at the turn of the twentieth century in his witty *Microcosmographia Academia*.

Max Weber

Another tradition focuses on the negative consequence of the state's role in academies. Of Weber, it can be said that he concerned himself with the purpose of the university in a given social context. This is best seen in Weber's discussions of the problems of the German university in the last decades of the nineteenth century and the early twentieth century. Much of Weber's attention was concerned with the academic in the face of political and bureaucratic authority.

First, he considered the social context of academia that he saw in the former Imperial Germany under Bismarck, shortly prior to Weber's time. Weber saw, in that era, German university professors deceiving themselves over the merits of their social impact. Second, Weber contended that similar shortcomings occurred once again in his own era. For Weber, vital scholarly traditions were in a state of decay; instead of those traditions, a set of compromised social circumstances developed: prestige and vanity became the purpose of many professors.

Shils (1974) describes Weber's concern, *viz.* some professors had failed to develop insight into an 'enfeebling influence' from those professors' 'readiness to bow before the prestige and power of the imperial monarchy and its political and administrative agents' (2). Weber presented a lecture to an association of students of the University of Munich in 1919, his *Wissenschaft als Beruf* ('Science as a Vocation') lecture (Weber 1922). This lecture is, for Shils, 'one of the deepest and most moving confessions of faith in the value of science and scholarship coupled with a tragic awareness of their limits' (3). Shils suggests that the German problem lay squarely upon academia at the time, an argument which he puts in the following terms:

> The capitulation of so many German academic figures to the Nazi regime may be plausibly interpreted as evidence of the correctness of Max Weber's diagnosis regarding the complaisance of the German academic profession in its eager subservience to the authority of the state and the erosion of its moral rectitude (Shils 1974, 2).

Antonio Gramsci

Yet another tradition highlights the negative consequences of a deluded academy with a focus on the dangers arising from scholars employing the academy as an instrument to overthrow society and radically change the social system.

The idea of harnessing the universities as a means to achieve radical social change became an issue during the early twentieth century. It was popularised by Antonio Gramsci via his concept of cultural hegemony. Gramsci contended that a non-violent political overthrow of an existing hegemonic social system could be achieved with education. One has only to achieve an ideological win in territory within a country's educational institutions. Several English translations of *Prison Notebooks,* written between 1929 and 1935, are available (e.g., Gramsci 1971) or see Lears (1985).

A more subtle variation of this position has since been taken up by those who promote politics on campuses currently with social change as their goal. They seek to impose their own hegemonic system within the academy itself. This re-wiring of the role of the university as an instrument of 'social justice' or 'social change', rather than as means to pursue truth and to educate the young in the canon, has particularly led to the negative consequence of closing down the free exchange of ideas and silencing those who dissent from the radical social justice script.

Dissent, debate and intellectual conflict lie at the heart of appropriate scholarly practice and academic work-a-day, as human welfare is usually affected by the outcomes. For instance, the debates of the medical fraternity can determine the diagnostic and therapeutical processes in medicine that lead to whether a person lives or dies; economic debate can determine the economic welfare of a nation; and so on. Intellectual conflict in the academy elicits triumphs and tragedies outside of the academy. Debatable premises can also transfer to society prematurely.

The risk is heightened when a particular set of factors congeals through time, thrusting debatable scholarly premises out of the academy and social dogma permeates:

> Intellectuals are perhaps more susceptible than other classes in society to the rhetoric of revolutionary change, especially when what is promised is nothing less than a radical transformation of all existing human relations and social institutions. The seeking after political Utopia, indeed, has been for some centuries a major activity of Western intellectuals, whose hopes have been pinned now on this, now on that revolutionary movement or personality. These hopes, needless to say, have been repeatedly dashed – revolution turns to orthodoxy of another and sometimes more brutal kind, idealists are transformed into dogmatic functionaries or unprincipled opportunists; theory and practice part company. Yet the hopes themselves persist, and soon enough attach themselves to a new cause. Utopianism has become the surrogate faith of Western intellectuals, a faith that is not falsifiable by actual experience (Hollander 1977).

Klein and Stern (2005) and Gross and Simmons (2014) are recent accounts that bring empirical clout to the contention herein.

Hidden economic incentives

Behind a mis-directed academy is usually a set of economic incentives forming a mechanism that is overlooked. For instance, in Australia, the combination of the incentives driving the corporatised university along with high levels of government intervention in higher education sets in place particular economic forces that can scaffold academic social welfare dysfunction. Media commentary in Australia is currently noting this phenomenon (e.g., Gittins 2017; Creighton 2018).

The corporatisation of the university, a relatively recent phenomenon documented elsewhere (e.g., Keohane 2006; Reuben 1996, 2014), is characterised by corporate university managers. This role appears not to be equipped academically to manage intellectual trends such as those under discussion herein. Corporate university managers are adept in the skills for backing winning bets only.

These are complex ideas for the space here and the purpose here is to highlight the idea that academic dysfunction can exist and can pose a serious risk to social welfare. Let us next consider examples from recent decades.

When dissenting voices fail social progress

Scholarly dissent can generally be regarded as vital and useful. It supports academic work in all disciplines. It enables assessments of existing results to be aired, as disagreement hones arguments and methods, inaccuracy can be spotted, conclusions can be qualified and so on. Fresh thoughts happen, too. Thus, dissenting voices can guard social progress against flaws in research and teaching.

Unfortunately, not all dissent guards social progress. The point is illustrated by some circumstances in recent decades internationally when dissent has become dogmas. For instance, post-modern thought originally involved acts of scholarly dissent but some went further. Universities in Western democracies have generally swayed strongly towards influences from post-modernism and its intellectual complements. In the space here, 'the canon wars' serve as a starting point for describing what happened.

The canon wars were so named because they were direction-changing and territory-changing intellectual battles in the humanities. They were over which literary works, if any, are central to studies in literature. The stand-off originated in universities in the United States in the 1980s and spread to the rest of the world during the late-1980s and 1990s.

Although the canon wars started with some legitimate scholarly questioning of the literary canon, the battle appealed to wider interests. It was only a matter of a few years before 'the culture wars' developed into an international phenomenon in the West and the oft-heard expression, political correctness. It is said (Reed 2013; and Donadio 2007, for instance) that post-modernism won the canon wars and, with that win, came implications for ideas that were once the conceptual footings for Western thought, culture and morality. Some contemporary philosophers have little time for such over-influence, for instance:

> ... [I]t has left behind a generation of academics in the humanities disabled by their distrust of the very idea of truth and their disrespect for evidence, settling for 'conversations' in which nobody is wrong and nothing can be confirmed, only asserted with whatever style you can muster (Dennett 2013).

The focus replaces former emphases: specific cultural issues and group-defined identity problems occupy the policy agenda. A problem with this development is that identity politics is not a functional political framework for society and its economics is based on theft and retribution. That emphasis is not the same as the objective that maximises social welfare with redistribution that happens on an equitable basis. Under identity politics, some individuals are forced to shoulder the burdens of the wrongs of others; while some groups benefit from identity politics, that benefit arises out of opportunities that are unearned.

Current media comment occasionally affords illustrations of the ideological regime of theft that develops under identity politics (e.g., Dragovic 2018) but space does not permit examining the premises. An example of a change in the academy is useful. That change is about the foundation of inter-disciplinary study centres. Behind this development are ideological premises from Marxism and post-modernism that have melded into dogma in the academy and beyond it.

Study centres proliferated, first in the US, and then began emerging internationally.[4] Many study centres tended then to balkanise with the passage of time. They are like chameleons inside the academy. It is important to appreciate the significance of this type of variableness. Left-wing historian, Tony Judt, referred to the multiculturalism in American universities that created 'microconstituencies'. Judt observed that currently American universities are 'more like a supermarket – kids can take pretty much any courses they like: Jewish kids take Jewish studies, gay students gay studies, black studies, African-American studies. You no longer have a university, but a series of identity constituencies all studying themselves' (cited in Donadio 2007).

These changes happened alongside the coddling of the mind in modern universities. See Lukianoff and Haidt (2015, 2018), for instance. These authors contend that the post-modernist disposition of treating all opinions as of equal value causes this effect.

The tragedy for social welfare lies in the loss of the relevant framework for establishing social merit. During this fluid time, central ideological premises of these intellectual shifts became more dogmatic in the absence of the relevant conception that establishes social merit. The stepping stones towards the social optimum became immersed in tides of social ideology which also enabled a new status quo to become entrenched.

Entrenching bias

An entrenched status quo happens by way of an intellectual milieu gaining employment when people of similar persuasion predominate in the positions held. In the US economy, for example, this ascent is specifically noted about the media-entertainment-government-foundation-university sector (Kotkin 2014), which Kotkin calls the MEGFU. Kotkin charges the MEGFU with becoming a modern-day 'clerisy'.[5]

---

4 This is not to suggest that interdisciplinary study centres have no place in scholarly endeavour. The connotation intended is about the relatively non-disciplinary centres that are for studying anything – or everything.

5 'The clerisy' is the secular priesthood of America's 'progressive' elite, which Kotkin (2014) observes to be individuals feathering their nests at the expense of others.

In this short space, it is difficult to describe the phenomenon of dissenting voices failing social progress adequately without aggravating readers from both The Left and The Right. Each blames the other for the culture wars and political correctness. Accusations flow both ways as to which side is using which tool for political control. What once had been dissent over the canon inside the academy has become a developing intellectual milieu beyond the academy, having roots in post-modernism and now pervading across the latitude of the Left-Right spectrum.

The veracity and balance of the account above can also be debated; but let that debate happen separately. The purpose here requires discussion that sits above the usual polarisation. An illustration is available by seeing that a new set of forces underlay the tension that developed within the United Kingdom over Brexit.

Brexit became a tension between nationalists and globalists. David Goodhart (2017) refers to this split as having developed between the 'Somewheres' and the 'Anywheres'. This tension was driven by forces deeper than the reasons for international trade and those forces made the Brexit inevitable. Goodhart demonstrates that Brexit became a defeat for the 'cognitive elites', which he sees as the group dominating politics since the 1960s. This defeat, which affects economic welfare, appears to be a distinction that matters more deeply than that between The Right and The Left.

Mapping a flattened intellectual terrain

In the second decade of the twenty-first century, the appropriate place of dissent in universities is under insufficient scrutiny and only a few media outlets and some academic circles express any awareness. Some media commentary notes, for instance: 'Today, radical students with the support of some academics are in the forefront of moves, sometimes violent, to shut down debate. This is the case in Australia, North America and Western Europe' (Henderson 2017). Another is entitled, 'The campus mob came for me – and you, professor, could be next: whites were asked to leave for a "Day of Absence". I objected.

Then 50 yelling students crashed my class'. The author, an academic, elaborates on 'a tension that has existed throughout the entire American academy for decades' in the following terms:

> The button-down empirical and deductive fields, including all the hard sciences, have lived side by side with 'critical theory,' postmodernism and its perception-based relatives. Since the creation in 1960s and '70s of novel, justice-oriented fields, these incompatible worldviews have repelled one another ... [and]... rarely mix in any context where reality might have to be discussed (Weinstein 2017).

In the scholarly literature scholars on both the political Right and Left discuss a very similar concern. For instance, from The Left, there is Haidt (2012).[6] There is also, for instance, Cohen (2007) and Neiman (2008); and a decade ago from The Left, Richard Rorty (Rorty 1998) predicted the rise of a Donald Trump figure (Senior 2016). On the Right, there is Scruton (2016), for instance.

The relevance of this selection serves to illustrate briefly the political breadth: scholars on The Left cannot dismiss these critiques as merely some views being expressed by The Right, and the scholars on The Right observing this list cannot dismiss these critiques as views of The Left.

When the free exchange of ideas is discouraged, a specific intellectual risk is fostered which Mill warned of in 1840 in his Coleridge essay: 'In all intellectual debates, both sides tend to be correct in what they affirm, and wrong in what they deny'. For Mill, dissent is a vital element in knowledge formation:

> He who knows only his own side of the case knows little of that. His reasons may be good, and no one may have been able to refute them. But if he is equally unable to refute the reasons on the opposite side, if he does not so much as know what they are, he has no ground for preferring

---

6 Haidt has been examining the state of Western democracies more recently.

> either opinion.... Nor is it enough that he should hear the opinions of adversaries from his own teachers, presented as they state them, and accompanied by what they offer as refutations. He must be able to hear them from persons who actually believe them ... he must know them in their most plausible and persuasive form (*On Liberty*, II.23).

This phenomenon is more insidious than conventional Left-Right politics. Scholars from across the spectrum are noting that a preconceived view has developed inside the academy and beyond it and that it is a mind-set informing various areas of contemporary knowledge that is affecting national welfare already. This is a concern about dominating preconceptions that ought to be subject to much more scholarly scrutiny than is happening. Not a passing comment. These preconceptions form a set of beliefs about social welfare ascending in research and teaching in universities and schools.

It is timely for our focus to turn to the analytical foreshadowing of these assaults. They have their roots in the decay of intellectual rigour. An account is provided by Coleman (2002). The name that Coleman gives to this phenomenon is anti-economics.

Anti-economics

Anti-economics is a specific type of intellectual decay. It is described fully elsewhere (Coleman 2002) in an account from the eighteenth century to the present day. Coleman begins: 'From almost its beginnings economics has been shadowed by a kind of negative *Doppelgänger*, which has mocked, denigrated and wished ill on its positive counterpart. This clamorously hostile figure we will call "anti-economics"...'.

Although the germination of anti-economics often happens in universities, Coleman notes that anti-economics pervades societies as well:

> An anti-economist is whoever sees economics as a bane. To the anti-economist the offence of economics is that it

is harmful. (...) Its teachings must be discredited. (...) To the anti-economist there is no value to be salvaged from economics in its present state. (...) To the anti-economist the only way to discover economic truth is to throw out all economics and start again (7).

By way of a thorough treatise of the history of intellectual thought and ideas, Coleman shows also that anti-economics is not comprised of 'a single critique of economics' (11), or 'not, simply, "disagreement" with economics...' and 'not, simply, criticism of economics' (8). Instead, he finds anti-economics to be surprisingly heterogeneous: 'a heterogeneous aggregate of positions united only by finding economics deplorable' (11).

Thus anti-economics can be seen as a stock of hostility to economic concepts and that a critical mass of support for anti-economics will exist that will ebb and flow over time. Anti-economists even hold positions that are 'actually contrary to one another' (11), including those from the Left and the Right, the empiricist and the historicist, and so on.

With hostility to economics in any shape or form as the principal marker and unifying trait of anti-economists, various beliefs take refuge behind the hostility. These beliefs involve a long list of views that Coleman documents, including such accusations as economics being false, useless, harmful, methodologically inadequate, conceited, biased and bidden or that economic considerations are not important and can be overlooked or should not be important and should be overlooked. Let us pinpoint its relevance more precisely: is anti-economics post-modernism? No. Or Marxist? Often not. Is it apiece with a process of balkanisation in universities noted above? No, except insofar as the self-identified 'heterodox' see themselves like blacks, gays, etc. Is it concerned with bias? Yes, definitively so. Anti-economics defines the prejudice that economics confronts, a mental block, a mind-set, over how social merit is established.

One of Coleman's key findings is that the topography of anti-economics involves both public and private interests. Anti-economists include those 'hostile to economics on account of some supposed offence to public life...', which means 'the sense of offence at the harm done to the state of the world' by economics is one accusation, to those anti-economists offended by the supposed harm of economics done to 'the state of oneself' (Coleman 2002, 191). Coleman demonstrates that it is not only the idealist stance that can involve anti-economist, by the very act of being ideologues having high-minded objections due to being 'supposedly disinterested observers' but also the 'interested' enemies of economics with their 'doughty concern to defend one's own state'. In other words, Coleman's treatise enables the flesh on the bones of a singular, very stark notion that affects future economic welfare to be seen: 'Economics will always be dogged by interested opponents' (Coleman 2002, 196).

The case strengthens that a status quo has formed out of the defeats in recent intellectual battles in the modern Australian university landscape, and there are 'interested' losses in the ability to establish social merit. A further way to think about the co-occurrence of anti-economics and the canon wars is to conceive of the canon wars being like a coin, and anti-economics the coin's obverse. It is said that the winner of the canon wars was post-modernism,[7] and the win has had many implications for central ideas in Western thought, culture and morality.

Attention will turn now to an Australian illustration.

An Australian illustration: the 'economic rationalism' attack

Economic rationalism is a (mostly) derogatory term about the value of economics that was once on the lips of many Australians. It is a term for a point of dissent in the academy; the dissent gathered into a disproportionate attack throughout Australian society on the place of economics in Australia's future.

The attack commenced in the early years of the 1990s and, as it happens, the canon wars were under way as well. The Antipodean

---

7 See Reed (2013) and Donadio (2007) for instance.

focus on economic rationalism served in turn to spread a specific political view, *viz.*, that the place of economics in establishing social merit needed to be undermined.[8] Both the canon wars and the economic rationalism attack in Australia are cases of intellectual dissent having implications for the academy and, in turn, for social welfare.

The origin of the attack was in the actions of an Australian sociologist, Michael Pusey. Pusey had a very poor grasp of economics, although he and others thought he knew a considerable amount. A national mind-set over economics developed by coining an expression from the title of his book about some economic rationalism he believed he saw in Canberra (Pusey 1991), and then by propagating it like an advertisement jingle. Pusey's book construed a political phenomenon, purported neo-liberal economic rationalism, as having engulfed Canberra's policy apparatus.

On strategic grounds, one can regard the assault as a successful offensive. 'Economic rationalist' became a pejorative term in many circles. There was a prolonged assault on economics inside universities and beyond, also. Various forces of attack inside Australia's universities developed rapidly; however, the attack was most effective in the hands of the Australian media: everyday people in everyday conversations soon joined a melee having injudicious consequences for longer-term national welfare

For Pusey, and the others convinced of Pusey's views, the social costs of simplistic free market economic reform were then asserted often; with the assertion, the belief that the demise of economics as a discipline in Australia is warranted was disseminated by the media and by knowledge disseminators in Australian universities.

A Google Trends data count of 'Economic Rationalism' in Australia 2004-18 [9] reveals the term is now seldom heard. Generation Z may have never even heard of economic rationalism. Economic rationalism appears to be vanishing. Yet if it is so important for society, how

---

[8] Even some economists flourished during this period by referring to themselves as economic rationalists. This move afforded footings up some career ladders.

[9] The year, 2004, is the start of data of Google Trends data, not the start of the attacks.

can it happen that the concept withers? Or was the concept merely a vehicle for power.

With this attack having 'gone quiet', one wonders why. It is plausible that the defeat may have been adequate enough; the need to attack has faded. Its purpose to deride, undermine and diminish the important contribution of economics is achieved.

There is a hegemony that has formed in the vacuum left behind and it warrants scrutiny. There are many undiscussed consequences of this attack. One should also be mindful that verbal assaults on economists and economics as a discipline prove more destructive in some parts and places than in others.[10]

The intention is not to imply that dissidence has no place in economics. There is an historic record of economics in Australia being well-acquainted with dissidence of a productive kind. Historic shifts in Australian intellectual territory have had beneficial effects for Australia's social welfare. Dissident stances adopted by economists in past eras injected some overlooked matters into policy-making over Australia's economic welfare.[11] Such examples are the influences documented by Corden (1968), recorded also by the three volume *Surveys* of Fred Gruen (Gruen, 1978, 1979, 1983). A summary is in Norman (2007). There is a recent detailed documentation in Millmow (2017).

Social folly known of even in antiquity

Even the Ancient Greeks understood the complexities in establishing social merit, and the risks. That evidence is found in *Antigone* (441 BC) by Sophocles. The account provided here draws on the explanations of Yale professor of political philosophy, Stephen B. Smith (Smith

---

10 These assaults were intense on a regional campus and the long-term role that vital economic knowledge has played in the regional areas of Victoria is destroyed now. Economics education in regional schools and local university campuses had a crucial role for decades.

11 This 'voice' has attenuated in later decades. The decline is largely because of the ageing and death of Australia's past policy-transforming academic economists as well as to 'the rise and rise' of the consultancy.

2012, ch. 2). In Smith's interpretation, *Antigone* portrays Creon and Antigone as having legitimate goals and loyalties but each claim is quite different from the other.[12]

Conflicting claims are commonplace in society. The existence of a vexing social problem for Theban social welfare is soon apparent as *Antigone* unfolds. The fact of conflicting claims upon social welfare is the centrepiece of the plot. As the ambiguities and complexities of the social tension unfold, the alternative ways that the King of Thebes has available to resolve the conflict soon become the focus.

Creon symbolises a leader resolving the situation by entitling himself to crazed power. Dominance can simplify an otherwise complex social situation. Despite more problems arising for Thebes long-term than are solved (for Creon himself most starkly, too), Creon does not stay his hand. A widening circle of problems soon becomes apparent. Counting the corpses as the plot unfolds enables an unambiguous conclusion. The first corpse (precisely, Antigone's brother) that sets the plot in motion signifies an initial loss to economic welfare. See this as a loss from an early death of a young man, and also there is now a corpse that needs to be buried. Creon's outcomes are even measurable in Theban times! There is soon a second corpse (Antigone's). There is soon a third corpse (Creon's son; and then a fourth, his wife).

Losses to economic welfare from Creon's follies mount in this Theban theatre. How many corpses does the plot need before the impact on living standards of Creon's mind-set is noticed (and the paradox about Creon's vested myopia is that the corpses number not just his opponent's but his own son and wife)?

---

12 Antigone, daughter of Oedipus, has buried her brother, who was a traitor to Thebes, in defiance of the clear edict of the king, Creon. Antigone's pleas for her brother's corpse are not just personal; they represent profound temporal and spatial dimensions of the plot. To Creon, Antigone's convictions mean nothing and Creon's punishment for Antigone's disobedience is that she be buried alive. Creon's edict is not the end of the story because Antigone takes her own life. Creon's son, abhorring his father's cruelty, then commits suicide. When Creon's wife learns of the loss of her son, she, too, takes her own life. There, the play ends. By the time Creon realises his error, it is too late.

Here is a clash of social values between Antigone and Creon. It arises over Antigone's wilful, yet considered, act of disobedience to Creon. Antigone has deep convictions over family, kinship and the ancestral ties. These are in keeping with Ancient Greek values. *Antigone*'s Theban audience looked on while Creon resolves the social tension weakly by indulging might − the human capacity for cruelty and a propensity to blindness over one's actions.

The contrast of Antigone with Creon is the first instance of which we are aware of a character such as Antigone, an individual who acts upon a matter of principle or conscience. Antigone's *persona dramatis* is a stark contrast to Creon. Her actions portray an individual acting both within her human limits and upon her belief in divine principle.

This seemingly modern dilemma in establishing social merit is actually ancient! Is folly to rule society? Is despotism to rule society? Is dissent to be silenced? If not, then whose values are to count in resolving matters of economic welfare?

The point, here, is that even the Greeks knew about the conflict between two fundamentally different, i.e. alternative, moral codes or ways of life. This tension has to be resolved for social merit to be established.

The framework that Western civilisation enables

It should not be thought that Sophocles is the only writer ever to draw our attention to the two conflicting sets of values that *Antigone* portrays about society. Leo Strauss (1899-1973) and Hannah Arendt (1906-75) have both remarked on a conflict between two fundamentally different, i.e. alternative, moral codes or ways of life to be resolved in society (Havers 2004). Although Sophocles' play is the first known instance, it is not the only, or the last, instance. Both Strauss and Arendt have regarded Western civilisation as a dialogue around these two alternative sources of human motivation, and all the ambiguity and complexity that the dialogue embraces.

Strauss refers to these poles that are depicted in *Antigone* as 'the theologico-political predicament' of all societies. For Strauss, on the one hand, there is the existence of 'Athens', where authority is derived from man-centred conceptions and egotistically-based reason alone (Creon writ large); and there is 'Jerusalem' on the other hand, which represents the city of faith and the alternative source of authority (Antigone writ large). It is precisely that tension that affords us insight into the reality with which Sophocles will have confronted Ancient audiences of *Antigone*. This reality is contemporary. Theban plays were attended by audiences of tens of thousands.

Space is limited here and this chapter has already clearly affirmed that when anti-economics ascends, various misplaced beliefs about social merit predominate over how social tension is resolved. One can speculate whether modernity may be losing sight of a social reality known of in Antiquity. Strauss's argument is that Western civilisation cannot hold only to 'Athens', as reality becomes misconstrued, and that 'Jerusalem' is relevant also when establishing social merit.

Arguably some may still quarrel the concept of Jerusalem as hardly being of any assistance in any positive social science. Haidt (2012) provides some further persuasion. Haidt explains political differences with empirical evidence based on moral foundations theory. This theory postulates that there are at least six inherent moral foundations upon which cultures develop their moralities. There are spectrums which provide the dimensions of morality on which individuals form their positions towards social behaviour: care *versus* harm, fairness (equality) *versus* cheating, liberty *versus* oppression, loyalty *versus* betrayal, authority *versus* subversion and sanctity *versus* degradation.

Haidt's findings are evidence of the contemporary clash: The Left tends to endorse two foundations only, primarily, care and equality, whereas The Right endorses all six foundations more equally. Haidt finds empirical evidence also on a narrowing of the moral palate in the current era.[13] Haidt's results are important for our times: the value judgments on which conflicting views on political questions are

---
13 The narrowing of the moral palate is not new: the roots of this narrowing are found in Bentham and Kant.

resolved are vital to establishing social merit. Haidt's results suggest that the foundations may be destabilising.

There are obvious implications for social welfare. Strauss and Arendt have foreseen grave risks in losing a sense of 'legitimate and stable political authority' (Havers 2004, 19). Both Strauss and Arendt argue that this loss constitutes a nihilistic threat to Western democracy. Strauss and Arendt both contend that aligning only with 'Athens' misses the tension between the two poles of 'Athens' and 'Jerusalem' that exists in productive interaction in the passage of Western civilisation.

The Australian policy issue

The focus for reform is found in the content of policy and the direction of policy. The goal of striving to excel does not have to diminish in a university sector. Recent empirical evidence about the crisis in universities internationally concludes with the charge of bias having a footing in the academy, a serious bias requiring a policy response:

> Orbiting all of these debates about the future of higher education in the United States, and in other countries as well, is the issue of professorial liberalism and political 'bias' in the academy. Many of the contributors to the volume address this issue in some form. Our view is that few questions of substance can be directed toward the future of the nation's colleges and universities that ignore the bias charge (Gross and Simmons 2014, 313-4).

Four areas at least are infected: the curricula in the academy and the academic standards; those teaching and researching in the academy; university management; and university policy-makers. Attention to developing the knowledge base about the phenomenon is warranted urgently. I refer here to knowledge that will empower these university groups to initiate the steps that will reverse this trend.

Welfare losses will continue into the future at a compounding rate as the current level of concern is insufficient: there is no response yet. Externalities of an intellectual kind will persist when poorly managed. Highly educated people are being gullible about the social impact of universities: intellectual externalities pervade in this morass. Managers of universities are applied economists and no manager is 'above' economics. Solutions are to be grounded in the conception that embraces the full social effect of universities upon social welfare, as presented in the second section above.

Ignorance, incompetence and intention are behind the deepening crisis. Recall Keynes (1936):

> The ideas of economists and political philosophers, both when they are right and when they are wrong are more powerful than is commonly understood. Indeed, the world is ruled by little else. Practical men, who believe themselves to be quite exempt from any intellectual influences, are usually slaves of some defunct economist (383-4).

A well-documented malaise clearly exists, and responding to it requires a shift away from partisan polemic. It is, in short, patent that policy-makers and decision-makers have been warned of the dangers of these transformations in the university sector. In Australia university managers are on inordinately high salaries for delivering responsibilities when social welfare clearly stands to lose in the set of circumstances that has developed: twenty-first century-type social welfare loss is happening now.

Conclusion

The crisis can be interpreted as simply a symptom of a more general intellectual decay in the academy. One manifestation of that general decay is the incapacity to engage or grasp the problems with establishing social merit; the fact that anti-economics is on the rampage in universities is only to be expected.

Living together in society involves endless nuances and ambiguities. Ideology that prevails is responsible for developing a social mind-set unable to resolve the inevitable conflicts and tensions of society. This mind-set is unseen for its dangers: the academy comforts and protects a mind-set when it ought to challenge it.

The fact that this type of situation can develop is known of: it was known of even in Antiquity. It is nothing new. The new challenge is for highly credentialed societies to see its twenty-first century expression. What else is new is a political framework that has been developing. Although this framework is believed in for improving the passage to the future, this belief is misplaced.

Rightful, proportionate and wise responses to our times are sought. Considering the state of the contemporary intellectual milieu, responses on two fronts are warranted. One front involves fostering the freedoms that will avert the propensity for education and research currently to entrench a bias that is incapable of establishing social merit. The other front involves persuading an entrenched intellectual milieu of some contemporary folly. Even though the challenges may seem insurmountable, the necessity and urgency of averting the forces bearing on both fronts cannot presently be overemphasised.

References

Bergson, A., 'A Reformulation of Certain Aspects of Welfare Economics', *Quarterly Journal of Economics*, 1938, 52(2), 310-334.

Cohen, Nick, *What's Left: How Liberals Lost their Way*, Fourth Estate, London, 2007.

Coleman, W. O., *Economics and its Enemies: The Story of Two Centuries of Anti-Economics*, Palgrave, Houndsmills, 2002.

Cook, Simon J., *The Intellectual Foundations of Alfred Marshall's Economic Science: A Rounded Globe of Knowledge*, Cambridge University Press, Cambridge, 2009.

Corden, W., *Australian Economic Policy Discussion: A Survey*, Melbourne University Press, Melbourne, 1968.

Cornford, F. M., *Microcosmographia Academia: Being a Guide for the Young Academic Politician*, 5th edn, Bowes & Bowes, Cambridge, 1953.

Creighton, Adam, 'There are Degrees of Fudging in Claims Made of University Funding', *The Australian,* 4 September 2018.

Dennett, Daniel C., 'Dennett on Wieseltier *v.* Pinker in the New Republic: Let's Start with a Respect for Truth', edge.org, 10 September 2013.

Donadio, Rachel 'Revisiting the Canon Wars', *New York Times*, 16 September 2007.

Dragovic, D., 'Religion Seeks to Unify, Where Identity Politics will only Divide', *The Australian*, 9 July 2018.

Gittins, Ross, 'Our Universities Aren't Earning the Money we Give them', *Sydney Morning Herald*, 29 May 2017.

Goodhart, David, 'Anywheres *vs* Somewheres: the Split That Made Brexit Inevitable', *New Statesman*, 17 March 2017.

Gramsci, Antonio, *Selections from the Prison Notebooks*, ed. and trans. Q. Hoare and G. Nowell Smith, Lawrence & Wishart, New York, 1971.

Gross, Neil and Simmons, Solon, *Professors and their Politics*, Johns Hopkins University Press, Baltimore, 2014.

Gruen, F., *Surveys of Australian Economics*, 1-3, Allen and Unwin, Sydney, 1978, 1979, 1983.

Haidt, Jonathan, *The Righteous Mind: Why Good People are Divided by Politics and Religion*, Pantheon, New York, 2012.

Havers, Grant, 'Between Athens and Jerusalem: Western Otherness in the Thought of Leo Strauss and Hannah Arendt', *The European Legacy*, 2004, 9(1) 19-29.

Henderson, Gerard, 'La Trobe's Dewar Shows How Radical Left Shuts Down Debate', *The Australian*, 3 June 2017.

Hollander, Paul, 'Review of *Utopia and Revolution*, by Melvin J. Lasky', *Commentary*, 1 May 1977.

Keohane, Nannerl O., *Higher Ground: Ethics and Leadership in the Modern University*, Duke University Press, Durham NC, 2006.

Keynes, J. M., *The General Theory of Employment, Interest and Money,* Macmillan, London, 1936.

Klein, Daniel B. and Stern, Charlotta, 'Professors and Their Politics: the Policy Views of Social Scientists', *Critical Review*, 2005, 17(3–4), 257-303.

Kotkin, Joel, *The New Class Conflict*, Telos Press, Candor, NY, 2014.

Lasky, Melvin J., *Utopia and Revolution*, The University of Chicago Press, Chicago and London, 1976.

Lears, T. J. Jackson, 'The Concept of Cultural Hegemony: Problems and Possibilities', *The American Historical Review*, 1985, 90(3), 567-93.

Lukianoff, Greg and Haidt, Jonathan, 'The Coddling of the American Mind', *The Atlantic*, 2015, 316(2), 42-53.

Lukianoff, Greg and Haidt, Jonathan, *The Coddling of the American Mind: How Good Intentions and Bad Ideas are Setting up a Generation for Failure*, Penguin, New York, 2018.

Mill, John Stuart, *On Liberty*, Longman, New York, 2006.

Millmow, Alex, *A History of Australasian Economic Thought*, Routledge, New York, 2017.

Nath, S.K., *A Reappraisal of Welfare Economics*, Routledge & Kegan Paul, London, 1969.

Neiman, Susan, *Moral Clarity: a Guide for Grown-up Idealists*, Harcourt, Orlando, 2008.

Norman, Neville R., 'The Contribution of Australian Economists: the Record and the Barriers', *Economic Papers*, 2007, 26 (1), 1-16.

Pigou, A. C., *The Economics of Welfare*, 4th edn, Macmillan, London, 1932.

Pusey, M., *Economic Rationalism in Canberra: A Nation-building State Changes its Mind*, CUP, Melbourne, 1991.

Reed, Matt, 'Remember the Canon Wars?' *Inside Higher Ed*, 11 April 2013.

Reuben, Julie A., *The Making of the Modern University: Intellectual Transformation and the Marginalization of Morality*, The University of Chicago Press, Chicago, 1996.

Reuben, Julie A., 'Challenging Neutrality: Sixties Activism and Debates over Political Advocacy in the American University', in Neil Gross and Solon Simmons eds, *Professors and their Politics*, 217-40, Johns Hopkins University Press, Baltimore, 2014.

Rorty, Richard, *Achieving our Country: Leftist Thought in Twentieth Century America*, Harvard University Press, Cambridge MA, 1998.

Scruton, Roger, *Fools, Frauds and Firebrands: Thinkers of the New Left*, Bloomsbury, London, 2016.

Senior, Jennifer, 'Richard Rorty's 1998 Book Suggested Election 2016 was Coming', *New York Times*, 20 November 2016.

Shils, Edward, 'Introductory Note', in Max Weber, *The Power of the State and the Dignity of the Academic Calling in Imperial Germany: The Writings of Max Weber on University Problems*, 1-3, The University of Chicago Press, Chicago and London, 1974.

Smith, Stephen B., *Political Philosophy*, Yale University Press, New Haven, 2012.

Weber, Max, 'Science as a Vocation' 'Wissenschaft als Beruf' from *Gesammlte Aufsaetzezur Wissenschaftslehre*, 524-55, Tubingen, 1922.

Weinstein, Bret, 'The Campus Mob Came for Me – and You, Professor, Could be Next', *Wall Street Journal*, 30 May 2017.

13

The Exposed Academic and the Disappearance of Disciplines in the Managerial University

John Lodewijks

Books like *Australian Universities: A Portrait of Decline* (Meyers 2012) and *Whackademia: An Insider's Account of the Troubled University* (Hil 2012), and articles titled 'Institutional Breakdown? An Exploratory Taxonomy of Australian University Failure' (Clarke 1998) and 'Dumbing-down in Australian Universities' (Murray & Dollery 2006) suggest that the quality of university education is being eroded on multiple fronts. This chapter examines the impact on, and actions by, three players in this developing saga: academics, students and university administrators.

Academics

Academics can tell that the students they are teaching have changed. They lament falling standards and declining attendances in lectures. 'Blended learning' approaches are increasingly foisted on staff, even though it is not at all clear that it saves any time or effort on the part of the academic, and anecdotal evidence exists that it consumes more time than traditional chalk and talk in the pre-electronic age. Many academic staff are perplexed about the new student landscape and the extra demands being placed on them. More so, this is happening in an environment of significant enrolment increases and higher student-staff ratios. The additional students often lack basic literacy and numeracy skills so that their preparation to enter higher education is deficient. Increased student numbers have led to a fall in the quality of education and in assessment standards.

Academics also face increased accountability for the volume and quality of research outcomes. The Excellence in Research for Australia (ERA) outcomes has effectively placed researchers 'on notice'. In addition, academics are required to devote more attention to quality learning outcomes and are extensively audited to demonstrate these outcomes, not least by the daunting Australian Universities Quality Agency (AUQA) Audits that have now been replaced by a national regulatory authority for higher education, the Tertiary Education Quality and Standards Agency (TEQSA).

Academics are being hit on two fronts, in quite a confronting way, to improve both their teaching and research outcomes.

Students

Two detailed studies published by the Australian Academy of the Humanities as part of a 'Mapping the Humanities, Arts and Social Sciences in Australia Project' provide us with a clear picture of the impact on universities of the expansion of student numbers (Dobson 2013; Turner and Brass 2014).

Over the period 2002-11 student numbers grew by 36%, student load by 40 % but the size of the total academic workforce in Australia only by 27%. Non-research postgraduate enrolments increased by 44% across the university sector. The humanities, arts and social sciences (HASS) disciplines teach the majority of students in the Australian higher education system maintaining a share of around 65% of all enrolments, and 63% of student load (Turner and Brass 2014, 12). The growth in student enrolments over the last decade has been fuelled by growth in international enrolments across the whole sector, and the area of most substantial growth has been in Management and Commerce (107%). The HASS sector is large and diverse – covering fields from economics, psychology, geography and demography to linguistics, archaeology, history, arts and media studies. Within the HASS, Management and Commerce had the largest share of enrolments in 2011 (26%) followed by Society and Culture (21%).

Both of these reports note that the demand-driven system has resulted in the rationalisation of offerings in certain fields, the mergers of disciplinary units, such as schools and departments, and a reduction in the geographic spread of HASS programs across the nation. In particular there has been a contraction of disciplinary presence from the regional or non-metropolitan campuses to the metropolitan and Group of Eight (Go8) universities. Certain disciplines – Anthropology, Political Science, Archaeology, Sociology, Economics, for instance – are now overwhelmingly concentrated in Go8 universities. Another trend has been that the number of majors available within the BA degree has declined as well as the number of 'tagged' degrees (i.e., Bachelor degrees named after a particular specialisation, such as a Bachelor of Economics).

The inequitable distribution of HASS programs across metropolitan and regional centres is an issue of key concern. There is evidence that entry scores are dropping and numbers declining in HASS programs in regional universities while enrolments in these fields of education are becoming increasingly concentrated in the metropolitan universities and the Go8 universities, with consequent reductions in the range of opportunities available to those in regional Australia. Responsibility for discipline offerings is largely left to individual universities or groups of universities to address, but is the education market delivering what the nation needs? Subjects where the demand from the student market may not be high may still be of national, strategic, or academic importance. Course rationalisations are not always going to be in the national interest nor, indeed, in the interest of particular disciplines or fields of education (Turner and Brass 2014, 31).

There is a risk that if student choice continues to determine discipline offerings, HASS teaching would contract to the metropolitan universities, and perhaps even only to the Go8. There is evidence that in some universities there has been a gradual institutional disinvestment in HASS fields of education. In particular, regional universities are becoming more oriented towards offering training programs targeted towards specific professions rather than the more generalist degrees.

So far we have documented the growth in student numbers and the rationalisation of course offerings in certain fields. In addition, the uncapping of university places has led to a decline in entry standards in a number of universities across Australia. It is clear that there are widespread declining university admission standards in the lower ATAR level universities. This has been even more noticeable in the more competitive markets in Sydney and Melbourne, compared to the areas of fewer university choices. It should be noted that while it appears that the higher ATAR (usually Go8) universities may have increased their entry requirements in some cases, it is important to remember that most universities now offer up to 10 bonus points that they will allocate to students. This would suggest an additional erosion of standards that is not reflected in the published ATAR scores. It is no coincidence that as universities have aggressively expanded enrolments, with the extra students less prepared than earlier cohorts, these students have found that the intellectual demands and quantitative requirements of courses like economics pose a major deterrent and they are far more comfortable enrolling in other business programs. Maxwell (2003) describes this nicely as a 'hardening of the discipline' coming up against the 'softening in preparation of students' combined with the rise of more fashionable fields of study which students perceive as being 'more suited to their vocational needs'.

Students' motivation to learn is being significantly undermined. Many students must work to be able to afford a university education and this work is mostly in casual, unskilled employment that adds little to their intellectual development. As a consequence, students are withdrawing from face-to-face engagement with their classes and with the university environment more broadly except for experiences they perceive (correctly or incorrectly) to enhance their 'work-readiness'. This reduction in engagement is reducing the development of the intellectual skills they once would have been able to take into the workforce.

Finally, we need to examine the learning and teaching 'innovations' that are so heavily spruiked in universities. Educational theorists, who advocate the explicit recognition of the learning process, and university administrators, who must appear to be proactive in educational development within their institutions, are pressuring staff to change the way they teach these students. The changes involve criterion-based assessment, curriculum redesign and quality assurance. Academics are required to do assessment mapping and scaffold learning outcomes throughout programs and courses and relate these to graduate attributes. In turn course outcomes need to be externally benchmarked to discipline academic standards.

Some of the frustration and annoyance related to this process is articulated by Oslington (2012):

> The current obsession with learning objectives and graduate attributes is essentially about describing what universities are doing in language fashionable among the current regime of educational bureaucrats ... lots of meetings, paper, and box ticking ... this guff has little to do with the quality of what goes on at the educational coalface ... I have never met a student who has actually read the guff in a course outline – at most they have a bit of a giggle before turning the pages to the course content and assessment. There is no real evidence that the current obsession with process makes any difference to the quality of education.

'Blended Learning' is all the rage in many Australian universities. While universities are keen to harness new technologies in the provision of education, the application of Information Communication Technology (hereafter ICT) to teaching is not without complications and difficulties. The developing literature that tracks the use of ICT in education certainly emphasises the *potential* for valuable contributions.

However, that same literature also raises some significant concerns and limitations in the ability of ICT to improve educational outcomes. If there is one underlying moral of this literature, it is that the appropriate use of ICT in higher education is yet to be discovered, and that a hasty application of such technology is likely to be fraught with problems. Moreover, these blended approaches seem to be steadily displacing tried, tested and successful strategies for managing teaching programs.

For example, studies of podcasts in comparison to traditional lectures find that while initially appealing to students, there was no significant difference between the achievement of students who used podcasts and those who did not. This is not to suggest they had a negative impact on student learning—the podcasts simply did not make a significant improvement in student outcomes. Furthermore, although some responses to the podcasts were positive, the students themselves did not suggest that podcasts should replace lectures at all, and should remain a supplement only. Moreover, students who have poor attentional control, or who are susceptible to external distraction, are likely to be disadvantaged in mobile multimedia learning environments where distractions may be high.

There is no doubt that more and more use will be made of mobile technology for educational purposes. Although this area of education practice is still evolving, even at this early stage there are some salient lessons that can be learnt from the literature. To begin, mobile technology is likely to be popular with students, and the perceptions of students are important. If they are enthusiastic about the use of a technology in their learning, they are no doubt likely to obtain a better outcome. However, the student perception cannot be the sole focus. Much attention also needs to be devoted to measuring outcomes that are derived from the use of technology and that is, at best, mixed.

Despite these cautionary tales, blended learning is promoted everywhere. It has been alleged that blended learning designs are central to securing a sustainable future for teaching units. Administrators may perceive blended learning as a means to cut costs. However, blended learning is not necessarily cheaper than face-to-face learning and we may well ask if our students fit the profile of the motivated, self-directed and reflective students that the blended learning approach assumes. Experiences with non-face-to-face learning do indicate serious concerns with retention and failure rates unless students are mature and self-disciplined.

The literature indicates we should be very careful before we leap head-first into blended learning. This has not happened. Lectures are under threat and being abandoned. Student contact hours are being reduced and class sizes increased. There is currently considerable concern in Australian universities around blended learning and staff workload. Blended learning facilitators and quality assurance officers have been hired in great numbers to torment staff, and curriculum mapping projects are all the rage. Moreover, there are many other changes afoot in the teaching and learning space that absorb the time of academics. There is the threat from massive open online courses (MOOC) and the ever accumulating documentation required, often to satisfy external agencies like TEQSA that we are fulfilling our requirements under the Higher Education Standards Framework.

The inevitable blended-learning tsunami and the increased bureaucratisation of teaching are apparent to all. It may be necessary to join the blended learning movement to survive as our traditional teaching styles are increasingly under threat. The hurried application of ICT strategies dispense with tried and tested traditional approaches to learning, in pursuit of the rapid adoption of new fashions and trends in higher education offerings and pedagogy, often without clear or convincing evidence in support of the changes.

The onus seems to fall completely on academic staff when it comes to achieving quality outcomes. In truth, when it comes to learning outcomes there is only so much that even the most dedicated and well-meaning staff member can do, especially when students are spending less time on the campus and more hours in paid employment, and where their studies are being increasingly compartmentalised in a hectic schedule of non-study activities. Moreover, the attitudes and motivations of students often appear antithetical to traditional concepts of scholarship – note the increased incidence of plagiarism and contract cheating – and the scholarly purpose of universities to broaden one's mind and to explore ideas in a critical and creative way. Many students seem solely employment focused, and view a university education as a paper-chase at minimalist effort and with modest targets where bare passes are satisfactory.

Administrators

George Morgan, in a media piece, 'Australian universities are drifting to mediocrity' (*Sydney Morning Herald*, 3 May 2017), noted that most universities employ more administrators than academics, particularly middle managers brought in to make the university more 'lean, agile and competitive' while it is the remuneration of the most senior administrators that raise eyebrows. He goes on to say that corporate-style management has proved to be highly inefficient and that there needs to be more academic oversight to curtail the 'excesses, caprice and follies of managerialism'.[1]

It is commonly perceived that the modern university has lost its way and poor decision-making by managers, who are often not academics, has led to undesirable consequences. Corporate managerialism has replaced collegial systems of university administration. The ability to enact spending cuts without collegial discussion or oversight is seen as a prerogative of governing bodies. Decision-making characterised by short-termism and extreme risk aversion on the part of the university is another noticeable development.

The decline of collegiality in favour of executive managerialism is widely lamented in the higher education sector. There is nostalgia among faculty for a 'golden age of collegiality' that had been replaced by the Australian university phenomenon of a corporate managerial culture. In a struggle for survival in competitive student markets, with no shelter for poorly subscribed courses or research not funded from grant income,

---

1 For the development of this argument, see Ginsberg (2011).

higher plane considerations of scholarly pursuits were seen as self-indulgent. Harry Clarke (1998), in a strident polemic, 'Dumbing-down in Australian universities' had previously written that:

> Courses are established to be attractive to students (now described as 'clients' or 'customers' of the university) by having apparent vocational appeal with unchallenging subject matter and assessment.... Academically weak students, facing the option of choosing between challenging, analytical courses or descriptive, narrow courses with little intellectual challenge, tend to go for the latter if that is where they see apparent vocational opportunity.

Murray and Dollery (2006) comment that administrators sometimes acted despotically, without regard to logic and fairness, and the costs incurred of organisational restructures were often far in excess of any derived benefit. Others blame rent seeking educational bureaucrats who provide the appearance that the quality of education is checked and standards upheld. These bureaucrats have established a cottage industry for themselves and, to further their ends, they push for unified standards and methods, a one size fits all approach. This allows them to tick off boxes set against each course and lecturer. It is a mistaken concern for homogeneous inputs instead of looking at outputs. These concerns relate to a fixation with *Performance Metrics* via an *Audit Culture*.

Today we witness an intensification of outcomes-based performance management in many universities and particularly management by metrics. Journal rankings are routinely used as management tools for evaluating staff research performance. ARC research grants are another metric. They are used as proxies for research quality. Administrators want simple management tools for performance reviews and promotion applications to assess their staff members' research output or teaching performance (using student feedback scores). The judgment and experience of seasoned academics, in a consultative and collegial interaction with colleagues, is being consistently replaced by the administrator's performance metrics.

A case in point is the rounds of the Excellence in Research for Australia (ERA) audit organised by the Australian Research Council. Serious concerns have been raised about the adequacy of the ERA audits to judge the full breadth of economic research accurately and fairly (Bloch 2012). For example, the ERA1 audit showed that two-thirds of universities that were assessed in applied economics, as well as the overall economics discipline, were rated as 'below world standard'. The implication of ERA1 was that Australia generally is very poor in economics research by world standards.

At the two digit level (14 Economics) 40% of assessable economics units were given the lowest possible rating of one representing 'well below world standard'. By comparison, in the Humanities and Creative Arts, less than 10% of institutions received a one ranking across all fields, including Law. The overall average for economics was 2.4 and only 2.1 in Applied Economics. In Applied Economics only four out of 35 universities got a 4 or a 5 ranking. Note that applied economists account for 66% of all Australian economists, 80% of the research grants and 76% of the publications. Are we really that bad? Of course not.

An increasing proportion of universities' research funding is based on ERA outcomes and, hence, there is reduced funding within universities for low-ranked research codes. As such, the perceived 'value' of academic economists in many universities is very low and, if they perform 'below world standard', or even just at that standard, why persist with them when a better return on research resources can be obtained in disciplines with far higher ERA rankings? The end result is that these ERA exercises rank the quality of economics research far lower than an objective assessment of the data (see Davidson 2013).

Research evaluations depend significantly on journal rankings. In the ERA1 exercise only 28% of applied economics journals ranked A or A* (the top journal quality ratings). In the second ERA round explicit journal rankings were dispensed with. This was in response to clear and consistent evidence that the rankings were being deployed inappropriately within some quarters of the sector, in ways that could produce harmful outcomes, and based on a poor understanding of the actual role of the rankings. One common example was the setting of targets for publication in A and A* journals by institutional research managers. There is now far less tolerance for self-directed research that is unrelated to external funding and not supported by citation and impact ratings.

The challenge of private providers

On 12 April 2017 the federal Department of Education released the Quality Indicators for Learning and Teaching (QILT). Perhaps not surprisingly, private institutions like the University of Notre Dame and Bond University had the most satisfied students while six of the Go8 universities performed well below the national average. The University of Technology Sydney had the lowest score reflecting a shift in 2016 from semester to trimester teaching periods, and from traditional lectures to interactive tutorials.

Often it is a new entrant to an industry that disrupts the incumbents and takes market share. There has been a rapid growth of new for-profit entrants into the higher education market. An article dated 17 May 2017 in *The Australian*, 'TEQSA report shows students favour private degrees', reported that undergraduate student numbers in commercial colleges rose almost one-fifth between 2013 and 2015, while postgraduate numbers more than doubled. In contrast, our universities had a 1% decline in commencing student load in 2015.

Education private providers have been in the news repeatedly for all the wrong reasons. With private providers there is always the threat that, in the triangle between students, academic standards and the bottom line, the first two will be dominated by the third consideration. We have seen ample evidence of that in the media reporting. But let us not be blinded by these fiascos from seeing the positives that also emerge and may in the future present an increasing challenge to our bloated public universities.

Working in a private higher education provider, S. P. Jain Global, offering Australian accredited degrees, is an eye-opener for someone who spent over 30 years in the public university system. What has been achieved is quite remarkable in many ways, not least the logistical feat of moving hundreds of students from one country to another in the pursuit of global education, driven by the passion and vision of the institution's President. It is certainly not a perfect workplace by the standards of the public universities. Many academics would not last long in this environment and there is rapid staff turnover. Yet, in terms of cost efficiency, prompt decision-making in a system devoid of bureaucracy and over-paid administrators, and innovative education platforms, there is much to be learned from this private provider.

S. P. Jain Global is a small, young and an innovative business-school with a unique multi-country model. The School has steadily been growing in terms of educational courses, students, faculty and infrastructure. In a short span time, S. P. Jain has introduced top quality courses recognised by governments, accreditation agencies and industry. It receives no government funding whatsoever. The only revenue is student fees – 99% of our students are international and we are expensive! Hence our institution is exceedingly student-focused and students have a great deal of influence in the institution, particularly with respect to learning outcomes. The students are very demanding, expect an engaged learning environment with the emphasis on practical application and real world skills. They will not sit idle through Death by PowerPoint or by doing the exercises at the end of each textbook chapter.

Our selection of academic staff is primarily on their engaged teaching ability. That being said, we are still more research-intensive than most other private providers. The average annual publication rate exceeds two journal articles for the 30 permanent academics and that includes a number of A-ranked ABDC journals. Most of the articles are applied business projects and many are co-authored with our students.

As a private provider S. P. Jain is very lean. There is no fat in the organisation. Most staff wear multiple hats, performing a variety of tasks. There is no deadwood. This has its own costs in terms of work-life balance and stress. Decision-making is exceedingly fast. There are no tedious, long-winded academic committee deliberations that postpone decisions or move them on to another bureaucratic committee. If a good idea comes along, and the President of the organisation is in agreement, it gets implemented the next day.

While far from a perfect institution, there are lessons to be shared from the experiences of a private provider.

Conclusion

This chapter has raised a number of concerns about modern higher education in Australia. The additional pressure on academics undermines rather than enhances the quality of core services that they can offer students: the teaching of discipline-based content. The acutely conflicting demands on academic time is undermining the quality of what they can deliver in the class room. The cumulative nature of pressures being placed on coal-face academics derives from the managerial prerogatives at the top of decision-making, the performance metrics that now dominate staff appraisal, the lack of preparedness of many students for higher studies, and the shift in teaching away from the conventional classroom. The challenges provided by private universities and other providers of higher education attest to the problems in the public university system.

References

Bloch, H., 'An Uneven Playing Field: Rankings and Ratings for Economics in ERA 2010', *Economic Papers*, 2012, 31(4), 418-427.

Clarke, H., 'Dumbing-down in Australian Universities', *Quadrant*, 42 (9), September 1998, 55-59.

Davidson, S., 'Excellence in Research for Australia: An Audit of the Applied Economics Rankings' *Agenda*, 2013, 20(2), 5-20.

Dobson, I. R., *Mapping the Humanities and Social Sciences: Analysis of University Statistics 2002–2011,* Australian Academy of the Humanities, 2013.

Ginsberg, Benjamin, *The Fall of the Faculty: The Rise of the All-Administrative University and Why it Matters*, Oxford University Press, New York, 2011.

Hil, R., *Whackademia: An Insider's Account of the Troubled University*, New South, Sydney, 2012.

Lodewijks, John, 'The Elephant in the Room: Conflicting Demands on Academics in Australian Higher Education', *Australasian Journal of Economics Education*, 2011, 8(1), 17-40.

Lodewijks, John and Heath Spong, 'Pedagogy, M-Learning and Financial Stringency', *Australasian Journal of Economics Education*, 2013, 10(2), 1-23.

Lodewijks, John and Tony Stokes, 'Is Academic Economics Withering in Australia?', *Agenda – A Journal of Policy Analysis and Reform*, 2014, 21(1), 69-88.

Lodewijks, John, 'The History of Economics "Down-under": Repulsing the Barbarians at the Gate', in *Reclaiming Pluralism in Economics*, Jerry Courvisanos, James Doughney and Alex Millmow (eds), Routledge, London, 58-75, 2016.

Lodewijks, John, Tony Stokes and Sarah Wright, 'Economics: An Elite Subject soon only Available in Elite Universities?', *International Review of Economics Education*, 2016, 23, 1-9.

Maxwell, P., 'The Rise and Fall (?) of Economics in Australian Universities', *Economic Papers*, 2003, 22(1), 79-92.

Meyers, D., *Australian Universities: A Portrait of Decline*, AUPOD, e-book, www.australianuniversities.id.au, 2012.

Murray, D. and B. Dollery, 'Institutional Breakdown? An Exploratory Taxonomy of Australian University Failure', *Higher Education Policy*, 2006, 19(4), 479-494.

Oslington, P., 'The Approaching University Degree Bubble', *Quadrant*, 2012, 49, 150-52.

Turner, G., and Brass, K., *Mapping the Humanities, Arts and Social Sciences in Australia,* Australian Academy of the Humanities, Canberra, 2014.

14
Introducing Competition Policy into Higher Education
Potential to Create Genuine Diversity

Paul Oslington

For many years Australia's higher education system has been a story of organisational uniformity, intellectual uniformity, declining academic standards, lack of innovation, rent-seeking and high costs. Without competition from new entrants it is hard to see this story changing much in this bureaucratic- and union-dominated world.

Australia's higher education system has so far been dominated by what are denominated as public universities.[1] The few private universities we have (such as Bond and Notre Dame Australia) were created by State parliaments under regulatory arrangements that no longer exist.[2] The current regulatory regime was created in 2011, following the Bradley Review of Higher Education completed in 2008. Under this regime, the Tertiary Education Quality and Standards Agency (TEQSA) administers rules for accrediting new universities set by the Higher Education Standards Panel (HESP), which is made up of mostly university experts.

Australian policy-makers and those who work in public universities

---

1 The language of public and private is used here because it is standard, but the language reveals part of the problem. Perhaps public universities would be better described as bureaucratic-political, and private universities as truly public because of their reliance on appealing to a public beyond the bureaucrats and politicians for their survival.
2 Glyn Davis (2017) provides a good recent history of Australian higher education policy. Andrew Norton (2016) provides a snapshot of the current state of the system.

find it difficult to conceive of anything else.[3] Most of the people in the room tend to be alumni of Australian universities. The universities maintain large public relations departments and multiple well-funded Canberra lobby groups. University experts stack the policy advisory committees. There are cosy arrangements between the higher education bureaucracy, university management and the unions. Australian newspapers and websites which rely on university advertising are reluctant to antagonise those who send money their way. A game of mates?[4] Perhaps even a cartel?[5]

The consequences of the lack of competition

These cosy arrangements have left Australia with a lack of competitive neutrality between private and public providers and high barriers to entry for potential new providers. What are the consequences of this lack of competitiveness for students and the wider public?

One consequence is a *lack of diversity*. We have around forty public universities that are remarkably similar in structure and aspiration. And their marketing slogans: I doubt even many university staff presented with a list of universities and their marketing slogans would be able to match very many in a blind challenge. Throwing in a few slogans from the random slogan generator would be much better value for universities than their expensive consultants. Variation is mainly the extent to which universities live up to their claims to research quality, and in their financial position. This closely tracks their age.

---

3 It is interesting to contrast Australia's higher education policy arrangements with school policy arrangements, which are some of the most neutral, between public and private schools, anywhere in the world, and quite supportive of new private entrants. The potential for schools in Australia to take advantage of this has been limited by bureaucrats and unions.

4 Frijters and Murray (2016) briefly discuss the university dimensions of Australia's game of mates, their elegant expression for cosy and lucrative web of government-corporate relationships that strips wealth from ordinary Australians.

5 Other cartels could only dream of a government that fixes prices for them, erects almost insurmountable barriers to entry, and even heavily subsidises their operations.

It is hard not to think this institutional monoculture is part of the reason we have an intellectual monoculture. Take the examples of the education faculties in our universities and their attitude to phonics education, as highlighted by Buckingham (2009), or the approach to religion in our universities, as discussed in Oslington (2014).

Another consequence is a *lack of innovation*. One of the lessons of economics about innovation is that it tends to come from new firms entering a market rather than existing firms.[6] Depending on the structure of the market, innovation will spread to the incumbent firms, with some incumbent firms who fail to adapt exiting the market. The lack of possibility of entry does not bode well for innovation in higher education in Australia.

As well as organisational innovation in higher education, there is also the question of whether large bureaucratic and mostly comfortable institutions are a good environment for generating innovation and collaboration with industry that Australia needs.

The potential for organisational and product innovation in a moribund industry is nicely illustrated by the recent history of the religion industry in Australia.[7] It was a market dominated by a few large longstanding organisations (the Anglican, Catholic, Methodist, and Presbyterian churches), which were being abandoned by their customers from the 1970s. Then, along came a new entrant, Pentecostalism, with a radically different organisational structure and leadership style, offering a product much more appealing to contemporary Australians. Interestingly, the two largest Pentecostal churches, Hillsong and C3, were started in Sydney by immigrant New Zealanders, outsiders who saw the possibilities more clearly than any of the executives of the incumbent organisations. The Pentecostal movement has now passed the Anglicans to be the second largest Australian religious group measured by attendance, behind the Catholics whose numbers have

---

6 Palangkaraya, Spurling and Webster (2016) survey the literature on firm level innovation.

7 The literature on the economics of religion is discussed by Iannaccone (2012) based on an Economic Society of Australia conference keynote address.

been held up in recent decades by large migration inflows.[8] The story of the innovation and growth at Hillsong is told by Riches and Wagner (2018), and I have offered some reflections on the reasons for the growth of the movement in Oslington (2016), including the role of Alphacrucis, the national college of the movement.

Rent seeking. In a protected market, especially one where large government subsidies are on offer, rent seeking is likely to be much more lucrative for university administrators than efforts to innovate or improve the quality of teaching and research. Rents can be taken by administrators as high salaries, perks, large administrative entourages, or some combination of these. And it certainly looks like there is no shortage of takers in contemporary Australian universities.

Unionisation. One of the curious features of the Australian higher education system is that all universities have enterprise agreements with the academic union. The union enjoys a legislatively enforced monopoly position in Australian higher education. Academics may choose to join (and around 20% do) but, regardless of whether they join or not, the union negotiates pay and conditions for everyone who works at the university. These enterprise agreements are extremely detailed, covering staff workloads, union representation on various university decision-making bodies, promotion committees, union consultation about any workplace change, access to university resources for union negotiators, compulsory contribution to a superannuation fund connected with the union, arrangements for various services to be provided by union-controlled entities, and so on.

All of this adds up to high costs to students and taxpayers. Fees are high, but even more damaging are the incentives for incumbent universities to enrol as many students as possible to gain the government subsidies for enrolments. Hence the large marketing budgets. In many cases, students are persuaded to enrol, despite there being little chance of them completing or benefiting from higher education. The otherwise laudable policy of income contingent loans

---

8 NCLS Research (2001-16).

for students[9] magnifies the effects of the perverse incentives to enrol students, who are ill-equipped for university, by pushing the private costs for students forward into the uncertain future.

It is hardly surprising that the quality of higher education in these circumstances is deteriorating, especially at the bottom end of the system. The incentives to erode quality in search of the government dollar are just too strong for university administrators to resist. Evidence of this includes declining employment rates and starting salaries for graduates relative to non-graduates. Results of the recently introduced government survey of teaching quality, Quality Indicators for Learning and Teaching (QILT), also shows that the few private institutions allowed into the system hold the top places in the rankings, above any of our public universities.[10]

What can be done?

Facilitate new universities. The combination of Australia's underdeveloped culture of educational philanthropy and the hostile policy environment make it extremely difficult to start new universities. The Higher Education Standards Panel (HESP) sets the rules for accreditation of new universities, such as having three broad areas of study, degrees up to doctoral level, and substantial research capacity. Besides the category of 'university', there is the strange category of 'university college', which is a swamp designed by the university experts who wrote the original standards to ensure no new entrant passes through. HESP is currently reviewing provider categories, and should rewrite the category of 'university college' to fit high quality private providers who have no interest in the breadth or research requirements of universities, but deserve a title that allows them to compete in education export markets with lesser overseas institutions. This change would

---

9 Chapman (2006) discusses income contingent loans. Under the Australian income contingent loan system the university gets paid up front for the enrolment, while the student repays the loan to the government over a long period if their income is above a threshold.

10 QILT Reports are available at https://www.qilt.edu.au/

also allow institutions, which have been granted self-accrediting status by TEQSA in recent years, to apply directly for university status when they meet the requirements, thereby opening up public universities to real competition.

Restructure public universities to facilitate takeovers and exit. In the current environment, there seems to be an implicit political guarantee that no existing university be allowed to go to the wall, and certainly not a regional university, or university in an outer metropolitan marginal seat. What about forcing the incumbents to adopt governance arrangements that facilitate the transfer of control to a new management where the university is consistently making losses (which requires exceptionally awful management under the current regime of regulation and subsidies for public universities) or underperforming in other ways. Such changes in governance arrangements may preserve the institution's not-for-profit status. If so, what is the incentive for a new management to take over the institution? It might be the lure of the monopoly rents on offer, which are taken by managers of not-for-profit organisations as inflated salaries and perks, in contrast to being taken as profits by the owners of a for-profit organisation. Or it might be a public-spirited consortium of locals who believe they can do a better job of running their university than the incumbents. Either way the threat of takeover can discipline the incumbent management and improve outcomes, even if takeovers do not happen.

Fight the threat of tying accreditation to enterprise agreements with unions. One of the insidious trends in public policy is tying government contracts to so-called 'best practice industrial relations arrangements', which is code for an enterprise agreement with the relevant union. This gives the union massive power over the organisations, and it is not difficult to see this leading to ever more intrusive and efficiency destroying enterprise agreements with already cowering university managements. It is something to be vigorously resisted by taxpayers and students.

Reform undergraduate domestic student degree funding. The logic of the demand driven system links government subsidies to enrolments in accredited degree programs. This should apply regardless of whether the accredited degree program is in an institution that is public or private, university or not. At present this is not the case and needs to be fixed. Removing the iniquitous 25% FEE-HELP loading on the debts of students who choose private providers is also needed.

A more radical reform would be to replace FEE-HELP with student debt bonds sold on financial markets. This would cut out the government as a loss-taking middleman and make higher education institutions responsible for the student debt generated by their degree programs. Instead of subsidies for enrolments and FEE-HELP funding flowing from the government to institutions, the institution would sell bonds representing the repayments on the student debt on financial markets. The government would still set the rules of the income contingent loan scheme, still set repayment thresholds and interest rates (perhaps in relation to some market benchmark), but financial institutions would bid for the debt of various institutions' degree programs. There would be no government guarantee offered on the student debt.

With this reform, there would still be the option for the government to provide supplementary funding to courses that have public benefits in excess of the private return to the student (such as nursing or teaching) or which are judged important for other reasons. The point of the bond scheme would be to price the private returns from higher education properly.

Financial markets could be expected to price the private return on degrees (based on likely incomes for the graduate) reasonably accurately because actuaries they employ are trained to make these calculations, and the large sums involved mean it will be a thick market (in other words, a market where there is enough trading volume). To facilitate the market, the government may even continue to recover income contingent loan debts through the tax system and transfer the funds to the financial institution which has bought the debt from the university.

The main advantage of this reform is that university administrators would get immediate signals of the worth of the degree programs they are offering. It is important the signals are immediate, so they affect current administrative behaviour, making administrators think twice about behaviour that reduces the value of degrees to boost student numbers.

The prices obtained for the student debt generated by various university degree programs would be public knowledge. This would provide potential students much better information about the worth of alternative degree programs than problematic information currently supplied by published minimum ATARs for entry into degree programs, or by the information provided by commercially published guides. This is so especially as these guides rely on advertising from the universities and, in some cases, are even owned by the universities. Better information would improve student choice. Better information could potentially reduce the attraction for universities to spend large amounts on advertising.

A wise colleague suggested the price obtained in financial markets by some institutions for some degree programs would be derisory. I can think of business degree programs of a few universities for which I would hesitate to offer twenty dollars for the student debts generated. Financial markets may even price the debt generated by some degree programs at zero, after administration costs.

If financial markets do not value the income earning potential of certain degree programs highly, that would be a much-needed wake-up call for some administrators in the sector. No doubt the reform proposal would go down like a lead balloon with university Vice-Chancellors, however.

Open PhD funding through the government's Research Training Scheme to all accredited PhD programs. As PhD Program Director at Alphacrucis for the last three years, I have spoken with many students who would have enrolled with us if they could bring with them the government living-allowance scholarships only tenable at universities, or if we could match the zero-fees offer from universities who receive approximately $50,000 per-student government subsidies. Our PhD completions attract a government subsidy of $0 even though accredited by TEQSA according to the same standards. This is not just a fairness issue but an efficiency issue. Students choosing an inferior PhD program at a public university because of the government subsidy means the government is not getting the best value it can for the limited research dollar it has to spend. Funding all accredited PhD programs regardless of the institution they sit in would improve efficiency and be budget neutral, as the number of students would not change but are simply reallocated between institutions.

Open ARC research funding to private providers. Again, the principle is that all accredited institutions should have a chance to compete for government funding, with the best researchers and projects winning. The research environment is already a large part of ARC assessment processes, so the complaint from incumbent universities that they offer a better environment for projects is already dealt with. Allowing all researchers regardless of institution to apply would be budget neutral as the available pot of money for which they are competing remains constant.

Politics

There have been several failed attempts to open public universities to competition in the past. Each has been defeated by a coalition of universities and higher education unions. There has been the $100,000 university degree scare campaign and the VET FEE-HELP debacle. This latter was a failure of regulation rather than of competition. Vice-Chancellors are quick to invoke it when opening universities up to competition is discussed, even though they know that VET markets and regulatory arrangements are very different to higher education.

Vice-Chancellors and unions are also keen to point out the evils of private ownership. But the distinction between public and private is increasingly vague. For instance, the governance structures of ACU and Notre Dame are indistinguishable; yet one is regarded as public and the other private. The real difference is that one began under older regulatory arrangements than the other.

It is not legal ownership but regulatory arrangements and the social character of the goods that matters (as pointed out by Marginson 2007). Even the distinction between not-for-profit and for-profit is shady, and is perhaps just a matter of whether rents are cashed out by management above the bottom line as salaries and perks, or more transparently taken below the line as profits.

Conclusion

The potential gains from completing reforms like those discussed above are huge. Competition alters the cost and quality benchmark for public universities even if private providers remain small. Altering the cost and quality benchmark for universities means budget savings for government, savings and quality gains for students, and the potentially large export earnings generated by new private universities.

The Vice-Chancellors squealing loudest about the threat of competition from private providers are identifying their institutions as the most vulnerable to competition from private providers on anything like a level playing field. The louder they squeal the clearer is the need for a good dose of competition in teaching and research in Australian higher education.

References

Bradley, Denise et al., *Review of Australian Higher Education,* 2008.

Buckingham, Jennifer, *Schools of Thought: A Collection of Articles on Education*, Centre for Independent Studies, Sydney, 2009.

Chapman, Bruce, *Government Managing Risk: Income Contingent Loans for Social and Economic Progress,* Routledge, London, 2006.

Coleman, W. O. (ed.), *Only in Australia. The History, Politics and Economics of Australian Exceptionalism,* Oxford University Press, Oxford, 2016.

Corden, W. M., 'Australian Universities: Moscow on the Molonglo', *Quadrant,* 2005, 44(11), 7-20.

Davis, Glyn, *The Australian Idea of a University*, Melbourne University Press, Melbourne, 2017.

Frijters, Paul and Cameron Murray, *Game of Mates*, Publicious, USA, 2016.

Harper, Ian, et al., *Review of National Competition Policy*, Australian Government, Canberra, 2015.

Hilmer, Fred and Independent Committee of Inquiry into Competition Policy in Australia, *National Competition Policy*, Australian Government, Canberra, AGPS cat. no. 9321328, 1993.

Iannaccone, Laurence, 'Extremism and the Economics of Religion', *Economic Record*, 2012, 88, 110-15.

Marginson, Simon, *Markets in Education*, Allen & Unwin, St Leonards, N.S.W., 1997.

Marginson, Simon, 'The Public/Private Divide in Higher Education: A Global Revision', *Higher Education*, 2007, 53, 307-33.

Melleuish, Gregory, *Australian Intellectuals: Elitist, Adversarial and Damaging?*, Connor Court, Ballan, Vic., 2013.

NCLS Research, *National-Church-Life-Survey*, 2001-16. Reports at https://www.ncls.org.au/

Norton, Andrew, *The Unchained University*, Centre for Independent Studies, Sydney, 2002.

Norton, Andrew, 'The Future of Higher Education: Better but Not Necessarily Faster or Cheaper', *Policy*, 2013, 29(2), 10-14.

Norton, Andrew, *Mapping Australian Higher Education*, Grattan Institute, Melbourne, 2016.

Oslington, P., 'The Place of Religion and Theology in the National Research System', CHASS Forum and Workshop on ARC and Theology, Canberra, 2013.

Oslington, P., 'Religion and Australian Universities: Tales of Horror and Hope', *The Conversation*, February 2014.

Oslington, P., 'Dose of Competition Can Lift Higher Education Productivity and Quality', *The Conversation*, September 2014.

Oslington, P., 'The New Normal? Pentecostalism Overtakes Anglicanism', *ABC Religion & Ethics*, 26 August 2016.

Palangkaraya, A., T. Spurling and E. Webster, 'What Drives Firm Innovation?', Australian Council of Learned Academies, 2016.

Parker, Stephen, et al, *Reimagining Tertiary Education: From Binary System to Ecosystem*, KPMG Report, 2018.

Riches, Tanya and T. Wagner (eds), *The Hillsong Movement Examined: You Call Me out Upon the Waters*, Palgrave Macmillan, Melbourne, 2018.

Shergold, Peter, *Learning from Failure: Why Large Government Policy Initiatives Have Gone So Badly Wrong in the Past and How the Chances of Success in the Future Can Be Improved*, Australian Public Service Commission, Canberra, 2016.

Warburton, Mark, 'Beyond the Demand Driven Obsession and Policy Impasse', *Campus Morning Mail,* https://campusmorningmail.com.au/news/beyond-the-demand-driven-obsession-and-policy-impasse, 2017.

Withers, Glenn, 'The State of the Universities' in *Through a Glass Darkly: The Social Sciences Look at the Neoliberal University*, edited by M. Thornton, ANU Press, Canberra, 103-17, 2014.

Acknowledgements

This work arose from the Freedom to Choose conference of 2017 on the state of universities. It took place at the University of Notre Dame Australia, Fremantle, and was overseen by Gregory Moore. The encouragement of Ron Manners and the Mannkal Economics Education Foundation is gratefully acknowledged, as is the invaluable editorial assistance with the manuscript of John Nethercote and Michael Gilchrist.

William O. Coleman
Editor
Sydney, New South Wales
June 2019

Contributors

Professor James Allan, a Canadian by birth, has been Garrick Professor of Law at the University of Queensland since 2004, following appointments in Hong Kong, New Zealand, Canada and the United States. His books include *Democracy in Decline; A Sceptical Theory of Morality and Law;* and *Sympathy and Antipathy: Essays Legal and Philosophical.*

Professor Emeritus Charles Beach is a professor of economics at Queen's University, Canada. From 1995 to 2002 he was editor of *Canadian Public Policy/Analyse de Politiques.* He has jointly edited *Higher Education in Canada* and co-authored *Are We Becoming Two Societies? Income Polarization and the Myth of the Declining Middle Class in Canada.*

Dr Stephen Chavura has lectured on political thought and history at Macquarie University and Campion College. His book, *Tudor Protestant Thought, 1547-1603*, was published in 2011.

Dr William O. Coleman is Reader in Economics at the Australian National University. His books include *Economics and Its Enemies*; *Giblin's Platoon: the Trials and Triumph of the Economist in Australian Public Life*; and, as editor, *Only in Australia: the History, Politics, and Economics of Australian Exceptionalism.* He is the editor of *Agenda: a Journal of Policy Analysis and Reform.*

Professor Emeritus Peter Drake studied at the University of Melbourne and the Australian National University before his appointment as Professor of Economics at the University of New England, where he was later Deputy Vice-Chancellor. Subsequently, he was inaugural Vice-Chancellor of the Australian Catholic University. His books include *Economic Growth for Australia* (jointly); *Currency, Credit and Commerce*; and *Arndt's Story: The Life of an Australian Economist* (jointly).

Professor Gigi Foster, Director of Education at the Business School, University of New South Wales, studied at Yale and the University of Maryland. She recently co-authored *An Economic Theory of Greed, Love, Groups and Networks* and is the joint editor of *The Economics of Multitasking*.

David Martin Jones is Professor in the War Studies Department, King's College, London, and Honorary Reader at the School of Political Science and International Studies, University of Queensland. He has authored *Sacred Violence: Political Religion in a Secular Age* and jointly wrote *The Rise of China and Asia Pacific Security* and *The Political Impossibility of Modern Counter-Insurgency*. He holds a PhD from the London School of Economics.

Professor John Lodewijks is Dean of the S. P. Jain School of Global Management and Adjunct Professor, UNSW Business School. He was previously Director of the Centre for South Pacific Studies at UNSW, and Head of the School of Economics and Finance at the University of Western Sydney. He has been editor of the *History of Economics Review*.

Professor Frank Milne is BMO Professor of Economics and Finance in the Economics Department of the Queen's University, Canada. He been a consultant to the Bank of England and Special Advisor to the Bank of Canada. His publications include *Finance Theory and Asset Pricing* and, as joint author, *Current Directions in Financial Regulation* (2005).

Professor Paul Oslington is Inaugural Dean of Business and Professor of Economics at Alphacrucis College, Sydney, and was previously Professor of Economics at the Australian Catholic University, 2008-13. His books include *The Theory of International Trade and Unemployment* and *Political Economy and Natural Philosophy: Smith, Malthus and Their Followers*.

Professor Emeritus Steven Schwartz, FASSA, is a Senior Fellow at the Centre for Independent Studies and the former Vice Chancellor of

Murdoch, Brunel and Macquarie Universities. He recently retired as chair of the Australian Curriculum, Assessment and Advisory Authority. Born in New York City, he took degrees at the City University of New York and Syracuse. His academic appointments include Professor of Psychiatry at the University of Queensland, along with visiting positions at Stanford, Harvard and Wolfson College, Oxford. His books include *Classic Studies in Psychology* and *Pavlov's Heirs*.

Michael Sexton has been Solicitor-General of New South Wales since 1998. He previously taught law at the Australian National University and the University of New South Wales. His books include *Illusions of Power*, republished as *The Great Crash; War for the Asking: Australia's Vietnam Secrets*; *The Legal Mystique: The Role of Lawyers in Australian Society* (jointly). He recently published his autobiography, *On the Edges of History: A Memoir of Law, Books and Politics*.

Dr Barry Spurr is Literary Editor of *Quadrant* magazine. He was Professor of Poetry and Poetics at the University of Sydney, the first professor of poetry in Australia. Among his many books are *Anglo-Catholic in Religion: T S Eliot and Christianity*; *See the Virgin Blest: Representations of the Virgin Mary in English Poetry*; and *Lytton Strachey*. In 2016 a book of essays and poems was published in his honour, *The Free Mind*.

Dr Ruth Williams is currently Honorary Senior Research Fellow, Department of Mathematics and Statistics, La Trobe University Bendigo, and has had appointments at La Trobe, Griffith and Victoria Universities. In addition to her more than 50 journal articles, she is joint author of *The Economics of Mental Health Care: Industry, Government and Community Issues*.

Professor Alison Wolf, Baroness Wolf of Dulwich, is the Sir Roy Griffiths Professor of Public Sector Mangement and Director, International Centre for University Policy Research, at King's College, London. Her publications include *Review of Vocational Education* ('The Wolf Report'); *Improving Skills at Work*; and *The XX Factor*.

www.ingramcontent.com/pod-product-compliance
Lightning Source LLC
Chambersburg PA
CBHW070018010526
44117CB00011B/1631